When Gary Rosberg and I first talked about this book, I realized he had something to convey to many hurting people. I had the irresistible urge to say, "If you write it, they will read."

Dr. Steve Farrar
Author of *Point Man*

Dr. Gary Rosberg has written the friends' and lovers' guide to reconciliation—a handbook for relationships that will stand the test of time.

Tim Kimmel
Author of *Little House on the Freeway*

Gary Rosberg has been a popular speaker at our conferences for several years. His message, now in this book, will help you learn to resolve conflict. Whether you need to "close the loop" of broken relationship with a spouse, parent, child, co-worker, or a friend, this will give you some clear, practical, healing steps to take.

Dennis Rainey
Author of *Building Your Mate's Self-Esteem*

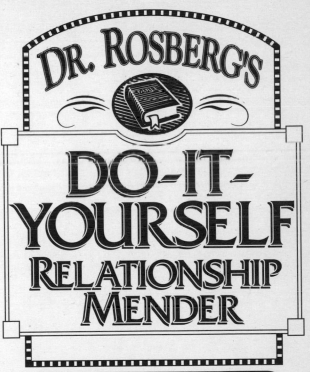

DR. ROSBERG'S

DO-IT-YOURSELF RELATIONSHIP MENDER

DR. GARY ROSBERG

FOCUS ON THE FAMILY

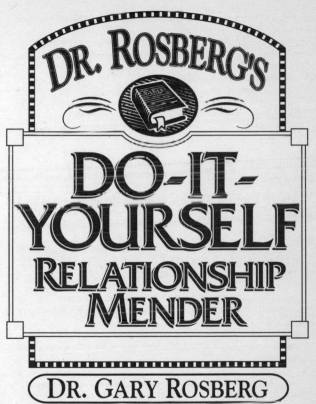

DR. ROSBERG'S

DO-IT-
YOURSELF
RELATIONSHIP
MENDER

DR. GARY ROSBERG

Tyndale House Publishers, Wheaton, Illinois

DR. ROSBERG'S DO-IT-YOURSELF RELATIONSHIP MENDER
Copyright © 1992, 1995 by Dr. Gary Rosberg

Library of Congress Cataloging-in-Publication Data

Rosberg, Gary, 1952–
Dr. Rosberg's Do-It-Yourself Relationship Mender / Gary Rosberg
   p. cm.
   ISBN 1-56179-760-X
   1. Conflict management. 2. Interpersonal conflict.
   3. Interpersonal relations. I. Title.
HM136.R67   1992
303.6'9—dc20

                 92-24478
                 CIP

A Focus on the Family Book Published by
Tyndale House Publishers, Wheaton, Illinois 60189

Unless otherwise noted, Scripture quotations are from the HOLY
BIBLE, NEW INTERNATIONAL VERSION®. Copyright © 1973,
1978, 1984 by the International Bible Society. Used by permission
of Zondervan Publishing House. All rights reserved.
Scripture quotations designated NASB are from the New American Standard Bible, © 1960, 1962, 1963, 1968, 1971, 1972, 1973, 1975,
1977 by The Lockman Foundation.

Some people's names and certain details of case studies
mentioned in this book have been changed to protect the privacy
of the individuals involved.

This book was originally published under the title *Choosing to
Love Again.*

Editor and Study Guide: Larry K. Weeden

Printed in the United States of America
99 00 01 02 03/10 9 8 7 6 5 4 3

To you, Mom, for teaching me laughter and joy.
To you, Dad, for teaching me compassion
and integrity.
Thanks for believing in me.

To my daughter Missy, for keeping laughter
and joy in my life.
To my daughter Sarah, for keeping compassion
and integrity in my life.
Thanks to both of you girls for believing
in your daddy

And most of all to my wife, Barbara, who daily
gives me the encouragement of a cheerleader
and the love of the ages. I am your greatest fan,
Barbara. Thank you for
paying the price and believing in me,
and most of all for introducing me to the Savior.

CONTENTS

ACKNOWLEDGMENTS

Writing a book is a little bit like birthing a baby. You start out looking at pictures of other babies and watching other parents with their babies, and you smile. As the pregnancy progresses, your body changes, you stay up late at night, and you experience what our birthing teacher called *discomfort* and what Barbara more appropriately called *pain*. Yet there is pure joy and humility in the birthing room as you hold the baby you have carried for months.

This book also started with a smile, went through a long gestation period, had incredible labor pains, but has ended with great humility, joy, and many smiles. And just as a baby doesn't come into today's culture without a lot of people's involvement, from the family to the doctor's office and through the delivery room, neither has this book. It takes a team to birth a baby. It also took a team to birth this book. I want to honor my team.

DENNIS RAINEY AND THE FAMILY MINISTRY TEAM: You gave me the platform with the Family Life Conferences that has changed our lives and, we pray, many of the lives of couples who have attended. Barbara and I are humbled to be on the team. Thank you for believing in Barbara and me.

STEVE FARRAR: From the day we sat in my dining room and you asked that simple question "How do you help people resolve broken relationships?" to today, you have believed in me and this book. Your encouragement that "this book will be published" never wavered. You are a special friend, Steve.

JOHN TRENT: From my trips to Scottsdale for Mexican meals, brainstorming, and encouragement to three CBAs, you have believed and cheered me on. I know that without you on the team, I would still be on the bench, watching the rest of the guys play.

DAVE BOEHI: The "coach." You challenged, tugged, and pulled the best I had to give. You are numero uno in my book. Without you, this book never would have been written.

TIM KIMMEL: You challenged me to bleed all over this manuscript. I did. Thanks for helping to pave the way.

FRIENDS AT FOCUS ON THE FAMILY: The privilege of working with all of you has been one of the greatest experiences of my life. Thanks to Janet Kobobel and Sandi Shelton for believing in this project. You two are terrific! Also thanks to my editor, Larry Weeden. Your feedback and encouragement helped me to keep stepping up to the plate when I wanted to toss off my batting helmet and say "Enough!" I also tip my hat to Gwen Ellis and Al Janssen for taking on a rookie author and giving me a shot at sharing my heart on these pages. Jeff Stoddard, you brought the loop alive in the artwork. You saw things I couldn't see. Now we all can see them. Thanks. The folks at Tyndale: You are up to the plate now. Thanks for helping me to get this book out there to minister to families. And also my deepest appreciation to Rolf Zettersten and Dr. James Dobson for your obedience to God in ministering to families throughout the world. We all need you.

I also want to honor some people in Iowa who could play on any writer's "all-star team."

Jerry Foster, Mike Colby, and Tim Vermillion: three men who since 1978 have met with me weekly as we have grown together. Thanks for the encouragement and accountability. See you at lunch Tuesday!

Dr. Tom and Patty Evans: Thanks for being a safe place for Barbara and me to let down and take risks. You always call at just the right time. You are loved.

The men of CrossTrainer Men's Study: Wednesday mornings are the highlight of my week. You have been great encouragers through this process and have taught me well. Guard your hearts, men.

The staff of America's Family Coaches and Family Legacy Counseling: Thank you for your support during the writing of this book. Go team go!

Pastor Quintin Stieff and our friends at Valley

Evangelical Free Church in West Des Moines: There isn't a better home team in the league. Thanks for ministering to the Rosbergs. We need you.

And to a very special group of people who taught me how to restore broken relationships: to the hundreds of people I have had the privilege to sit with in counseling. You taught me how to close loops. I just wrote down what we learned together. Stay faithful, and watch God be glorified.

Most of all: Barbara, Sarah, and Missy. Thanks for greeting me at the door each night with "Dad's home." You have sacrificed more than anyone. Yes, Missy, my book is now done.

PREFACE

A father knocks on his 16-year-old son's bedroom door after a stormy weekend. "Son, let's talk," he says.

A wife rolls over in bed to check the clock for the umpteenth time. It's 1:30 A.M., and she hasn't slept a wink. Unbeknownst to her, neither has her husband. "Honey, let's talk" are welcome words in a relationship feeling the coolness of night even though it's August.

A colleague taps you on the shoulder after the business meeting, stepping up to the plate to reconcile the icy relationship the two of you have experienced lately. "Let's talk," she says. "We both know we have an issue that needs to be addressed. Our relationship is too important to leave the way it is."

You call your mother after last Christmas's disaster. You've tried to steer clear of the blowup, but you and she know you're just avoiding it. "Mom, I know you're hurt," you say. "Let's talk this thing through. Life is too short . . ."

"Let's talk." They are the two words that need to be heard more between husbands and wives. The two words dads and daughters need to say on the edge of the bed after they've had a shouting match about boundaries that aren't being kept. The two simple words moms and sons need to share during cookies and milk after school or over coffee at breakfast tables during trips home. "Let's talk." From boardrooms in executive suites to elders' meetings in churches. From neighborhood fence discussions between friends to long-distance calls to siblings seldom heard from. From kids that live far away and parents that live right around the corner.

"Let's talk" means something. It means that the relationship is worth the keeping. It means that even though the issue at hand needs to be resolved, the relationship is paramount. "Let's talk" helps to strengthen relationships that are already on the right path and to give life to those that have been dying on the vine.

But even though "Let's talk" gets the ball rolling, it's only the beginning. And if you're anything like the many people I counsel and speak to in audiences all around the country, we all need to learn how to "close the loop" of unresolved conflict. That's why I wrote this book—to encourage you and those you care about, and to give you the practical tools of reconciliation. So let's not only talk; let's also forgive. I'm going to show you how. Thanks for joining me.

PART 1

THE PAIN OF BROKEN RELATIONSHIPS

MOVING VIOLATIONS

I talk to people like you every day. Good people. They tell me about their struggles, their fears, and, above all, their hurts. They're people who have been violated.

Most marriage surveys reveal that the biggest problems for couples are dealing with communication and resolving conflict. My own experience bears this out, but I wouldn't limit those problems to married couples. Whatever your season of life and wherever your time is spent, you work with people. And conflict is inevitable in any relationship.

I call these conflicts *moving violations*. It's kind of like driving down the street a little too fast, looking in the rearview mirror, and bingo! A police officer writes a ticket that puts a dent in your miscellaneous budget. It hurts.

Relational moving violations hit us a lot harder—and where they really hurt—in our hearts.

Have you ever been hurt? Laura has. She thought when she met Dave that he was it—the man for whom she'd been waiting. God had held her back from committing to any other man so that He could save her for Dave.

They dated and fell in love. It seemed so right. Dave would send Laura little notes and call her unexpectedly just to say hi. The flowers and gifts kept on coming. At first she feared it wouldn't last, but eventually she began calling old college friends to tell them the good news. She celebrated the "perfect match" with co-workers. Mom and Dad were looking forward to the parental review at Thanksgiving.

Laura knew that giving herself sexually to Dave was not condoned biblically, but she was in love. It seemed so right, and she didn't want to lose him over something she would gladly give him after marriage anyway.

Then, out of nowhere, Dave began to pull away and lose interest. Laura never saw it coming. When the relationship suddenly ended, she felt tainted and used. A moving violation.

Have you ever been hurt? Karla has. She and Jody met in college and became fast friends. They got along so well that the biggest thing they ever fought over was where to eat pizza after the game on Saturday night.

After they both graduated and got married, they continued to do things together, although the relationship seemed different. Jody had changed so much. It was becoming harder and harder for Karla to trust her. Seemingly little and unimportant rifts started to strain the friendship. No matter how hard Karla tried to resolve conflicts with Jody, any time a third friend got involved, Jody "snapped, crackled, and popped."

Then one Thursday afternoon, Karla received a phone call from another friend, Liz, and realized Jody had undermined Karla's relationship with Liz. In her jealousy, Jody had ruined another friendship.

"Why couldn't we all be friends?" Karla said. "Right underneath my nose, yet I never saw it coming." She didn't know what to do. There was no way she and Jody could ever talk about it. She didn't want to hurt Jody's feelings; they were friends. A moving violation.

Have you ever been hurt? Jack has. He had a 22-year marriage, 4 kids, a mortgage, and college tuition on the horizon. His answer to the pressure of making ends meet was to work harder and longer hours.

3

He knew he was too busy with his job: scratching and clawing his way to the top, trying to beat out the competition, staying late nights at the office, and missing recitals and ball games. After years of driving himself, he was beginning to realize that at the end of the rainbow, things wouldn't be so great as he had hoped.

But he never thought his 16-year-old son, Matt, would start experimenting with alcohol and sex. The hurt and accusations played over and over in his mind, like a broken record: *I never would have done this to my father. . . . Kids today don't respect their parents. . . . After all I've sacrificed for him. . . . Doesn't he know I work so hard for him, his sisters, and his mom?*

He and Matt were isolated from each other, scared, and hurt. Their lives were flying out of control. Like many men, both were too proud to reach out, to listen, to try to keep the team together with two out in the bottom of the ninth. A moving violation.

Have you ever been hurt? Cindy has. Here she was, 39 years old, a professional with a good credit rating, a college degree, great friends, a strong faith, and the respect of her peers. But when she visited her parents, it all went down the tubes. Mom still treated her like little Cindy, the 5-year-old. She could never measure up.

"When are you going to get married?"

"Why don't you ever call home? Your sisters and brother call every day, yet you never pick up the phone."

"Hazel's daughter, Joy, is taking them on another vacation. Hazel is so excited."

Cindy couldn't take the fight for control. "I can't even stand calling her on the phone, let alone going to visit," she said. A moving violation.

Have you ever been hurt? The Thompsons have. Jan and Tom looked great on the outside. Thirteen years of marriage, a couple of kids, and a house in the suburbs—they had it all. Or so it seemed. Behind closed doors, the tension was mounting.

They argued continually, especially over parenting responsibilities. Their tempers flared, the kids sensed the loss of laughter their parents once had, and things seemed to have changed. What once was a vital relationship with daily communication, frequent date nights, and spontaneity had now turned into a marriage without joy.

Conflicts came and went without resolution. Offenses seemed to build upon each other and lose their distinction. Jan and Tom dropped the word *forgiveness* from their vocabulary. Isolation had crept into another home, creating an emotional separation. Without assistance, the Thompsons would soon see their names in the newspaper in small print under the heading "Divorces." A moving violation.

Have you ever been hurt? Mike has. He worked hard for his good job—four years of college, and then graduate school. After three transfers, he finally landed a management position in one of the top businesses in his industry.

Then he found himself working for Bill, and no matter how well he did, Bill let the criticism fly. Nine out of ten comments Bill made were negative. Yet Bill continually stole Mike's ideas for projects and claimed credit for them. Mike's ideas; Bill's signature. Mike felt used, and he didn't know how to change the situation. A moving violation.

Have you ever been hurt? Janice has. What seemed like an ideal marriage 23 years ago now seemed like a nightmare. Bills were left unpaid; the kids were rebelling; a 12-year-old car needed replacing. And then her husband took off with another woman.

How can I compete with a 25-year-old? Janice thought. *She seemed so nice when he hired her. I trusted her. When they took business trips together, friends raised eyebrows, but I thought, No, not Jeff. What a fool I was!*

Now Janice is a single parent, trying to make ends meet, feeling rejected, and hearing continual reports from so-called friends about the trips Jeff and his girl-friend are taking. Another moving violation.

Have you ever hurt or been hurt? Sure you have, and so have I. We've all been on the offending side of the conflict, holding the knife, and we've been on the receiving end, feeling the pain of hurt and disappointment.

Moving violations are offenses that betray the heart and send our emotions into a tizzy. They're hurts that throw us for a loop as we try to regain our equilibrium in a world that suddenly loses all sense of fairness. Some of the conflicts are minor, and some are major. In many cases, they were caused by parents who abused us emotionally, verbally, or, most tragic of all, sexually.

Offenses of the heart are common material for pastors, counselors, and everyday people. If we live in the real world, we see them all around us. Friends hurt friends. Parents hurt their kids. Wives and husbands hammer away at the hearts of the ones with whom they once shared wedding cake. Kids, young and old alike, shut out their parents.

Show me a relationship that has any time and experience to it and I'll show you conflict. It may be overt and loud or quiet as a smoldering fire, but strife is inevitable. We are self-centered people; we've been going our own way since the beginning of time.

The real tragedy, though, is that so many people find themselves without a clue about how to regain the health of their relationships or to repair cracks in their hearts the size of the San Andreas Fault. Why? Because no one taught them how to resolve conflict. They didn't see it modeled in their homes as they grew up, and they don't see it modeled on television. So rather than heal the hurt, they allow their hearts to harden.

OPENING THE LOOP

Over the last few years, as I listened to and learned from hundreds of people in my counseling office, God kept tossing an idea into my head. It was loose at first—bouncing around in my mind like a ball in a racquetball court. I knew He was on to something. The idea had potential.

A common sequence of events seemed to occur with conflicts of various kinds. The names and faces changed, but over and over I heard some of the same thoughts and experiences. As I analyzed this sequence, I developed my concept of "opening the loop." Here's how it works:

1. A conflict begins with an offense. Person A does something harmful to Person B.

2. This offense leads to an emotional reaction. Person B is hurt.

3. That hurt then leads to another common emotion: Person B becomes angry. And for many people, the sequence stops there. Out of fear, ignorance, or pride, Person B takes the wrong step and actually makes the conflict worse. Person B may attack Person A verbally or physically, may bury his or her anger and let it simmer, or may compromise and let Person A—the offending mate, child, or friend—have his or her own way. In whatever fashion, Person B—the hurt person—leaves the loop open.

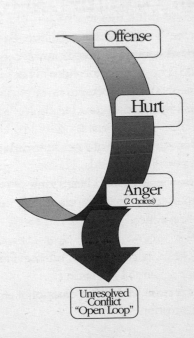

9

Many people have dozens of open loops in their lives. These unresolved conflicts build upon each other and lead to smoldering anger and bitterness. With each unresolved issue between them, two people grow more isolated from each other.

Sounds bleak, doesn't it? For many of the people I've counseled, that's how life seemed—grim and hopeless.

CLOSING THE LOOP

I used to think that at this point in my counseling career I would be burned out. But just the opposite has occurred. Despite my exposure to so much pain, I have incredible hope. That hope is not in my credentials, my techniques, or my person. It's in the revealed truth of the Bible. The Bible provides clear instructions for resolving conflict—for "closing the loop." And you know what? Those guidelines work.

1. Resolving conflict begins with *heart preparation*. Before approaching the other person, your heart needs to be made ready.

2. The second step is clear *communication*. Honestly describe your thoughts and feelings about the offense.

3. Next come clear *decisions*. Plan what to do to make the situation right.

4. Then comes the most important step, *forgiveness*. I don't know how counselors who don't show their patients how to ask for and grant forgiveness can get out of bed in the morning. Forgiveness starts the healing process, and true conflict resolution is impossible without it.

5. Finally, closing the loop requires rebuilding *trust*. Stopping with forgiveness won't do it, especially when the offense is major and habitual.

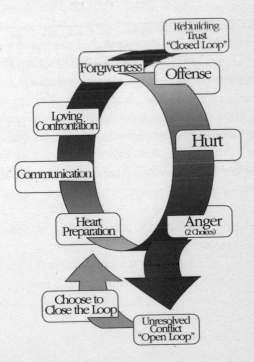

This concept of closing the loop in conflicts is both practical and biblical. I've used it with little kids, big kids, and adults. I have helped couples married 49 years and holding, couples getting married in a few days, and couples trying to heal their marriages after one partner has committed adultery. I have worked with executives worth millions and cocaine addicts who have lost everything. High-school kids who can't stand their parents have opened up and reestablished trust. Single adults in deep despair over unfulfilled dreams have risked piercing their protective bubbles to share the pain of their hearts.

There are days when I feel like tossing in the towel. And then, out of nowhere, as they say, something or someone will remind me of God's promise that He will never forsake us, and the hope is restored.

Through the rest of this book, I'll show you how to realize this hope in the conflicts you face. I'll explain what keeps us from closing our open loops, and then I'll take you through each part of the process, step by step.

This concept works. To show you how, we'll start by looking at the stories of two prodigals.

THE TWO PRODIGALS

Y ou're probably familiar with the story of the prodigal son:

> But while he was still a long way off, his father saw him, and felt compassion for him, and ran and embraced him, and kissed him. . . . "For this son of mine was dead, and has come to life again; he was lost, and has been found." And they began to be merry.[1]

This is a historic illustration for contemporary times: A father. A son. Resolution. Celebration. Closing the loop.

The hurt and pain abounding in families today is in many ways no different from what it was centuries ago. The Bible offers us hope, real hope, for restoration of broken relationships.

I began to see this passage in a different light as I started counseling people in how to resolve conflict. It's perhaps the best story in literature about a relationship that was broken and then restored, a loop that was opened and then closed.

The story began when the younger of two sons asked for his share of the father's estate. Then the offense continued: "Not many days later, the younger son gathered everything together and went on a journey into a distant country, and there he squandered his estate with loose living."[2]

Today he might have said, "Give me my money and I'm outta here." He wanted to break loose. No more working the land for him.

His father granted his request. He must have known he couldn't control that headstrong lad. His brother must have burned with his own resentment. Yet he stuck to the farm. Perhaps he knew his brother wouldn't survive.

So the lad was off, and I'll bet he had friends. Everyone likes a winner, especially one who's loaded. He was kind of like the only guy in high school who has a driver's license and his own set of car keys. He must have partied hard. Money ran through his hands like water.

The story doesn't say how long it took to use up his cash, but my guess is that it took only a few weeks or months. And then reality began to hit home.

At that point he could have returned home, but he probably was too proud. He likely told himself all sorts of things to help him rationalize why he left: *The old man isn't going to change. And that brother of mine, what a drag! I had to do it on my own. I wasn't going to die in that town.* His pride was strong, yet the attraction of the freewheeling lifestyle began to diminish as he realized the fast track only went in circles.

> Now when he had spent everything, a severe famine occurred in that country, and he began to be in need. And he went and attached himself to one of the citizens of that country, and he sent him into his fields to feed swine. And he was longing to fill his stomach with the pods that the swine were eating, and no one was giving anything to him.[3]

And what about the young man's father? Can you imagine the deep hurt he must have felt? The pain, the loss of separation. The grief over a son who rejected everything the father stood for: hard work, responsibility, righteous living. Yet he waited and probably looked daily, if not hourly, down the road to see if perhaps that day would be the day the boy returned.

THE TURNING POINT

Finally the son reached the end of his rope. He began to realize he had made a mistake. He had offended the very roots of his life, his heritage. It was time to make a choice. Would he leave the loop open forever—rationalizing his behavior, blaming others, feeling the inevitable self-pity and relentless guilt? Or would he start to close the loop and resolve the conflict?

> But when he came to his senses, he said, "How many of my father's hired men have more than enough bread, but I am dying here with hunger! I will get up and go to my father, and will say to him, 'Father, I have sinned against heaven, and in your sight; I am no longer worthy to be called your son; make me as one of your hired men.'"[4]

The son realized that humbling himself and confessing his sin was the only way to restore a clear mind and heart. By returning home, asking forgiveness of his father, and offering to make restitution for what he had lost, he sought to close the loop.

He didn't know how his dad would respond. Would he reject him? That's what he deserved. That's what he had done to his father. Yet he knew in his heart of hearts that he needed to go home. Pride began to give way to the honest expression of a broken heart. It was an incredible shift of the son's heart—from a demanding, self-centered view of life to a desire to restore a broken relationship.

And then an amazing thing occurred:

> But while he was still a long way off, his father saw him, and felt compassion for him, and ran and embraced him, and kissed him. And the son said to him, "Father, I have sinned against heaven and in your sight; I am no longer worthy to be called your son." But the father said to his slaves, "Quickly bring out the best robe and put it on him, and put a ring on his hand and sandals on his feet; and bring the fattened calf, kill it, and let us eat and be merry; for this son of mine was dead, and has come to life again; he was lost, and has been found."[5]

The father must have been looking for his son with some sort of first-century binoculars, knowing that some hour, some day, he would return. What gives me goose bumps is that when the father saw him from a long way off, he didn't wait for the boy; he actively went to him. He could have been self-righteous and turned his back, as so many fathers do. Instead he ran to him, threw his arms around him, granted him complete forgiveness, and restored him to fellowship. What a scene! The angels of heaven must have danced for joy as two souls who had been torn apart by pride were reconnected and their conflict was resolved. A loop was closed. Both father and son chose to heal the relationship.

ANOTHER PRODIGAL SON

That story is meaningful to me, not just for its clear demonstration of how to open and close a loop, but also for my personal relationship to it. I lived it. My story goes back to the 1960s.

"Gary, Dad's home," yelled my little brother, Jim, one Friday afternoon.

"Dad who?" I replied.

"Dad who? What do you mean? I said Dad's home, and he wants to see you in the kitchen now."

"Dad's home" at that time of day ranked right up there with "There's a pot of gold at the end of the rainbow" and "The Cubs won the pennant." In other words, it just didn't happen. In my house, Dad didn't come home until 5:30 at night.

So why was he home early that day? To explain, I have to fill you in on what had occurred a short time before. I was 15 years old and a "rock star." You laugh, but no one told me back then that it wasn't true. I started out in a garage band during the Beatlemania craze of the sixties, and by the time I was a freshman in high school, I was into the world of after-the-game dances, sock hops, bar mitzvahs, and teen clubs.

Earlier that afternoon, I had been cutting the grass, a chore I deplored. I had put it off, and the grass was long. I also had a gig that night, and normally I would rest during the day when my band was to play at night. I wanted to be inside, practicing my keyboards, keeping my fingers loose, and acting cool. My attitude was in the pits, which was normal for me. Mom returned from running errands, looked at my work, and said, "Gary, you're going to have to cut the grass a second time. You let it go too long, and once around won't get the job done."

On my list of least-favorite things to do, Mom's "cut it again" ranked with painting the house, looking for my lost dental retainer in the garbage can, and taking my little brother to the movies. So I replied as any other rock star would: "No." One word. Simple. Direct.

Mom came a little closer as she walked through the turf, blades of grass sticking to her ankles. "What did you say, Gary?"

"I said no, Mom. I have a gig tonight. I need to rest."

"I am not going to tell you again, Gary. Cut it over, before your father gets home."

I hated those words: "before your father gets

home." So for the third and final time, with all the brilliance I could muster, I said, "No. If you want it cut again, cut it yourself."

There were three major problems with that statement. Number one: I shouldn't have said no to my mom even once, because it was disrespectful. My dad taught me that. Number two: Mom didn't know how to operate the old mower. Number three: My mother was and is my father's first priority, and rightfully so. I didn't need a detective to help me deduce that I was now in deep weeds.

Mom walked over to me, looked me in the eyes, raised her hand, and slapped my face. She had never done that before. Oh, she had spanked me when I was a little shaver, but she had never slapped me.

"Mom, don't do that," I said. Once again, straight and to the point.

Her face was set. She looked deep into my eyes and said it again: "Gary, cut the lawn over."

"No."

With that, Mom raised her hand again and swung a second time, only this time I put my arm up to block her hand. In my best Clint Eastwood fashion, I said, "Mom, don't slap me again."

Now, mistake number 36 within this episode was touching my mother in any way other than a hug or a kiss. Her anger, hurt, and deep disappointment shifted to shock. "Get to your room," she ordered. "Now!"

Well, that was one way of getting out of cutting the grass. Up to my room I went; there was no way I was going to defy that last order. About 45 minutes later, I heard those three dreadful words: "Dad is home."

A KNOCK-DOWN-DRAG-OUT FIGHT

What happened next changed my life profoundly. You see, a loop had been open for months. Actually, it was more like a series of loops. Time after time I had disappointed my parents with failing grades, broken promises, flippant and disrespectful attitudes, and rude behavior. A confrontation was inevitable.

As I approached the kitchen, Dad's back was to me. Mom was dead quiet, and she looked down to avoid eye contact with me. It was so still, like the quiet before the storm. As Dad turned around, I could see the anger in his eyes.

Then he said 22 words that would pierce my soul in a painful yet cleansing way: "Son, you can mess with anyone in the world—me, your brothers, your friends—but you will never mess with your mother."

"Dad, I just held up my hands."

"Gary, you never raise your hands to her. She is your mother." And then he added his final words: "I have had it with you. Now you can mess with me."

What happened in the next few minutes left me with the most ambivalent feelings of my childhood. Dad and I went at it—a knockdown-drag-out, man-to-man fight. Arms and legs flailed as Dad's two years of frustration with the monster my rock-and-roll career had created came to a head. My dad loved me enough to let me know enough was enough. I had gone too far.

As I lay on the floor, my dad on top of me, holding me down, my mom cried and begged us to stop. Jim looked on in horror, learning his own lesson.

"I'm moving out!" I declared. "You can't do this to me!"

"Fine, Gary, I'll get your suitcase," Dad said. That statement captured my attention. He got up and went to the attic to find my suitcase, while I headed to my room and started packing. I grabbed my bell-bottom jeans, Ringo boots, hairbrush, gig clothes, and my Beatles poster.

"Where are you going?" asked Dad as he dropped off my bag.

"I'm moving to Old Town in Chicago. They'll want me there."

It wasn't enough that I had maintained a cocky attitude for two years. It wasn't enough that I had raised a hand to block my mom's frustrated slap. It wasn't enough that I had rolled on the floor with a frenzied dad. I had to throw one last punch and hurt them more deeply. By going to Old Town, I was declaring, "You and Mom failed. I'm going to the hip culture, where people will care for me."

AN UNFORGETTABLE SIGHT

Dad left my room. I continued packing, looking at the bedroom I had inherited from sister Gail after she got married and moved out. I took one last look at my junk: books, records, posters, the wallpaper I always hated anyway. Then I did a curious thing: I lay on the bed one last time, taking five minutes to stare at the ceiling, almost as if to drink in some last few minutes of security from what I knew was home.

A few minutes later, I headed to Dad's bathroom to get my English Leather cologne. Even a runaway needed to smell good. And for some reason, as I was digging through the medicine cabinet, I went to the window. I don't know what drew me there, but I'll never forget what I saw. I peered out the venetian blinds and saw the huge flower garden my mom toiled in, the gas grill, the magnolia tree that had just blossomed, the basketball hoop where I dreamed of touching the rim. And then I looked over to my dad's car.

There was Dad, gazing out over the yard as well. In my cynicism, I figured he was probably thinking that now he would have to cut it. In reality, he was probably wondering what to do. As I watched, he leaned on the hood of his Dodge Charger, dropped his face into his hands, and began to sob.

He wept. Right there, in broad daylight, all six feet, three inches of him.

I wish I could bottle what occurred in my heart during the next few minutes. It was as if God told me, "Gary, My son, enough is enough. It's time to let go of the pride, the arrogance, the power of hurting others. Time to let go of doing it your way. You have broken your father's heart. Go to him, just like the prodigal son."

I had never seen my dad cry, let alone sob. To realize I had caused this deep pain was too much. I went downstairs, out the front door to avoid my mom and brother, and straight to him. He saw me coming. He waited. I remember saying simply, "I'm sorry, Dad."

We hugged. And as we sat and talked, I learned something. I learned that Dad was letting me go my own way because I had to learn to set boundaries, just like the prodigal.

I wanted to go home. Just as the prodigal son's father did, my dad welcomed me with his response, although it had a twentieth-century slant on it: "Son, you can have your choice of discipline. You can have one month of early curfew, or we can forget the whole thing."

I couldn't believe my ears. I deserved a life sentence in Leavenworth Federal Penitentiary, and here he was ready to wipe the slate clean! But somehow I realized what I really needed.

"Dad, I'll take the 30 days of discipline."

He looked mildly surprised and said, "You don't have to."

"Yes, I do."

My life changed after that summer day. The arrogance began to diminish, honor for my parents was restored, and the loop began to close. I was home. We still had disagreements during the rest of my adolescence, but I never questioned my esteem for Dad (or Mom). He had welcomed me home.

That event is the reason I wrote this book. Loops can be closed. Relationships demand it. Jesus modeled it, and our hearts need it. It just takes someone willing to assume the risk of closing the loop to begin restoring a relationship.

Excuse me, I need to go call my dad.

PART 2

OPENING
THE LOOP

CHAPTER 3

INTERNAL BLEEDING

D r. Rosberg, I can't believe I could ever hurt this bad." I was only 15 seconds into an appointment with a man whose world had fallen apart. Phil's wife, Susan, had betrayed him. She had seemed to be the perfect Christian wife and mother. As Phil said, "Everyone thinks she is such a great person." Yet for two years, she had played a one-sided game of charades with Phil.

"Tell me what happened," I said. I knew that what was coming would not be pretty. I've been there before, scores of times, listening to people who have just had the rug, pad, and floorboards yanked out from under them.

"I was in one of the kids' rooms, looking for some white socks for my daughter, when I found it."

"What did you find?" Now my heart was pumping.

"On the closet floor, I found a bag. You know, one of those dozens of bags lying around that you take to the beach. I thought there might be one of those missing socks in the bag, the ones that never make it from the bag to the washer.

"In the bag was a note from Tim. Tim and Susan work together. You've probably even heard his name around. The note unraveled stuff that first made my head spin. Then I thought I was going to throw up. There I sat, in my baby daughter's closet, reading a lousy note that had been written to my wife."

"What did you do?"

"I was blown away. I felt as if someone had taken a two-by-four to my stomach. I was sweating. I didn't know what to do. I knew that as soon as I got up and left that closet, I would have to face the reality that my life was completely changed. All of a sudden, the junk that cluttered the closet floor was like a bunker protecting me from the truth of the war I didn't even know I was fighting in my own home."

"Did you go to Susan?"

"At first I just walked through the house. I looked around at all the stuff. I felt stupid. I even feel stupid telling you."

"Go ahead, Phil. You're doing fine."

"I looked at each of the kids' rooms. As I looked at their junk, memories flashed through my mind. It was just like what they say happens before you die— my whole life passed before me. I saw souvenirs from the ballpark. Pictures on the walls. Swimming trophies. Buttons and old school papers lying around. Stuff that represented us. A family. A family that I thought made sense."

"Then what?"

"Susan walked into Christopher's room, where I was standing, and came up behind me, all smiles. As I turned to her, it was as if I was in slow motion. Like in the movies, when a guy is out in the field and hears his love calling to him, and he turns to run to her. When I turned around, I first looked into her eyes. Not a clue. There wasn't anything but joy. You know what I thought about at that instant? I wondered if she pretended it was him when she looked at me. I knew that as soon as I opened my mouth, my world was going to be completely different.

"She could tell that something was wrong. 'Phil, what is it?' was all she said.

"'Susan, I know.'

"That's all I had to say, Gary. As soon as I said that, the blood drained from her face. Tears rolled down her cheeks, and she dropped her head and turned away."

"What were you feeling at that point, Phil?"

"It was strange. On one hand, I wanted to reach out to her. That was my job. You know, all that stuff about comforting each other. On the other hand, I wanted to wring her neck. I have never felt that type of confusion in my life. We both stood there. It was as though we were frozen in time.

"We looked at each other, both of us crying. I haven't done that in years. It was like a time warp. Susan was the first to speak. She said she wanted to tell me everything, but she was scared. Then she asked if I wanted her to move out. That was such a strange question to hear her ask me. I knew that things weren't perfect at home. We're like everybody else. I mean, we fight over bills, toys, my sports—the regular stuff. But to hear her say, 'Do you want me to leave?' I never imagined in my wildest dream—or nightmare, actually—that I would ever hear those words come out of her mouth."

BLINDSIDED BY OFFENSES

I'll return to Phil and Susan's story in a later chapter, but for now, look at his last statement: "I never imagined I would ever hear those words come out of her mouth."

I wonder how many times I've heard things like that from people I'm counseling?

"I can't believe he did that."

"I can't believe I said that."

"I can't believe we've actually let our marriage get to this point."

Two people begin a marriage with such a bright future, such an incredible feeling of love, such high hopes. But within a few years, they find themselves on their way to divorce court, filled with a bitterness and anger they never believed possible.

So many people are shocked that their marriages don't work out, but they shouldn't be. Have you ever talked to engaged people? Have you seen that glazed look in their eyes? Have you heard someone say with a straight face, "I don't see any weaknesses in my fiancé," and actually mean it?

Over and over, people like Phil and Susan come into my office. After the glow of the honeymoon or the first year of marriage begins to wear off, they start rubbing each other wrong. They offend each other. They hurt each other. And those offenses blindside them; they're not prepared for the conflict that inevitably enters their marriages.

In this chapter, I want to cover the first two stages of the loop. Inevitably, a conflict begins with some type of offense. It may be anything from a disagreement over which way to hang toilet paper (the wife grew up letting the paper come off the top; the husband's mother always had it emerging from the bottom) to a cruel comment about the other person's weight.

Sometimes offenses come out of nowhere, and you wish they would find their way back there. They jam, they sting, and other times they just plain overwhelm us.

A loved one who betrays you.

A parent who rejects you.

A colleague who mistreats you.

A neighbor who avoids you.

A friend who lets you down again.

A child who doesn't call.

A spouse who refuses to try again.

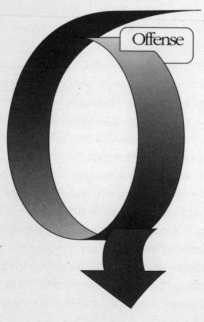

Offenses come in all shapes and sizes, but they all wound. Just as physical trauma penetrates our human skin, so relational offenses penetrate our emotional skin. In fact, the impact can be like sending a cannon-ball through the heart of an unsuspecting bystander.

One night, as I rolled over in bed, I noticed the hallway light was on. Barbara wasn't lying next to me, so I knew something was wrong. I knew she was hurt, but I didn't know it was "that bad." Earlier in the evening, we had experienced one of our own conflicts. While trying to resolve it, I had reached into my memory bank and pulled out a zinger, wounding the one I most love. Even with my training and experience in helping others, I sometimes blow it as well.

I ventured out of the coziness of the covers I had spent the last four hours warming up and went on the search. I found Barbara in the guest bedroom. Alone. Wounded. Self-protecting. It had been a long night for the one with whom I had exchanged wedding vows 16 years earlier. It was time for me to tune in and carry out that vow of "for better, for worse." This was not one of the fun times of marriage. Instead, it was a time when I needed to close my own loop. My selfish nature needed to give way to my role as helpmate. Mr. Potato Head wasn't good enough that night. Barbara needed a little of Dr. Welby.

The offense is usually a distinct event. If it's dealt with immediately, it may not have any lasting conse-quences. But in most cases, the person who was offended has time to think about it and stew over it. What develops is the emotion of hurt. Not anger or rage. Not bitterness and resentment. Those come later if the hurt is not dealt with.

Hurt acts as a barometer measuring our response to the threats of our world. Hurt is the emotion of vulnerability: It leaves us wide open, feeling as if our hearts have been yanked out, our tenderness shaken, and our equilibrium upset.

Sometimes we don't recognize the emotion right away. And when we do, many of us hide it. We don't tell others when they've hurt us; we don't want to appear vulnerable to them. So we submerge the emotion and act as if nothing happened.

This is where true fear can sink roots in the fertile soil of a wounded heart. We've all felt it in the past.

THE INEVITABILITY OF CONFLICT

I haven't said anything profound so far. Offenses and hurt are normal parts of marriage (or any other relationship). The problem is that too many couples don't realize this and, therefore, aren't prepared to handle them when they come.

Conflict is inevitable because any two people bring two distinct backgrounds and personalities into a relationship. As they adjust to each other, those differences can lead to all kinds of problems. Let's look at some of the common differences that lead to conflict—and therefore offenses—specifically in a marriage relationship.

FAMILY BACKGROUND

Decades ago, most people married others in the same small geographic area. Their socioeconomic backgrounds were similar, and their families probably knew each other. But one by-product of our increasingly mobile society is that men and women are moving away from home and meeting each other in other settings, like college. And their backgrounds may be totally different.

I'm not saying this is bad; it's just a fact of life. Let me describe one couple whose case is typical. Ron comes from the Pacific Northwest, Ann from the Southeast. They met in California as new employees of a large company.

Ron's father is a successful salesman whose income increased steadily as the years went by. The family wasn't rich by any means, but they were comfortable. They lived in a large suburban home, took nice vacations around the country, and were even able to keep up a vacation home on the coast.

Ann spent her first few years on a farm before her family moved to a large city. Her father worked in a factory; he didn't make a lot of money, but the family wasn't poor, either. They had what they needed—a home, enough food, and money in the bank to take care of future needs.

Ron had a secure home life. His parents loved each other and helped their children any way they could. His relatives seemed to have stable families as well.

Ann recalls that her childhood years were alternately secure and chaotic. Her parents loved Ann and her two sisters, but they fought a lot and had some rough years during Ann's early childhood. Somehow they never divorced, but they really never learned how to love and appreciate each other.

Ann's family always vacationed within 300 miles of their home. Some of her relatives lived in stable families, while others battled the typical problems of many families—divorce and alcohol.

The only time the two families met was at Ron and Ann's wedding. Today Ron and Ann live in the Midwest, and they feel as if their two families not only live on opposite coasts, but also in different worlds.

These differing backgrounds inevitably lead to some offenses and difficult decisions. Every year, for example, they're faced with a host of decisions about Christmas. Who should they give presents to? How much should they spend? They're on a limited income, so these are important choices. Ron's family spends more for Christmas gifts, and he often feels pressure to give equally expensive gifts in return. More than once, he has offended Ann by wanting to spend more on his parents than they spend on hers.

And where should they spend the holidays? Each one loves to "go home," but Christmas with their families is more difficult now with the pressures of long-distance travel and young children added to the picture. Ron declares that he doesn't like going to her home because "there's always too much chaos and cigarette smoke." Ann, on the other hand, feels Ron needs to learn to live with the situation, and she wonders how many more years she'll even have a chance to spend Christmas with her parents.

Ron and Ann are fortunate, because their faith and commitment to their relationship have smoothed over many conflicts. For some couples I counsel, decisions like these spark major offenses and terrible arguments that return year after year.

PERSONALITY DIFFERENCES

She's outgoing; he's an introvert. When they go to a party, she quickly starts talking with different groups of friends, while he scans the room desperately for one guy he can talk to. Her idea of recreation is talking to friends, while he likes curling up with a good book or watching a movie.

During courtship, many couples see personality differences as attractive. They see how their personalities complement each other. But sometimes those differences also grate on the nerves, especially after the wedding. The introvert wants to leave the party early and resents the extrovert's wanting to be the last person out the door. The perfectionist wonders why this laid-back slob of a husband can never pick up his shoes, while the slob wishes his wife would relax for once.

The more we understand how God made each of

us into a unique individual, the more we'll be able to appreciate our personality differences instead of wishing our spouses were more like us.

How do we learn to understand these differences? Numerous personality and temperament tests are available to help a couple understand each other. The one I use most often and recommend is the "Marriage Profile" developed by my friend Charles Boyd in conjunction with Performax International.[1] The best book I've seen on understanding personality differences and how they affect everyday life was written by two great encouragers to me, Gary Smalley and Dr. John Trent. It's called *The Two Sides of Love* and has been used widely to help couples and families get a clear handle on how to develop intimacy.[2] I use these two tools weekly, if not daily, in my own counseling practice to help others grow.

DIFFERING VALUES AND PHILOSOPHIES

As our society slides further and further from its original Judeo-Christian base, conflicts sparked by differing worldviews and philosophies become more common. Take the workplace, for example. Many businesspeople run into conflict with co-workers or partners who have no qualms about lying, cheating, or misleading customers to win accounts or increase sales. If people of integrity stand up for righteousness and honesty, they may be blasted for having a holier-than-thou attitude.

In marriage, differing values often arise in interfaith marriages—between, say, a Jew and a Roman Catholic. Should they attend services? Where? What do they teach the kids?

Even when both partners are committed Christians, differing values on some issues lead to offenses. Molly and Tom met and fell in love as college students involved with a Christian group on campus. They were certain their shared beliefs would give them a solid marriage, and they were right. But for two years, the choice of where to attend church was a source of real pain.

Molly grew up attending a small church. It was the only church she had ever known, and all her brothers and sisters continued attending even after they started families of their own. She loved her old pastor and the old hymns she had known all her life.

Tom, meanwhile, attended a large church that featured nontraditional worship. He preferred more-contemporary songs and a relaxed atmosphere. When he attended Molly's church, he felt stifled by the traditional service and thought the people needed to "loosen up and enjoy themselves for once."

When they married, Tom felt Molly should go to his church and was hurt when she said she didn't feel comfortable there. She, in turn, was hurt that Tom didn't see the need to keep up her family legacy at her church. Eventually, their arguments moved beyond the location of worship and touched on areas such as marriage roles ("Shouldn't Molly follow me to my church?") and sincerity of commitment ("Those people at Tom's church care more about raising their hands than they do about evangelism").

MALE-FEMALE DIFFERENCES

A discussion about differences between men and women often focuses on the cause of such differences—is it "nature" or "nurture"? For the purpose of this book, however, the cause is not as important as the fact that differences do exist. Dr. James Dobson discusses male-female differences in his book *Straight Talk*:

> Anyone who doubts that males and females are unique should observe how they approach a game of Ping-Pong or Monopoly or dominoes or horseshoes or volleyball or tennis. Women often use the event as an excuse for fellowship and pleasant conversation. For men, the name of the game is conquest. Even if the setting is a friendly social gathering

in the host's backyard, the beads of sweat on each man's forehead reveal his passion to win. This aggressive competitiveness has been attributed to cultural influences. I don't believe it. As Richard Restak said, "At a birthday party for five-year-olds, it's not usually the girls who pull hair, throw punches, or smear each other with food." [3]

Men and women differ in many areas, but I'll mention just one that commonly leads to offense and hurt: sexuality. Men are easily aroused by sight. We are also more quickly aroused than our wives. Women need more touching, caring, and relating.

This one difference has complicated lovemaking throughout history. I wonder how many men have bruised their wives by rushing through sex? How many women have developed hardened and bitter hearts? How many mothers and aunts have told young brides-to-be, "You won't enjoy it, but that's normal. Sex is really more for the man anyway."

Smalley and Trent write in their book *Love Is a Decision*: "To most women, sex is much more than just an independent physical act. It's the culmination of a day filled with security, conversation, emotional and romantic experiences, and then, if all is right, sex. For the average man, you can reverse the order—or just

44

skip everything that comes before sex!"[4]

I'm not real proud of our gender here, men, but it's true. To enjoy the physical relationship with our wives, we need to meet their needs as women. When there is conflict in the relationship and we then desire sexual intimacy, we're out of sync with women's feelings.

One man told me how he experienced this difference between men and women one summer day. He cut the lawn, paid some bills, had a disagreement with his wife, ate a burrito, and then suggested he and his wife be sexually active that night. As he told me his story, he looked puzzled. He then asked, "What's the problem with that, Gary?"

"Everything, to the typical woman," I responded. "What did she say?"

"I couldn't believe it. She said, 'You want to do *what* after what happened today? Now that we're talking about it, let's discuss what happened three weeks ago.'

"Three weeks ago? I can't remember what happened two hours ago," this typical male responded.

Men and women are different. What's the implication for sexual intimacy and conflict? Quite simply this: Before two bodies touch, two hearts need to touch. If there is conflict between a husband and wife, the conflict needs to be resolved before both parties can enjoy sexual intimacy.

THE WRONG TRAINING

Offenses and hurt—the first two stages of opening the loop—are inevitable in marriage. The question is, what steps do we take to resolve the problem and restore the relationship in love?

My experience is that a surprisingly large number of people have no idea how to resolve the conflict in their relationships. As I'll explain in the next two chapters, they've been listening to the wrong voices all their lives.

CHAPTER 4

HAVE YOU EVER HEARD VOICES?

I s this heaven?"
"No, this is Iowa."

That's a classic line from *Field of Dreams*, a movie filmed in my home state of Iowa. In the picture, a farmer named Ray Kinsella, played by Kevin Costner, is walking through his corn crop when he hears a voice saying, "If you build it, he will come." Ray has never heard voices before, and he thinks it's time to call a counselor.

Eventually he figures out that if he builds a baseball diamond in the middle of his cornfield, the famed Shoeless Joe Jackson of the infamous Chicago "Black Sox" of 1919 will appear. Well, build it he does, and sure enough, Shoeless Joe comes. Joe even brings other players, and Ray continues to hear voices throughout the movie, leading him on a number of adventures.

The point is that Ray heard a voice and followed its message. And I believe you and I hear from a number of voices as well. I don't mean the kind that come from talking ears of corn, but the kind that speak out to us from our culture and family upbringing.

Sometimes these messages are loud and blatant, like a strong midwestern storm. Other times, they're subtle and persuasive, like summer breezes. Either way, they do speak to us and influence us in ways we rarely recognize.

Many people wonder why they have such a difficult time resolving conflict. The reasons are that they've never been taught how to do it right, and they've never seen it done right. All their lives they've heard voices giving them all kinds of information and strategies for relating to others and resolving conflict. And they're dismayed to find that much of it doesn't work.

VOICES FROM OUR CULTURE

Have you ever been confused by too much advice? Perhaps you were driving in a city you had never been in before, and you got lost. You pulled up to a gas station, approached the attendant for directions, and he, along with three customers, began to give you confusing instructions for how to get to your destination. Voices.

Or maybe you were in the midst of an important career decision that involved moving to a new city. You asked for feedback from friends and family, and you were hit by a barrage of opinions:

"You need to stay here and give your kids a stable home."

"It may be a good time to look for a fresh start."

"Wouldn't that be a big risk for your career?"

"You won't get ahead unless you're willing to take risks. Maybe now is the time."

"These are bad times with the economy. Do you think you can afford such a move?"

"You can't afford not to make this move."

More voices.

When I close my eyes and try to remember the first time I was really confused, I recall the third grade. We were learning how to tell time, and this was before the days of digital clocks, so you had to learn it the old-fashioned way.

One morning we had a test. Our teacher, Mrs. Bowman, handed out a mimeographed sheet, hot off the presses with that odor that only a child of the fifties and sixties can remember. On the sheet were eight clock faces, and under each was written a time of day. It was our mission, whether we chose to accept it or not, to draw the two hands of a clock on the face, indicating the time described.

As soon as we finished the test, we could go outside for recess. I remember Larry and Eddie finishing in about 1.3 minutes. "Simple!" chirped Larry as he turned in his paper.

"What a breeze," said Eddie.

I remember Jill counting on her fingers. I recall Johnny looking up at the clock on the wall and pointing to the hands on the clock, calculating something in his mind. Each child in the class had determined his or her own way of answering the test.

One by one, the kids whipped off the assignment, walked up to Mrs. Bowman's desk to turn in their test, and headed outside to the jungle gym. Everyone but me. I was confused. The longer I sat and looked at the sheet, the more I clutched. It's my first memory of anxiety—I sweat, shook, and thought I would throw up all over my desk.

Every 5 seconds I looked up at Mrs. Bowman, who glanced from me to the clock, eager to escape the classroom herself. After about 15 minutes, finally admitting failure, I quietly turned in my test and walked outside. What did I feel? Confusion, embarrassment, humiliation. You see, I knew the assignment; I was just confused about how to complete it.

Whether you realize it or not, you've been hearing different voices all your life, giving you direction on how to resolve conflict. From television, magazines, movies, friends, and many other sources, you hear a myriad of ways to deal with conflict. And chances are that few of those voices gave you sound, biblical guidance.

VOICES FROM THE PUBLISHING WORLD

On a recent Saturday morning, I asked Barbara to accompany me to a bookstore to purchase some popular magazines. I wanted to see what the latest word was from the world of pop psychology on how to resolve conflict. I was in a good mood as we headed into the store. But in the next 30 minutes, as I browsed through 15 to 20 titles and tables of contents, I found myself beginning to get a little bit ticked. Here are some of the article titles: "Why I Date Your Husband"; "Sleeping with the Enemy: How to Fight with the Man You Love"; "Salvaging the Troubled Relationship: When It Is Up to You"; and "Good Girls, Bad Girls."

I spent a few days reading through those magazines, and I didn't like what I found. In her *Mademoiselle* article "Sleeping with the Enemy," Kim France wrote,

> It's not a party until someone breaks a glass, and it's not a relationship until you have a fight. In fact, the occasional

lovers' brawl is an essential part of a successful romance. It's healthy. It's emotionally cleansing. Besides which, did you really think you could have all that steady sex at no cost? Of course not— you play, you pay.[1]

How about *Cosmopolitan*? In "Salvaging the Troubled Relationship," Sue Bowders wrote, "For many, the only choice is to start afresh with a more liberated male. But according to experts, you do have the power to bring a stubborn man to the negotiating table."[2]

She then went on to recommend these conflict resolution strategies: "Overcome urges to play 'good girl.' (If you're already what insecure men call a bitch, great. If you're not, you need to reform)."[3] Her other recommendations? "Earn and control your own money, make an unexpected sexual request, dress sexy—for you, carve out your own space, and develop your own quirks."[4]

From Peter Gerstenzang's article "Good Ways to Say Bad Things" in *Cosmopolitan*, we get this volley of insults between Chloe and Peter:

"You know, Chloe," I said, "I've always really loved the way you treat people. You're about as kind and considerate as

Lady Macbeth on a 'good' day."

Chloe said nothing, but her eyes were as wide and heartbreaking as Bambi's. Dinner was served. Then it was "her" turn.

"There's something I've been meaning to tell you, Peter," she said. "The way you stuff your mouth with food compares favorably to a prisoner who's just been released from Devil's Island."[5]

I had enough! If you're like me, your first inclination would be to throw the magazines down. But I kept reading, and it got worse. Magazine after magazine and book after book, we're sold a hedonistic, self-oriented approach to life:

"Look out for number one."

"If there's a problem, walk away from the relationship."

"If the relationship you're in isn't satisfying, get out and find another one."

"There are no moral rights or wrongs. You need to decide what's right for you."

These are powerful, convincing weapons of propaganda. And these are the very sources that millions of men and women use as their guidelines for dealing with life's hurts and conflicts. Message upon message penetrates a person's mind, planting weeds that grow and entangle us so that we can't decide who is right and who is wrong.

The influence of magazines, however, is nothing compared to that of television.

VOICES FROM THE TUBE

I grew up watching "Howdy Doody" and "I Love Lucy." I laughed at "Get Smart" and put my six-guns on to watch "Bonanza."

My generation was the first to hang around the black and white RCA and then move up to the color version. You know you've been around a while when you can remember the wonder of your family's getting its first color television set.

There's another fact about my generation, the baby boomers, that is pretty sobering: We are divorcing each other at a higher rate than any previous generation in American history. Take a look at what happened to our divorce rates:

U.S. DIVORCE RATES, 1960-80[6]

Year	Divorces	Rate per 1,000 population, married women over 15 years old
1960	393,000	9.2
1965	479,000	10.6
1970	708,000	14.9
1975	1,036,000	20.3
1980	1,189,000	22.6

What do these figures mean? Consider that in 1960, the earliest baby boomers were 14 years old, too young to marry. So the 393,000 divorces that year involved the parents of baby boomers. But during the next 20 years, as baby boomers reached their late teens and then their 20s and 30s, the divorce rate skyrocketed. It began stabilizing in the 1980s, but it still remains far higher than it was for previous generations.

I'm sure many factors led to this incredible rise in the divorce rate. But I ask myself, "What made this generation so different? Why did the change occur so fast and so clearly with one group of people? Why do baby boomers have so many more problems in resolving conflict and committing themselves to their mates?" I can't help but think that television may be one of the biggest culprits.

Studies document the large number of hours children spend in front of the television. The shows and commercials they absorb play a huge part in their upbringing—perhaps as big a part as their parents and teachers. And when the messages emanating from the tube—hour by hour, day by day, year by year—all give them the wrong messages about how to relate to other people and resolve conflict, is it any wonder they reach adulthood with big gaps in their emotional and social skills?

To get a firsthand picture of what television tells its viewers, I decided to devote one day—December

9, 1991—to watching the tube. I wanted to view some of the ways television portrays interpersonal relationships and conflict resolution. I also wanted to see how watching TV influences our perception of everyday life. I started at 6:20 A.M. and had finally had enough at about 10:00 P.M.

The morning has an array of news shows, so that sounded like a good place to start. Do you think any conflict is reported in the news?

6:20 A.M. Charles Osgood, on "The CBS Morning News," reported that the Israeli negotiators showed up five weeks late in Washington, D.C., for the Mideast peace talks. Why? They were miffed that the United States didn't give them enough of a say-so on the time of the meeting. The Israelis and Arabs hoped to start negotiating the next day. But now a new conflict was started regarding whether they would meet in one room or two. Sounds just like home, doesn't it?

9:00 A.M. "The Phil Donahue Show" featured women who were sexually harassed by landlords. The program included women raped by landlords, women threatened with eviction if they reported the harassment, and university students who were sexually abused. More conflict and more voices about how to respond. The audience suggested strategies ranging from suing the landlords and universities to "getting a man to protect you."

12:30 P.M. On "Days of Our Lives," Carlie wanted to marry Bo, but she was still married to Victor, so she was trying to get the marriage annulled. But Victor was not a happy camper, so he decided to deal with his conflict by hiring someone to rig an elevator cable to break, sending Bo to his death. That's definitely one way to resolve conflict. The only problem was that Carlie was on the elevator instead. Oh, by the way, Bo is Victor's son. Bottom line on this one was that Victor said he would do anything to keep Bo from Carlie.

1:30 P.M. "Another World" gave us more misguided love, jealousy, and hatred, ending with a knock-down-drag-out fight between two women who were supposed to be trying on wedding dresses.

Enough? Well, the day wasn't over yet.

3:00 P.M. "Sally Jessy Raphael" featured Nola and Ron, who were in the county jail. Why? Put your seat belt on: Ron was charged with raping Nola's 11-year-old daughter—with Nola's permission. Why did she give permission? So that her daughter could carry Ron's child because Nola couldn't have any more children. The daughter bore a child at age 12.

4:00 P.M. "The Oprah Winfrey Show" dealt with jealousy and how it affects relationships. Oprah covered the gamut from workaholic husbands and husbands who were jealous of medical personnel in the labor and delivery room to men who were jealous of their hairdresser wives' running their fingers through other men's hair.

There was a report of a man calling his wife ten times in five minutes to check up on her.

Not to be outdone by their daytime warm-ups, the evening situation comedies also spoke loudly to our culture about conflict.

7:00 P.M. On "Evening Shade," Miss Ava, the prosecuting attorney, had her father's stripper girlfriend arrested for doing her act in their small Arkansas town. The townsfolk all responded differently, and Miss Ava was questioned by her dad about her motives: Was she really having the woman arrested because it was a criminal issue, or was it because she disapproved of her dad's dating a stripper?

8:00 P.M. "Murphy Brown" teaches the put-down method of resolving conflict. Opening line: When the pregnant Murphy walked into the TV studio where she works, she declared, "The nerve of some people! The parking attendant said my face is getting fat. Jim, what do you think?"

"Ask Frank, Murphy. I'll have a better answer after that," said Jim sheepishly.

When Frank agreed with the parking attendant, Murphy retorted, "Great! Next thing you know, I'll be booked as an act at Sea World."

The beat goes on and on and on.

Let's say you just spent a day tuned in to the tube as I did. You watched show after show, drinking up (both consciously and subconsciously) the messages from all those programs. Then, at 10:30 P.M., when a conflict rears its ugly head between you and your spouse, what do you rely on? Do you handle it like Murphy Brown earlier in the night—with put-downs and wisecracks? Do you hire a hit man (or at least think about doing it)? Do you sleep with your spouse's best friend to gain revenge or to soothe your emotions?

Chances are that your children are being even more profoundly influenced by what they see on television. Sandy Rovner of the *Washington Post* recently wrote about complaints from a mental health group over how anger was handled in soap operas:

> They're the kind of scenes that are staples of daytime soap operas. Travis is furious with Erica because she is still involved in her ex-husband's life; Gina is angry because the rich Capwells can give her son Brandon more than she can; Bianca is ticked because Courtney keeps answering for her before she can get a word in edgewise.
>
> Granted, these aren't real people in real situations, but for millions of Americans—some 20 million a day, of whom 14 million are women—these soap families provide models of ways to deal with anger and other emotions.[7]

The article goes on to describe how two students at Cornell University spent a summer watching "Santa Barbara," "All My Children," and "As the World Turns," among others. They monitored who got angry, why, at whom, and how the anger was resolved. They found that incidents portraying an angry person as a hero rose from 69 percent of the time to 82 percent of the time over the course of the summer.

Some studies have shown that television shows provide role models for young people. Not long ago, the Brown University *Family Therapy Letter* described an Australian study that found 50 percent to 75 percent of Australian children said their ideal role models were media figures rather than their parents.

In the study, published in the *Australian Journal of Psychology*, 313 children in the fifth to ninth grades were surveyed. More than 75 percent of the boys, 63 percent of the older girls, and 45 percent of the younger ones chose media figures as role models. The authors noted that in a 1956 study, before many Australians had television sets, parents and surrogate parents were chosen as the people the children most wanted to emulate.[8]

One more thing struck me during the day I watched television: God was never in the picture. I suppose I shouldn't have been surprised. There were shows portraying problems of adultery, murder, rape, sex with a minor, international kidnapping, arrests, wisecracks, and insults. But not once did I hear any mention of a biblical and healthy response to the pain of the human heart.

Now multiply the power of the voice of one day of the tube by thousands of hours of exposure and you can see why it is critically important that we learn biblical approaches to challenging the drowning messages of a culture dying before our eyes.

VOICES FROM OUR FRIENDS

"I wouldn't put up with that. Why don't you get out?"

"You deserve better than her. My old lady would be out on the street."

"I'm worried about you. Why don't you leave him? It would be better for all involved. You know, sometimes things just don't work out. It's not your fault."

Have you ever noticed that when you have a conflict with someone and it's hard to talk with the person, you often find someone else to talk to instead? It's natural. We all need to vent our feelings, talk about our frustrations, get advice. That's what friends and family are for.

The problem is that many of these people have

grown up hearing the same voices as you. They may have failed at relationships as well. Since they care about you, these well-intentioned friends will jump to the punch lines of self-protection: "Leave." "Fight back." "Call an attorney." "What about your pride?" "When I was a kid . . ."

These are the voices of people who, many times, are continuing to work through the pain in their own relationships. Often they'll unknowingly push issues onto you that they haven't dealt with themselves. As a result, when you're hurting, chances are that your friends will give you one of two messages: "Get out" or "Don't let him [or her] do that to you."

"Get out." Simple and clean. And when those two words are uttered, it can send a chill of fear and insecurity down the spine of the best of us. "Get out." It sounds so decisive and easy—if you leave, you don't have to feel the pain anymore.

Leaving may stop one kind of pain, but here's the hitch: Avoiding conflict leads to the death of a relationship. And the death of a relationship usually hurts far, far more than working through the conflict. Some of us have many bodies in the paths behind us as a result of listening to the voices that tell us to get out.

"Don't let him do that to you." That's the voice of protection. This type of soured perspective is often favored by people who have been worn down by offense after offense throughout their lives. Their advice is to get back at the person who hurt you. Revenge. An eye for an eye.

It can range from back stabbing and gossip to hiring a hit man. It occurs in our offices, church hallways, and family rooms. Parents fight back with each other; bosses, employees, and friends let each other have it. When an offense occurs, we often "put up our dukes" and get ready to defend our positions.

VOICES FROM SECULAR COUNSELING

I spent about ten years in college. In fact, I'm still paying off my college loans at the rate of $67.01 per month. I earned an undergraduate and two graduate degrees. I also taught college classes part-time for five years. So the college scene isn't alien to me.

In my doctorate program, I was trained in "humanistic counseling." I was taught that humankind is basically good, and that if a counselor provides a positive orientation for change, people will seek the good in themselves and become the best they can be.

I am deeply concerned about the impact my training had on me. Why? Because it's seductive. As I often say, the further I get from my training, the better off I believe I am. Is this because my professors were bad people or educators? No, neither could be further from the truth. They were excellent. There's a more fundamental reason.

The problem is that secular counseling discourages the client and therapist from centering on the very source of change that can ultimately free us: Jesus Christ. To conduct therapy without God and the Bible is like jumping on a trampoline without a spotter. Nobody is there to catch you.

Counselors all over the world provide therapy from a secular perspective. They've been taught that people only need to look inside themselves and rely on their innate goodness to solve their problems. And if that doesn't work, they just need to alter behavior to bring about positive change. The idea that people were created to have a relationship with a living God is seen as part of the pathology, or illness, that a person needs to be freed from rather than the very answer to our deepest needs.

Can Christians benefit from counseling with a non-Christian? Sure, in some cases, as long as they realize they may be fundamentally opposed to the counselor's entire frame of reference. If that's the case, they need to filter the "voice" of the counselor through their belief system.

But the problem doesn't rest only with the voice of the non-Christian counselor. It also rests with many Christian counselors. Why? Because often when they purport to conduct counseling from a Christian perspective, there's actually little emphasis on a biblical or spiritual orientation.

Some of the methods for resolving conflict taught by secular counselors are good; some are not. One ingredient that's often missing is forgiveness. As you'll read later in this book, forgiveness is a key step in resolving conflict from a biblical perspective. Yet this step is often ignored altogether in the secular world.

VOICES FROM THE CHURCH

Another voice that concerns me is the voice of the church. Sometimes it may also send out information contrary to the teaching of the Bible. And since this voice carries the weight of authority, many people assume it's always correct.

Take, for example, the issue of headship and submission. Many Christians, especially men, point to Paul's teaching in the book of Ephesians to support their view that men should dominate their wives, and that wives should submit to their decisions in any conflict or difference of opinion.

I hear many men quoting the verses about submission, but few mention the verses that come next:

> Husbands, love your wives, just as Christ
> loved the church and gave himself up

for her to make her holy, cleansing her by the washing with water through the word, and to present her to himself as a radiant church, without stain or wrinkle or any other blemish, but holy and blameless. In this same way, husbands ought to love their wives as their own bodies. He who loves his wife loves himself. After all, no one ever hated his own body, but he feeds and cares for it, just as Christ does the church—for we are members of his body. [9]

My friend Robert Lewis describes the difference between a "lording leader" and a "servant leader" in his book *Rocking the Roles*:

The lording leader loves to give orders. He's the boss. He has to have control. He makes all the decisions; everyone else just carries out his directives. If anyone questions his decisions, he silences them with another string of commands. That's because he's not interested in questions, suggestions, or better ideas. He's only interested in action, in getting things done his way. . . .

The lording leader becomes defensive when his wife challenges him with her own thoughts and view. He views everything from a win/lose perspective. He can't stand to be wrong and let his wife be right. He certainly can't admit to her when he's wrong. So he browbeats her into going along with him, and manipulates her into granting his wishes.[10]

I've seen many marriages damaged by husbands who used their role as the head of the home to club their wives with their control. This not only can cause long-term bitterness and damage to the relationship, but it also can harm the woman's relationship to God.

A NEW VOICE

Let me add one final voice to the chorus, a voice I wish I heard more: "Close the loop. Choose to heal the relationship."

Resolve the conflict. Face the fear, and slay the dragon rather than feeding it to the point where it overwhelms you. That's the type of advice I wish friends gave each other more often. It's good to get the advice of friends and counselors as long as that advice is wise. The Bible says to seek counsel from many.[11] But we need to be certain the voices are mature and wise, helping us to restore relationships, not voices that are confusing their own unresolved issues with ours.

Each of the voices from our culture is persuasive. We're shaped by the media all day long, often without our realizing the impact. And where the media drop off, the voices of our friends pick up. Our culture tells us to conquer, to manipulate, or to walk. And just when those voices tend to quiet, the small voices from our past, our families, tend to pick up. In the next chapter, I'll look at the profound and long-lasting influence of those voices from within our families.

CHAPTER 5

VOICES FROM OUR FAMILIES

For many of us, home is where the heart is. When I think of my family, I remember holiday dinners, storytelling, parents who talked to each other and even listened, and basketball games in the backyard. I remember school pictures, weekends at the lake, a snoring dad, and a mom who greeted me when I came in the door. I remember a dad who sometimes asked hard questions to help shape my character, brothers who made me crazy, and a sister whom I teased unmercifully but loved devotedly.

Those are just a few of my memories, which all seem fresh after celebrating my parents' fiftieth wedding anniversary recently. As my parents discussed how they wanted to celebrate their golden anniversary, the options ranged from a megaparty to an open house to a family vacation. But my folks, in typical fashion, resisted the pressure from friends to have a blowout celebration and chose to spend the time with just their family. They spent a year planning a celebration for their four kids, spouses, and grandchildren. Their family that began with just 2 people is now up to 18. Home really is where my heart is.

Unfortunately, many other people do not share my sentiments. For them, the very mention of the words *family* or *parents* stimulates other kinds of memories—of absence, of loss, of pain. Many people work all day long to block out memories of their homes in order to cope with the pain in their hearts.

During my years as a counselor, I've come to appreciate the incredible power parents have to mold the lives of their children. Whether you realize it or not, many of the patterns of your life—the decisions you make, the way you react to certain situations, the way you relate to others, your unconscious needs and drives—were shaped by your parents, your parents' parents, and so on. We tend to pass the legacy from generation to generation.

Many of us recognize this in others. We see how they're repeating behavior patterns, both good and bad, that they learned from their parents: the woman who repeats the perfectionism about housework that she once hated in her mother. The man who finds solace in alcohol, just as his father did. The boy who tries to win the approval of a father who never seemed satisfied with even the greatest accomplishments, and who then grows up to place the same unrealistic demands on his own children.

Sadly, many people fail to notice the same types of inherited problems in themselves. It's not until they end up in a counselor's office, trying to sort out the messes of their marriages, that they're willing to take a hard look at themselves to discern why they act as they do.

Someone asked me recently, "Out of all the married couples you counsel because of the difficulties they're having in resolving conflict, how many need to understand and deal with the patterns they learned during childhood?" The answer is more than 90 percent. No matter what kind of home you grew up in, chances are you're bringing something unhealthy into your marriage—that's how powerful sin is. And when you put two people together from difficult backgrounds, chances are that a crucial element in helping them learn to resolve conflict is understanding where they've come from and then unlearning certain patterns of behavior.

The Gospels show how Jesus utilized a teaching tool that blended word pictures with God's truth. He called them parables. In one of His most memorable, He spoke about land, seeds, and different types of soil:

> A farmer went out to sow his seed. As he was scattering the seed, some fell along the path, and the birds came and ate it up. Some fell on rocky places, where it did not have much soil. It sprang up quickly, because the soil was shallow. But when the sun came up, the plants were scorched, and they withered because they had no root. Other seed fell among thorns, which grew up and choked the plants. Still other seed fell on good soil, where it produced a crop—a hundred, sixty or thirty times what was sown. He who has ears, let him hear. [1]

Jesus used that story to illustrate the different kinds of human hearts. But I think the soils also portray different types of homes. Take a look around you. What we see in our culture are countless homes that have been abused and stripped of the nutrients that aid a child's healthy growth.

The crux of this first parable was not the seed. It signified the good news of the gospel, and it was all the same seed. The message never changed. Instead, the focus was on the ground where the seed fell. The ground was indeed different. Families can also be different, like the ground that receives the seed.

Let's review four types of families.

THE "GOOD" FAMILY

"As he was scattering the seed, some fell along the path, and the birds came and ate it up."[2]

Have you ever said about a neighbor, "Oh, the Andersons are such good people! They're an impressive couple, and they have a lovely family. Everyone likes them."

We all have neighbors like the Andersons, don't we? They're nice people. They make a good living and keep their lawns mowed and trimmed. They're also well-intentioned and loving parents.

There's only one thing they miss: a personal relationship with Jesus. These are people who may have heard the message of the gospel but have never let it penetrate the soil of their hearts. Some may even attend church and be highly moral people.

But they either don't recognize their need for a relationship with Jesus (because the voices of our world are drowning out the truth), or they hear it and don't care. They turn a deaf ear to the truth and decide to just live their lives for themselves, casting off "religious stuff" as either an encumbrance from their parents' generation or as hype from a bunch of "religious nuts." This is perhaps the most difficult home of all to understand, because the family members may not realize how needy they are.

Increasingly, the Andersons of our culture fail to set adequate boundaries for their children. (Many Christian parents fall short in this area as well.) They're the ones in restaurants who think Jenny is so cute as she throws food all over any patrons within 20 feet. Often insecure themselves, they may overreact to their own parents' "authoritarian" parenting style and swing to the other extreme, withholding discipline altogether.

How do they deal with conflict? They teach and model what appears to be a healthy strategy: Fight fair, negotiate, and compromise. It sounds good until you look at the base of their philosophy. The Andersons operate according to the popular "50-50 plan" in marriage,[3] the "You do your part and I'll do mine" philosophy.

Relationships become a matter of trade-offs and compromises, with people keeping score so one person never gets more than the other. The goal is to meet each other halfway. The only problem, as Dennis Rainey writes in his book *Lonely Husbands, Lonely Wives*, is that "it is impossible to determine if your mate has met you halfway. Because neither of you can agree on where 'halfway' is, each is left to scrutinize the other's performance from his or her own jaded perspective."[4]

There's a lack of serving and submitting to each other in the Anderson home. In its place is a strong emphasis on getting what is rightfully yours. Yet someone is missing—a Person who lives in the middle of Mom and Dad, who is deferred to. I don't mean the children, which in most homes appears to be the case. I mean a relationship with Jesus Christ, a union with a God who loves us and gives us direction through the Bible.

As the kids go from childhood to adolescence in this good home, they tend to either "do their own thing" in rebellion or jump through the right hoops to please their parents. Either way, the Anderson kids tend to grow up to be me-oriented adults. When they leave their parents' homes and go into adult relationships, they bring along the same value set they grew up with, the "I am number one" mentality.

Bad people? No, not really. In fact, many people who grew up in good homes are very generous. They participate in activities to help others, and they love their families. But there's a lack of a deep understanding of who God is. The seed that falls here really does get scattered along the path. No fertile soil is in sight.

THE "RELIGIOUS" FAMILY

"Some fell on rocky places, where it did not have much soil. It sprang up quickly, because the soil was shallow. But when the sun came up, the plants were scorched, and they withered because they had no root." [5]

The Armstrongs live down the street from the Andersons. In many ways they appear to resemble their neighbors, at least from the outside. But they offer a different twist: They're religious. In the Armstrong family, the word falls on "rocky places." The parents may have received Christ because they saw their need for a Savior. Or they may never have heard about a personal relationship with God. Because their hearts are not fertile, they miss the vibrancy and hope of a relationship between sinful humanity and a loving God.

The religious home is shallow and without root. Christianity is a set of rules, a code to live by. Parents like this remind me of the Pharisees in the New Testament. They were religious people who professed to know the truth about God. Yet Jesus challenged them, recognizing their zeal was superficial.

Because of their emphasis on rules, the Armstrongs live a life of rigidity. They never miss a Sunday morning, Sunday evening, or Wednesday evening church service. At home, they live by a rigid structure of roles. Dad runs the family with an iron fist, demanding submission from his wife and children.

Conflicts are either avoided out of fear or "settled" quickly as wives and children fall into line. The kids are expected to act like adults, even if they're only three years old. The authoritarian parents are harsh and demanding.

The children appear to be obedient, yet often their spirits are broken, and they lose their zeal for life. Or they comply behaviorally, but underneath the surface they're in full-blown rebellion.

The common line in a religious home is "Do what you're told." The Bible is used as a club. Wives are not allowed to question a decision by their husbands, because then they wouldn't be "submissive." Children cannot question any order because the Bible says they are to obey their parents.

In his book *Toxic Faith*, Steve Arterburn described one of the reasons children grow up with unhealthy perceptions of God and the church. He called it *toxic faith*, which he defined as "a destructive and dangerous relationship with a religion that allows the religion, not the relationship with God, to control a person's life." He continued by saying, "The toxic faithful find a replacement for God. How they look becomes more important than who God is. Acts of religion replace steps of growth. A facade is substituted for a heart longing to know God. The facade forms a barrier between the believer and God, leaving the believer to survive with a destructive addiction to religion."[6]

What would the Armstrong children's perception of God be? Typically they would see Him as waiting in the wings to catch them doing something bad so He could punish them. How would they see Dad? As the czar of the family, fully in charge and never to be questioned. How about Mom? She would be seen as the compliant, passive woman who keeps quiet so she won't rock the boat.

What's the implication for these children? They are typically starved, but not for food—they may be well fed and clothed. They're starved for genuine love and affection. They tend to be confused, because they see other kids around them being affectionately cared for by parents who allow their children to mess up. Mistakes are tolerated by parents of the kids they play with. Laughter comes easily. Not so in the religious home. These kids have holes in their souls that they will try to fill with anything from compulsive behaviors to alcohol and sex.

What happens to these children as adults? They tend to develop one of three types of family structures in their own marriages. One option is that they become overly compliant. They perpetuate the legalistic perspectives of their own parents, "doing the right things" because they're supposed to. They remain blind to the pain they experienced and convey the problems of their childhood families into the next generation.

The second option is that they may become overtly rebellious, doing anything they can to stay away from church and its influence. These adults have difficulty separating their experiences within rigid homes from the truth of a relationship with God. The mere mention of God may trigger an angry response because of the pain they feel. They may act up, trying to fulfill their deep needs for acceptance and love.

The third option is that they will live passive spiritual lives—neither hot nor cold but lukewarm.[7] They adopt an indifference to spiritual matters that erodes the foundation of the family. They may simply live life on spiritual automatic pilot.

Is there hope for those who have been raised in the rigidity of a legalistic home? Definitely. These people can develop a healthy relationship with God that is free from the punitive perspectives they experienced as children. They can learn that a balanced and healthy faith focuses on the God of the Bible, not on a distortion that others have constructed by putting God in a box and limiting Him to a bunch of rules.

THE "WOUNDED" FAMILY

"Other seed fell among thorns, which grew up and choked the plants."[8]

Thorns. Sharp, piercing, blood-drawing thorns. How many tiny seeds of faith and love have been planted in families, only to be choked by hard parental thorns? This happens when parents live out their own pain by controlling, abusing, or abandoning their children.

I call people in this third group the "walking wounded." They were hurt by growing up in homes with serious problems. This is a popular topic today; each week, you can find an article or television show discussing the most common types of abuse—alcohol and drug abuse, emotional and physical abuse, sexual abuse. Abuses like these leave terrible scars. Kids grow up never quite feeling accepted and loved the way God intended for them to be.

Others are wounded in less obvious ways. Some were raised by parents who didn't express love and nurturing—busy or aloof parents who were so occupied nursing or avoiding the scars of their own childhoods that they ignored their children. And some still deal with the loss of a parent through death or divorce.

"It's just the way it is, Dr. Rosberg," said Megan. She was a 32-year-old woman, frustrated and scared, who came in for help with the profound problems she and her husband, Ben, were experiencing.

Whenever Megan and Ben began to argue, Ben would get angry, and Megan would leave the room. She seemed to withdraw by instinct, and she had trouble getting a handle on why. She would run to her bedroom, telling Ben by the slam of her door that she needed some time. But Ben usually wanted to resolve the issue, and he wanted to do it right then. Sound familiar? The more she pulled away, the more he demanded they "fix it."

After several minutes of describing the situation, Megan commented, "It's just the way it is." And then, after a brief moment of silence, "No, it's just the way it was."

With that statement, Megan hit the proverbial nail on the head. She realized she was acting just like her mom.

Megan's father was an alcoholic who was subject to violent mood swings. When he and his wife argued, he would become angry, swear at her, and sometimes strike her. Over time, Megan's mother learned that the best way to avoid violence was to let him have his way. She would withdraw and do whatever she could to please him.

Megan had a powerful teacher on how to act when a husband gets angry—her own mother. She was following in the very footsteps she thought she would never emulate. She wanted more than anything to do it differently, but she was repeating the same pattern that wounded her own family.

To many of you, Megan's description rings clear as a bell. You've been there, and you're likely to go home and repeat a similar pattern tonight. You may be caught in a cycle of blowups that you never seem able to resolve. And when you fail to handle your conflicts in a healthy way, you feel guilty and hopeless.

That's the hard news. Now here's the good news: One of the nice things about learning how to resolve conflict is that even when we blow it, there will invariably be another chance later—this week if not this hour—to try again. It's never too late to learn effective ways to deal with the conflicts in our relationships.

THE "BIBLICAL" FAMILY

"Still other seed fell on good soil, where it produced a crop—a hundred, sixty or thirty times what was sown."[9]

The Blakes represent the biblical home. They live on the same street as Megan and Ben, the Armstrongs, and the Andersons. What makes them different? They have problems just like the other three families. Not only have they heard the truth, however, but it also has taken root in their hearts.

The Blakes have chosen to seek God in a way that is woven into the fabric of their family—not just on Wednesday night and Sunday, but throughout each day. They struggle with bills, pressures, and conflicts, but rather than let the conflicts drive a wedge between them, they use them as a force to drive them together. Their home is fertile soil. Mom and Dad work together to develop their home as a training ground, cultivating the soil, conserving it.

The Blakes had an old-fashioned conflict time during dinner one evening. Does it sound familiar? It did to me.

"Erin, you eat like such a pig. Look at the way you're eating your spaghetti."

"Dad, did you hear what Rachel called me? She called me a pig! I don't want anything to do with any of you." As the last words left Erin's tomato-sauce-covered lips, she stomped into the family room to finish her dinner.

"Come on, Rachel. Why did you say that? A nice, reasonably quiet dinner was just spoiled," said Father Blake. "You know Erin is sensitive about comments like that. Why in the world would you say such a thing?"

"Dad, didn't you see her slopping her spaghetti? Her head was almost in her plate! I think the way she eats is gross," retorted Rachel.

When Erin's parents approached the family room, it was clear that Erin had been wounded by the attack from her big sister and the apparent indifference of her parents. They knew a loop had been opened and that to help Erin deal with the offense, they needed to really hear what she was saying.

"Honey, can we talk?"

"Dad, I know you think I'm a pig, too. You think I eat too much, don't you?"

"Erin, no one said you eat too much. Your sister said your eating manners were 'like a pig,' not that you eat the amount of a pig. There is a difference, isn't there?"

Erin nodded.

"Erin, we need to talk this issue out." Turning his head toward the kitchen, he called, "Rachel, please come in here to talk this out with your sister."

As the family talked it through, several things occurred. Mom and Dad learned that Erin was feeling self-conscious about her weight. That's why she interpreted Rachel's comment the way she did. As the girls communicated, they began to feel heard, and their emotions began to quiet, allowing the conflict itself to resolve.

"Girls, when you say things to each other, the words can really wound, can't they?" Mom asked. "We all need to be careful how we talk to each other. And this is also good for Dad and me to see, because with all the tension we've been feeling in our family recently, we're getting sharper with each other."

Over the next several minutes, the Blakes experienced not only vital communication, but also some incredible releasing of offenses that had wounded each other. Genuine forgiveness occurred as they cleansed their relationships right there in that family room.

Obviously, the Blakes experience conflict just like any other family. But unlike many others, they have committed themselves to working out conflicts in a healthy way. They have learned how to close the loop.

You may be saying to yourself, *We could never do that.* Well, I couldn't disagree with you more. You can learn to resolve conflict, but only if you recognize the need for the presence of a living God who helps us to heal from the inside out.

CHANGING THE PATTERN

Over the last few years, I have heard similar complaints from people who grew up with the wrong type of family training:

"I just don't know how to do this."

"I don't know what normal is."

"No one ever taught us how to handle this."

You may feel the same kind of hopelessness, the same inability to change. My question to you is, "What are you going to do to alter the pattern? What kind of new legacy do you want to pass on to your children?"

The psalmist wrote:

> For He established a testimony in Jacob,
> and appointed a law in Israel, which He

commanded our fathers, that they should teach them to their children; that the generation to come might know, even the children yet to be born, that they may arise and tell them to their children, that they should put their confidence in God, and not forget the works of God, but keep His commandments. [10]

You can look at that passage as you would at a glass half filled with water. Is the glass half empty? If so, you can feel a tremendous burden of responsibility. But if you look at the glass as half full, the passage gives you hope that the future can be better than the past.

Listen to what pastor and author Charles Swindoll says about the influence of a family:

Whatever else may be said about the home, it is the bottom line of life, the anvil upon which attitudes and convictions are hammered out. It is the place where life's bills come due, the single most influential force in our earthly existence. No price tag can adequately reflect its value. No gauge can measure its ultimate influence . . . for good or ill. It is at home, among family members,

that we come to terms with circumstances. It is here life makes up its
mind. [11]

The biblical home is a place where convictions
are developed in the context of love and affirmation.
At times the training is done through formal devo-
tions, but even more important is how parents like the
Blakes use everyday life to capture moments to teach
and learn from their children what their heavenly
Father is teaching them.

Some of you grew up in biblical homes. For those
of you who did, I am thankful. Those of you who
didn't, however, need to commit yourselves to developing healthy patterns of resolving conflict.

The family you came from is important, but not
as important as the family you will leave behind. One
thing I always try in family counseling is to help
people identify what happened in the families they
grew up in that led to barriers to communication and
conflict resolution. We look for insight from the past,
share the emotional pain of it, and then move on
toward resolution and forgiveness.

The idea of biblical therapy isn't to camp out in
the problems of our lives forever, lying in the muck
and pain. We need to look below the surface, recognize the pain we may be experiencing, and then move
toward healing. Once we do that and then begin

modeling a more effective way of communicating and resolving conflict, we can bless the next generation. One way or another, we will leave our handprints all over the little personalities and hearts of our children. The only questions are: Do we want to leave a legacy that counts? Do we want to leave behind a next generation that will reach the world for Christ, or will we be passive and let them go their own way?

When my daughter Sarah was born in 1978, I read a newspaper article that said I could anticipate spending about $80,000 for four years of college education when she grew up. I remember choking on my Fruit Loops that morning. Eighty thousand dollars! At the time, I was earning about $12,000 per year as a probation officer.

I showed the article to Barbara, and her comment was, "I hope we have a crime wave so you can keep your job." That was encouraging. Well, we started saving, Sarah will be off to college in a few years, and I'm still a long way from saving all that money.

Anybody out there have the same dilemma? Many of you have a plan for your children's education and are saving for college as we are. But let me ask you this: What are you doing to give your children the spiritual training and skills they'll need to live in the next century? What kind of godly heritage are you leaving them?

Sound hopeless? Let me encourage you—the

situation is anything but! The answers are found in a relationship—not in a book or with a counselor or a pastor. They're found in establishing a home that honors God; a home where each individual is encouraged to develop a relationship with Jesus; a home where people make lots of mistakes and often fail each other but nevertheless recognize they have the power, through God, to be transformed.

Conflict is inevitable, but it's not inevitable that we be trapped in patterns of resolving it that were passed down from our parents. That's why I wrote this book—to give you a viable option of dealing with conflict by choosing to do the loving thing and closing the loop. In the next chapter, we'll consider the next step in that loop, which is dealing with the anger that follows the hurt of an offense.

C H A P T E R   6

THE BAKED POTATO SYNDROME

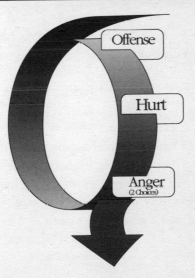

Offense

Hurt

Anger
(2 Choices)

When I order a baked potato in a restaurant, I love to stuff it with the works: sour cream, chives, butter, bacon bits, onions. I squish it all down, push it with my fork, and do everything I can to get as many ingredients in it as possible.

I've also been known to put a potato in the oven, turn up the heat, and let it bake too long. Guess what happens? It explodes. And it's messy.

Anger is much the same way. Sometimes we stuff it. At other times, we turn up the heat too high and blow it. I call this the "Baked Potato Syndrome."

The *Des Moines Register* took a poll of some elementary and junior-high kids about what makes them angry:[1]

"I get mad when my cat gets up on my bed when I'm sleeping and starts scratching and biting me."

> Jackie, 3rd grade
> Menlo, Iowa

"I was steaming mad when my parents went up north on a fishing trip without me."

> Ryan, 6th grade
> Emmetsburg, Iowa

"I thought I'd explode when my brother listened in on the phone when I was talking."

> Jenny, 5th grade
> Des Moines

92

"I thought I'd explode when I got to 3rd grade and found out we got homework!"

Sarah, 3rd grade
Manson, Iowa

I asked the same question of my daughter Missy, and she replied, "Dad, when you ask me if I brushed my teeth, I get temperish!" My older daughter, Sarah, surveyed six of her seventh-grade cohorts, and all of them agreed on one thing that makes them mad: "Josh." Apparently he's not the most popular boy in school. That's junior high, isn't it?

As Charles Swindoll says, "I don't know of anything more frustrating to deal with than anger (it makes me mad!). It has a way of disarming us, of robbing us of our testimonies. It injures our home lives and our relationships with co-workers."[2] It's an emotion that Christians often try to deny. In public, we keep it in check. But in the privacy of our homes, we feel free to let it explode, and it does so with grim consequences.

Anger is the next step in the loop of conflict. It's what grows out of the offense and the hurt. And it's what often prevents conflicts from being resolved peacefully.

Many psychologists today say it's good to express our anger. And we may feel better for a while after we "let it fly." "I'm glad I got that off my chest" is the common line. "I had to let her know how I felt. I'm supposed to express my emotions, aren't I?"

Yes, it's good to express our feelings. But when those feelings are expressed with hostility and pain, they cause more problems than they solve. Too often, anger is used as a weapon.

HOW HOT IS YOUR POTATO?

The following is a simple self-quiz to help you determine how you deal with the emotion of anger. Please fill out this 25-question inventory. Research on similar self-tests indicates that your first answer is typically the most accurate, so put down the response that first comes to mind.

Rosberg Anger Inventory

For each situation described, rate the degree of anger you think you would feel, using the scale below:

> 5= Major
> 4= Very significant
> 3= Moderate
> 2= Minor
> 1= None

1. _____Two days after your mate buys some expensive clothes, that same mate criticizes you for "spending too much money" on a new book.

2. _____Your parents forget your birthday for the third year in a row.

3. _____A man on the highway cuts in front of your car, forcing you onto the shoulder.

4. _____You observe a woman in a grocery store hitting her young child.

5. _____You learn your co-worker was promoted instead of you, even though you were clearly more qualified.

6. _____You lock your keys in the car 15 minutes before you need to leave for an important meeting at work.

7. _____You spill cranberry juice on your new white slacks.

8. _____You stand in line for more than 45 minutes to buy tickets to a concert, only to have the couple in front of you buy the last pair.

9. _____You open the freezer to get ice cubes for your iced tea, only to discover the tray is empty—again.

10. _____The telephone wakes you in the middle of the night. You answer it and learn it's a wrong number.

11. _____Your son rides his tricycle in the garage and crashes into your new car, scratching the paint.

12. _____Your bank calls and tells you it failed to

cover a check you wrote to your in-laws to repay some money you owed them.

13. _____ ² You start your new lawn edger and remember, as it begins to smoke, that you forgot to put in oil.

14. _____ ² After spending all day and evening working on your taxes, you arrive at the post office six minutes after midnight on April 16, and the workers refuse to postmark your envelope April 15.

15. _____ ³ Your child spills milk at the table for the second time in a week.

16. _____ ³ As you're feeling particularly vulnerable about aging, you notice your mate taking a second look at a younger person of your gender.

17. _____ ⁴ In the midst of a conflict with your spouse, he or she accuses you of "not walking with the Lord" and suggests you read some scriptures that would "help you change your behavior."

18. _____ ⁴ Hoping to finally have three minutes to yourself in the bathroom, you're interrupted by the kids for the third time.

19. _____ ⁴ You have moved three times in the last five years and finally have established a close friendship. Then your mate comes home and says, "We're moving again."

20. _____You're having guests over for dinner, and they arrive ten minutes early.

21. _____At a party, you overhear your mate joking about a particularly embarrassing private moment.

22. _____You start a new program in the church and are told you can't carry it out because "we've never done it that way before."

23. _____The day after you wash your car, it rains.

24. _____You walk into your family Christmas celebration having lost 20 pounds, and your brother comments, "Boy, have you gained weight!"

25. _____Your child is unfairly accused by the teacher of tattling on someone who has been taunting him or her for months.

After completing the Rosberg Anger Inventory, add up the scores from each of your responses. The lowest possible score is zero; the highest is 125.

You can interpret your total score according to this scale:

0-56   You have an extremely low level of anger and frustration. You may want to take your temperature to make sure you're not in denial and are still breathing!

57-69   You experience a low amount of anger.

70-94   Your anger level is average, and you respond to conflicts in a normal way.

95-106   You tend to have difficulty with anger and reacting aggressively.

107-125 You have a significant concern regarding anger. You would benefit from professional counseling to help you deal with conflicts.

Now that you've taken this inventory, you may have a better idea of how you respond to events that tend to trigger angry responses. Some of the questions would anger almost everyone because they trigger justifiable anger. Others most likely would not stimulate much of an anger response. As you learn to close the loop, it might be interesting to retake the inventory to see if your responses change in any way.

THREE KINDS OF HOT POTATOES

Anger can be categorized into three types of "hot potatoes." Each one has a different cause.

French Fries and Burgers

Some things just go together. Rodgers and Hammerstein. Summer and baseball. Salt and pepper. And french fries and burgers. To have a burger without an order of french fries seems an incomplete meal to me. We might say french fries are situationally specific to the main course of hamburgers.

In the same way, some anger responses are situationally specific to triggering events. They just go together, and you know it when it happens. Some situations that commonly trigger impatience and anger were included in the Rosberg Anger Inventory. In our home, anger usually rears its ugly head when we're hanging pictures, putting up the Christmas tree, or getting the kids ready for school each morning. (I've often thought someone could make a good living hanging pictures and erecting Christmas trees for people. And I just haven't seen any yellow pages ads for kid-starters—"How to jump-start your kids in 15 minutes or less.")

At our house, early mornings should be titled "Lost in Space." I get up at 6:00 A.M. every day of the week and follow the same routine. I take the dog out, do my morning study in the *One Year Bible*, hit the treadmill, and eat a bowl of cereal. I'm a wild and crazy guy who loves spontaneity, as long as it's not before 7:00 A.M. Then I shower and dress in six minutes, so I'm ready for my day by 7:15.

The problem is that my kids are in a different time zone. Instead of arising with the roosters, they would rather get up around lunchtime. Once I finally get them moving, the conflicts begin. They start look-ing for hair ribbons, stealing each others' panty hose, and searching for that particular blue sweater that is "Lost in Space."

I begin to get a little "temperish" myself and start pacing the kitchen, barking out orders from down-stairs: "If you don't hurry, you're going to miss your car pool." "Did you make your lunch yet?" "Don't forget to brush your teeth." Even as I'm making these comments, I find myself thinking I sound just like my parents. Some things really never do change.

Then, one by one, my three women come down-stairs. Missy is usually first. She has an unusual grimace she presents whenever she's either stretching the truth or getting frustrated; one of her eyes begins to blink. As she walks through the kitchen, she gives me the "old blinky eye."

Next comes Sarah, with that stern look that says, "Dad, do we have to go through this every morning?" Finally comes wife Barb, looking perfect with that beautiful smile. It drives me crazy! My heart is racing, my blood is boiling, and I find myself pulling out all the self-control I can muster to not howl at the moon, realizing it went down four hours ago.

At last they're out the door, and I can go to my study to write. But I'm now so exhausted that I'm ready to go back to bed and start over. Have you ever been there? Please say yes.

What flips your switch? A friend criticizing how you clean your house? Your teenager eating the last piece of pie you had been dreaming about all day? Your husband forgetting to call to tell you he would be late—again?

Or perhaps the open loops are closer to the heart: betrayal by a friend who went behind your back and revealed your private matter to another; rejection by your mother as she once again competes with you rather than encouraging you in the pursuit of your dreams; the letter you find in your wife's drawer from the man you thought was your best friend. Each is a specific offense producing anger.

Potato Sundaes

We all know that potatoes are either the main course or a side dish with a meal. They just don't cut it as a dessert. What would you do if the waitress at a barbecue restaurant put a potato sundae down in front of you? It would seem out of place.

Some anger responses are also out of place. Counselors call this type of anger *displaced*. Rather than confronting and dealing with the direct cause of anger, a person works it out indirectly.

Tim understands displaced anger. Whenever he and Jeannie have a conflict, she "forgets" to buy him pretzels at the store. What has that got to do with anger? Let me explain.

Tim and Jeannie have been married 13 years. He's an attorney; she's a chemical engineer. In a marriage counseling session recently, we identified a pattern: When a conflict arises in their home, Jeannie withdraws and does whatever Tim says, just as her mother did with her dad.

If she stands up to Tim, he just raises the volume of his voice until she gets the message of who is in control. She is not only dealing with her husband's anger in that situation, but also with the unresolved anger of her father. She gives in under the guise of being a submissive wife and backs off, feeling rejected, misunderstood, and powerless—powerless, that is, until she goes to the grocery store.

Tim loves this certain kind of pretzels. So before she goes to the store, he reminds her to pick up his favorite treat, and she nods in agreement. On the inside, however, she's thinking, *Sure, Tim, I'll get your pretzels—just as soon as you begin listening to me.*

The next day, as Tim goes to the cupboard to chomp on his pretzels, he asks Jeannie, "Where are my pretzels?"

To which Jeannie replies, "Oh, I'm sorry, I forgot them. I'll remember next time." An open loop. A potato sundae. Displaced anger. Jeannie feels blocked by her husband's and father's domination over her. Two generations of men, the most important men in her life, have not allowed her to express her heart.

Offenses occur. Displaced anger looms. Pretzels are "forgotten." Without the skill of expressing her anger to her husband, she conveniently displaces her anger week to week, and Tim takes years to get the message.

You're offended by your boss, so you yell at your spouse. You're angered by a spot on your shirt, so you drive too fast back to the office. You hear one too many complaints from the children, so you kick the dog. You displace your anger and take it out on someone or something else.

Au Gratin Rotten Potatoes

Some families grow up on leftovers, while others don't even know they exist. I used to have them as a child. Every once in a while, you could see Mom rummaging around in the refrigerator looking for some good, old-fashioned leftovers to serve her family.

I remember looking in the back of the refrigerator one time, and there it was: a dish with tinfoil on it. I was certain it was the leftover meatloaf, and I was ready for a sandwich. So I dug it out, hoping my brothers wouldn't see me and make me share it with them. I took off the tinfoil, and there it was: au gratin potatoes.

But these au gratin potatoes had something a little extra: mold. It was not a pretty sight. They had simply been left in the refrigerator too long.

Dealing with anger in a timely way helps to restore relationships. But when anger is shoved way back on the shelf and left too long, it can become chronic. And chronic anger is not a pretty sight.

Many people allow unresolved offenses to burrow deep into their hearts and memories. Those wounds generate an assortment of psychological and physical stresses, ruin a person's perspective on life, and eat away at the soul. People like this become loaded cannons, ready to be lit, waiting to see who ignites the fuse.

Let's look at an example of how one home created a lifelong response of chronic anger. Kathy was 34 years old the first time I met her. She had been on my schedule for four weeks, quietly waiting her turn for an appointment. After we got acquainted, she began to unravel a story that made my skin crawl. Since I had already done 16,000 hours of counseling by that time, that was quite a feat.

Kathy grew up in a large city. She lived in a regular house just like everyone around her. She had a stepbrother, a sister, and parents who both worked to eke out a living for a family of five. They were members of the church, patrons of the library, regular people—at least on the outside.

But inside those four walls, Kathy had lived a silent terror of sexual abuse at the hands of her stepbrother. It started out innocently enough with sexual play among neighborhood kids all trying to make sense of the changes occurring in their bodies. Yet what began as simple curiosity turned into madness.

For three years Kathy hid daily in a toolshed behind the garage, praying her stepbrother would not find her that day, not again. She hoped and prayed someone would find out. But fearing her family would be angry with her, she kept the secret. Now that secret was being exposed, and the emotion she feared most—anger—was about to be unleashed. In the office of a man she hardly knew, it was finally time to confront the pain in her heart.

Kathy had dealt with her pain and anger for almost 25 years by holding it in— stuffing it. People like Kathy typically want to repress painful memories, deny their existence, and hope and pray they go away. As Kathy shut out others, fearful of letting them get too close lest they find out her secret or hurt her again, she became isolated and withdrawn.

But the aroma of her baked potato emerged in many ways: compulsive eating, busyness, anxiety, rushing from church activity to homemaker activity, an unrelenting sense of shame, a fear of intimacy with her husband. Now she was experiencing the chronic anger caused by all those years of not resolving a terrible conflict.

HOW DO WE RESPOND WHEN THE POTATO HEATS UP?

As I explained earlier, people commonly respond to anger in one of two ways: They stuff it, or they explode. I've also noticed that the reasons they react as they do are often similar. Here are four types of people I observe:

The Self-Protector

Self-protectors have a difficult time acknowledging they've been hurt. If their tendency is to stuff anger, they'll act as though nothing is wrong or change the subject. Others will express their anger in an aggressive or hostile way rather than work through the offense that created the hurt. Anger distances people and keeps them away. Expressing hurt demands vulnerability.

Beth knows all too well that it's safer to show anger than hurt. As we sat in the mental health unit of a local hospital one night, I talked with her and her father. I had counseled Beth off and on for the last six years. Dad was passing through Des Moines and expressed a willingness to meet with her and me in a family therapy session.

As I entered the consultation room, I could see the pain that had existed in this family for all 29 years of Beth's life. She was adopted into the family at 4 months of age. Her father is an alcoholic. Her mom, a well-meaning enabler, didn't know how to help in a healthy way, so she unwittingly perpetuated Dad's illness for years. She thought she was doing the right thing by calling his workplace for him when he had too much to drink, by lying to relatives about why they never showed up for holidays. She believed it was a wife's duty to tell the kids to be quiet because Dad had a rough night and needed to sleep, even if it was 2:00 P.M. and he was lying on the living room floor.

On Beth's tenth birthday, her dad left. She reminded him of that fact as the worn-out father stared at the table and said, "I didn't remember it was your birthday, Beth."

"Oh, I remember, Dad," she said. "And the memory has come back on every birthday since that day. I remember Mom telling me you had to leave because you couldn't put up with us anymore."

This was a big step for Beth, acknowledging that hurt from 19 years before. As a child, she had learned to spew anger all around her rather than to ever express her hurt. Why? Because when she became too vulnerable, people left her. Her dad left, her grandfather died, her mom wouldn't return her calls. So every time she grew too close to a man, she sabotaged the relationship by blowing her stack. It was the only way she could stay in control and protect herself from being hurt. Now, with this important meeting with her dad, she was trying to break the pattern.

The Cannon

Other people express hostility because it's a powerful weapon. Quite simply, it works. When they begin to feel anger, they raise their voices, their bodies may tremble, and they shake, rattle, and roll because it gets the attention of those around them. I call them cannons.

Hostility is a powerful weapon. You've seen it happen. Two people disagree, and one of them explodes and attacks the other person. The attacker ends up "winning" the argument, not because his way is best but because the other person pulls away and gives in out of insecurity. It's hard to retaliate when someone blows up in anger; often people reciprocate with anger of their own, and the argument deteriorates into a shouting match. Most people, however, will back away because of their own insecurity.

I often see parents using this tactic with their children. Six-year-old Susie asks Dad, "Why can't we go to McDonald's tonight like you promised?" and Dad replies, "Because I said so!"

Susie starts crying and says, "But you promised!" Then Dad ends the discussion by raising his voice: "Don't talk to your father that way! Now go to your room until you can be a happy girl!"

The Conformer

Randy and Tanya exemplify another group of people who either stuff or vent their anger. Randy is the exploder, while Tanya is the stuffer. Both are conforming to lessons they learned from their culture or their families.

Randy is conforming to the societal myth about "real men." Many boys are raised to be tough, independent, and to never show emotion. "Big boys don't cry." "Act like a man." "Okay, that's enough. Now quit crying before someone sees you!" These messages tell men they can't be masculine and emotional at the same time.

One afternoon when I was about six years old, my older brother, Jack, and I were hitting baseballs at our backyard fence. I was standing a little too close to him. Being the "cool" little brother I was, I decided I would stand close enough to feel the breeze from the bat. But Jack's last swing hit me right above the left eye, opening a gash that took several stitches to close.

Jack's response? "Don't cry. And don't tell Mom." Naturally, I promptly did what any little brother would. I cried and told Mom. I also remember thinking, *Why don't I hit you in the head with a bat and see if you don't cry?* But Jack's remark illustrates the tug and pull many men, including Randy, feel.

In a similar way, Tanya grew up observing a mother who always repressed her anger, even during continual verbal assaults from Tanya's father. Her mother felt it was her duty as a Christian, that she needed to "submit" to her husband. She never questioned the way her husband wouldn't ask her opinion on important financial decisions, feeling it wasn't her role to "challenge his authority."

So as adults, Randy and Tanya find themselves acting out the parts that society, church, and family have trained them to play. And they wonder why they can't handle their anger.

The Denier

The fourth type of person dealing with anger is the denier. Lori is a good example. Rather than expressing hurt, she went right to the anger stage. The problem was that she simply didn't recognize when she was hurt.

Lori grew up in a home with three brothers who fought, parents who argued openly, and a dad who left whenever the temperature became too hot. Anger was the one emotion expressed. There was no modeling for the expression of hurt. Mom held her hurt inside. Lori's three brothers were "real men" being raised by a dad who only knew how to show anger in a hostile way, so hurt wasn't even recognizable. Thus, Lori learned to go right to anger as the only way to stand her ground in a hostile environment that didn't know how to legitimize the expression of hurt.

Lori developed patterns of spitting and spewing. Other people stayed at a distance because they felt they couldn't get close to her. She had a string of broken relationships; whenever conflict occurred, she became hostile and denied there were any problems. Lori lost friendship after friendship as people got tired of putting up with all her hostility.

After we talked about the patterns that tended to recur, Lori began to change some of her approaches to dealing with friends. The keys were learning how to work through her anger in nonhostile ways and facing the conflicts without denying their very existence.

THE DESTINY OF BAKED POTATOES

Unless a couple know how to work through their anger, they're likely to find themselves on an emotional roller coaster with no end in sight. McKay, Rogers, and McKay wrote in *When Anger Hurts:*

> Carol Travis (1982) notes that people who are most prone to vent their rages

> get angrier, not less angry. And the recipients of this rage have hurt feelings. The typical stages of a "ventilating" marital argument involve a precipitating event, an angry outburst, heated arguments, screaming or crying, a crescendo (perhaps including physical violence) and exhaustion, followed by withdrawal or apology. This cycle is replayed "ad nauseam," and no decrease in anger is apparent. [3]

The longer this cycle continues, the more the pressure hurts both people, whether they stuff their anger or allow it to explode. Over and over in my counseling, I've seen the same effects in people.

If we stuff our anger, for example, we'll probably begin to change, mentally and physically. Our outlook becomes tarnished, our countenance discolored, our sense of belonging futile and unfulfilled.

This is where unresolved anger begins to kick into bitterness and resentment. We see the world through dirty lenses. We become hardened and withdrawn, developing physical symptoms like headaches, muscular aches, colitis, ulcers, compulsive behaviors, and scores of other problems. In the process, we pull away from the person we're angry at, and our bitterness sours others as well. We end up lonely and isolated.

The results of venting our anger are not any better. When anger becomes a way of life, we develop the same type of bitter, critical attitude.

We can tell ourselves it's healthy to show anger, but research is beginning to recognize this philosophy as a myth. McKay, Rogers, and McKay wrote, "Experimental studies consistently point out that the popular remedy for anger, ventilation, is really worse than useless. In fact, the reverse seems to be true: expressing anger tends to make you even angrier and solidifies an angry attitude."[4]

Do you like being around people who are consistently angry? Of course not. People like that leave a trail of broken relationships behind them. McKay, Rogers, and McKay wrote, "A 1986 study by Susan Hazaleus and Jerry Deffenbacher revealed that 45 percent of angry male subjects had suffered a 'terminated or damaged' relationship during the previous year."[5]

Whether we stuff our anger or blow up with it, we arrive at the same dead end of isolation. We distance ourselves from the other person, whether it's a spouse, a friend, a parent, or a child. We wrap layer upon layer of protection around our hearts, and the relationship goes from a vibrancy of communication and joy to one that yields hurt and distance. Our hearts become hardened, and we pull away not only from each other, but also from a vibrant relationship with God. We might picture it like this:

THE GOOD NEWS

In his excellent book *Good 'n' Angry*, Les Carter wrote,

> Anger per se is neither good nor bad. It is how people use their anger that makes it positive or negative. Ideally, anger was given to humans by God as a tool to help build relationships. In its pure form, anger is an emotional signal that tells a person something needs to be changed. It was intended to be a positive motivator to be used in giving one another feedback about how life can be lived more productively. [6]

I agree. Anger can be a signal to us that something needs to be checked out. The machinery is breaking down somewhere. But as Steve Arterburn pointed out in his book *Toxic Faith,*

> In some expressions of the Christian faith, anger is a no-no for both men and women. Some believe that everyone must be completely loving and forgiving at "all" times and that anyone showing anger is not a good Christian and should work on the sinful attitude at the heart of the anger. But that belief is a distortion of how Christianity and reality are to be joined. Everyone, Christian or not, is going to experience anger. The sooner this anger is expressed and resolved, the better. Yet many angry Christians don't acknowledge they are angry, while they seethe with bitterness and resentment. And their denial of their feelings is ineffective and unnecessary. [7]

Everyone, Christian or not, *does* experience anger. It's a God-given emotion, part of the complexity of who we are as men, women, and children. It can be difficult to understand, but understand it we must if we're to achieve a sense of balance in our relationships. Anger doesn't have to be denied. It doesn't have to turn to bitterness and resentment. (In chap. 13, I'll describe in depth how to deal with hot potatoes.)

Anger hurts. But we can learn to deal with our anger effectively. We can learn to prepare the potato so that it's an integral part of a meal. We can learn how to season it so that it's palatable but doesn't become the object of our emotional binges. We can learn how to bake it long enough so that it's done but not overcooked, with the pressure building up and leading to an explosion.

PART 3

THE FORK
IN THE ROAD

DECISION TIME

I t's a beautiful spring day, the kind that beckons you to drop whatever you're doing and head outside. So you take off on your bicycle. As you shift gears, you listen to birds chirping and see squirrels chasing each other. Surveying the damage of the winter snow, you dodge the new potholes. As you hum to yourself, you see the sun breaking through the trees, its rays dancing off the leaves around you.

Then you come to a fork in the road. You may see it ahead, giving you time to slow down and approach it carefully. Or you may zip around the corner completely unaware, catching the fork right before you run into the trees. You come to a stop, or at least a slow approach, as you try to get your bearings.

Decision time. To your left is a well-traveled four-lane highway. Everybody else seems to be on it. It's the natural way to go, even though it's jammed with traffic. On the right is a narrow path. It winds up and down, yet it has that same light breaking through the trees, almost as if it's a light showing you the way.

Which way do you go? The scarecrow in *The Wizard of Oz* would tell you, "Some people go this

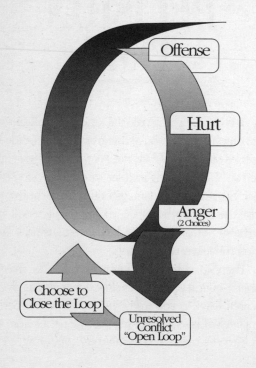

120

way, others go that way, and some go both ways." Isn't that the truth?

We all come to forks in the road. Sometimes we just put our heads down and barrel through. We don't even see the intersection. Other times we slow down, wondering which way to go. And still other times, we come to a red light, stop at the fork, and ask the tough question: "Which way do I really need to go?"

In a conflict, we come to a similar fork in the road. After the offense has led to hurt and the hurt has turned to anger, we're faced with a choice: Do we resolve this conflict, or do we let it pass? Do we close the loop or not?

Life is made up of many types of forks in the road. Usually they're called *choices* or *decisions*.

You go to the drive-through window at a fast-food restaurant and order two burgers, fries, and a Diet Coke. Simple enough. Zooming back to work, you reach into the bag: one burger, fries, and a Diet Coke. A dollar is down the tube. *Should I go back?* you wonder. *I'm going to tell them a thing or two!* But as you think about it, you realize your cholesterol level, the money, and the extra gas you'd burn driving back aren't worth it.

The boss is pushing you to fudge on the cost projections for a new contract. *Everyone else is doing it. It's part of the game in this business.* Or so you tell yourself. Another fork in the road.

Your kids are hammering each other, and you

have Excedrin headache number 362. Just give them the Popsicles, avoid the conflict, and retreat to the TV for the afternoon. Who wants to crawl into this conflict and deal with it?

With conflict, we often reach a point where we need to make a decision. Do we follow our natural inclination in the situation, or do we choose to take a risk and trust God by attempting to resolve the conflict? Do we enter the highway already crowded with unresolved conflicts, or do we take the narrow path toward the light?

Closing the loop in conflicts is never simple, and one reason is that each of us tends to react to hurt and anger in one of several ways. As a result of all the training I described in chapters 5 and 6, we all have learned certain styles of conflict resolution.

THE CONFLICT-RESOLUTION SURVEY

I often tell people that if there's a counselor in the room, there's a better than even chance you're going to take a test. Well, you're reading a counselor's book, so you know there's going to be a test, but let's call it a survey.

The following survey will help you identify your particular style of resolving conflict. Before you take the survey, identify one person with whom you are currently having a conflict. It may be a spouse, child, parent, friend, co-worker, or anyone else. Take the survey with that person in mind so you can identify how you relate to conflict with that specific individual. If you wish, you can go back and do it again with another relationship in mind. You may find that your conflict-resolution style is different with different people.

Here we go. Below you will find five boxes with a letter above each. Keeping that one relationship you just chose in mind, circle each word in every box that describes how you respond *consistently* to conflict in that relationship.

R

-Dominant	• Forceful	Purposeful
- Demanding	Task over people	-Strict
-Controlling	Win oriented	Take charge
- Inflexible	- Direct	- Competitive
Powerful	Decisive	

L

- Influencer	- Compromising	Seek tradeoffs
Optimistic	- Persuasive	Risk taker
Enthusiastic	Seek favor	Promoter
Smooth	- Motivational	People over task
Impulsive	Bargaining	

E

Nurturing	People oriented	Supportive
Sensitive	- Cautious	Agreeable
Loyal	Seek acceptance	Patient
Caring	- Desire security	Harmonious
Peacemaker	Status quo	

F

Passive	- Avoiding	- Easily frustrated
Emotionless	Sidestepping	Logical
Computerlike	- Critical	Black/White
- Tight emotions	Analytical	Thinker
- Rigid	Predictable	

W

- Compromising	Mediator	Seek solution
Good listener	Explore options	Resolve tension
Reflective	Flexible	Diplomatic
Facilitator	- Problem solver	Respectful
Seek consensus	Creative	

Now that you've finished circling the words, count the number you've circled in each box. Then double that number and write the new numbers down next to the corresponding letters below.

R: _16_ L: _8_ E: _4_ F: _10_ W: _4_

Next, take those same numbers and place them on the graph below. For example, if you scored 14 in the R box, you would place a dot on the R line right next to the number 14. If you scored 17 in the L box, you'd place a dot on the L line between the 14 and the 21, and so on. Continue until you have dots on each of the vertical lines.

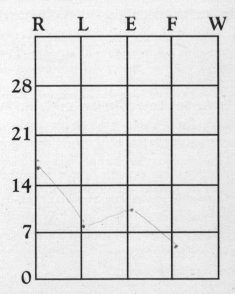

125

Now connect the dots! By following the path of the "peaks" made by the connecting line, you can see your typical style of conflict resolution, followed by your second-most-common style, and so on.

Now that you've taken the survey, let me tell you a little more about each style of resolving conflict. To illustrate each one, I'm going to take a trip down memory lane.

One of my favorite television shows as I grew up was "I Love Lucy." Lucy was also the childhood heroine of my wife, Barbara. Even today, if a rerun or special is aired, Barbara will race to the TV to watch and reminisce. She even gets a kind of glassy look of nostalgia in her eyes as she sits back and drinks up memories of simpler and more carefree days with the Ricardo and Mertz families.

If you recall, almost every episode of "I Love Lucy" focused on conflict. Lucy was always trying to get her way by manipulating Ricky or talking him into something. Ricky was usually bellowing in his Cuban accent, trying to keep Lucy under control. Fred just tried to avoid the whole thing, often shaking his head, probably thinking he was surrounded by a bunch of kids. And Ethel, the loyal friend to Lucy, would do just about anything to keep the peace, even if it meant giving in to others' wishes. Each of them represents one of the typical styles of conflict resolution.

THE RICKY RICARDO APPROACH:
WIN. "LUCY! I WANT TO TALK TO YOU RIGHT NOW!"

The people using this approach go into a conflict with one thing in mind: winning. The idea is to pull out all the stops and control others, making sure everything and everybody goes their way. These people rarely put much emphasis on the relationship itself, because they're too focused on the issue at hand and making sure they don't get the short end of the stick.

Is this style ever preferable? Sure. It works well in difficult situations when someone needs to take charge and get a job done quickly. There are times when a person doesn't have the luxury of getting other people's input, even though such decisions may be met with real resistance.

Ricky yelled, threatened, spit, and sputtered to get his way, and get his way he did. We all use his approach at times. But often we don't use it well—we try to control the situation and browbeat others into submission.

THE FRED MERTZ STYLE:
AVOID. "LET'S TAKE A NAP AND SEE IF THIS THING PASSES."

Fred always wanted everyone to settle down and relax. He probably would have described Ricky as always being hotheaded, Lucy as always stirring things up, and his wife as always going along with her friend Lucy. Fred would have preferred that they all have a nice, quiet evening. But with the powerful personalities of Ricky and Lucy around, things were seldom boring.

The Fred in us would like to stay away from conflict. In fact, the Fred in each of us would do just about anything to avoid it. By using this style, we end up placing a low priority on the relationship and also exercise low control needs. Freds just don't want any hassles. A nap sounds like a better way to deal with the whole thing.

How do the Freds of the world act in a conflict? They may leave the room, throw their hands in the air, shake their heads, or say things like "Here we go again."

Does this approach ever have benefits? Sure it does, especially if you're trying to deal with a powerful personality. If someone like Ricky is trying to overpower you, "pulling a Fred" can give you some time to think things through. But you have to be willing to get off the bench later and get back into the game, resisting the inertia that sometimes accompanies avoidance. Unfortunately, many people never do get back in the game. Withdrawing from conflict as a pattern can develop a hardened heart, and conflicts remain buried for years.

THE ETHEL MERTZ SOLUTION:
GIVE IN. "DON'T ROCK THE BOAT."

Remember Ethel? What a great lady! We all, at least silently, would like a friend like her who would stick with us during thick and thin and always be in our corner, no matter what. Whether Lucy was right or wrong, Ethel was there, defending her friend.

The Ethels are the pleasers of the world. They place their own needs aside and value the relationship above all else. In conflict, they tend to give in and do what the other person wants. By consistently burying their own feelings, however, the Ethels risk building up resentment under the surface. They feel as though others take advantage of them, but they can't seem to build up enough strength to take a stand.

Is this approach ever useful? Of course, especially when you don't place much value on the results. My mother taught me to choose my battles carefully, realizing that sometimes the relationship is more important than the issue. But when I went after something, she said, I should give it my all.

THE LUCY RICARDO APPROACH:
PERSUADE. "OH, RICKY, I HAVE SOMETHING TO TELL YOU ... "

Can't you just hear her? She knew exactly how

to twist a sentence, roll her eyes, look a little less than forthright, and get her own way. Lucy was a master of disguise not only in dress, with all the wild outfits she put on, but also in her communication style. When you get right down to it, she was a master of persuasion. She could sweet-talk Ricky and then give him a one-two punch to get her way. She was a combination of cute, manipulative, convincing, and endearing. And we all loved Lucy.

Even though Lucy won our hearts, she demonstrated a less-than-healthy conflict-resolution style. She was manipulative; she would do just about anything to win, much like Ricky, but she seemed to draw people closer to her in the middle of the conflict rather than dominating them. She would lie, needle, and convince those around her with a flair that only she could pull off. But I think there's a little of Lucy in all of us, and more than a little in some.

There are consequences to our behaviors, however. When we manipulate people, we may get our way in the short run, but they resent it. In the long run, it can damage relationships.

If we take a closer look at these four styles, we realize they all have their drawbacks. The chart below summarizes them.

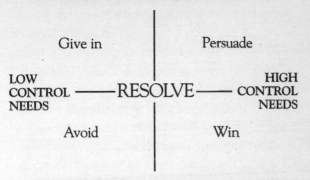

HIGH PRIORITY ON RELATIONSHIP

Give in   Persuade

LOW CONTROL NEEDS —— RESOLVE —— **HIGH CONTROL NEEDS**

Avoid   Win

LOW PRIORITY ON RELATIONSHIP

You can see that the win approach places a high priority on controlling the situation but a low priority on the relationship. The relationship is truly negotiable.

Avoiders don't put much emphasis on either the relationship or on establishing control. Instead, they tend to shut down and avoid dealing with the issue altogether.

Those who give in place a high priority on the relationship because they like to keep everybody happy, even at the cost of their own feelings. The downside is that although they keep others happy, they exercise low control over the issue at hand and tend to feel unhappy and used.

Then there are the persuaders, who place a high priority on people and use their ability to persuade and, at times, manipulate others.

THE WARD CLEAVER APPROACH:
RESOLVE. "LET'S TALK THIS THROUGH."

I racked my brain trying to identify a television character who embodied the right way to resolve conflicts. I finally thought of Ward Cleaver, from that classic show "Leave It to Beaver."

You remember Ward. He was the guy who always sat around the house in either a suit or a cardigan sweater, reading the newspaper and never going to work. He and June would listen while Wally and "the Beave" described the conflicts they had with Eddie Haskell, Lumpy, or Larry. Ward was an expert at coming up with just the right thing to say at just the right time. He would call friends' parents to close the loop, he would get the boys talking when they were mad at each other, and he saw right through Eddie Haskell's shenanigans.

Ward Cleaver exercised just the right balance between a healthy control need and a healthy priority on the relationship. He didn't try to win or avoid. He didn't persuade or give in. He hit the issues head-on in an endearing way that made all of America sigh with comments of "Isn't that Ward something?"

MAKING ALL THE WRONG CHOICES

When you look back over past conflicts, what patterns do you see? What style have you found yourself using most of the time? If you're like most people, chances are you haven't been resolving conflict in a healthy manner.

You've probably reached many forks in the road during conflicts. You know what decisions you need to make, yet you find you always have a difficult time actually doing it. If that's the case, the next three chapters will help you. I'm going to describe some different "red lights" that often prevent you from choosing the right path to close the loop in love.

CHAPTER 8

RED LIGHTS

In the summer of 1976, Barbara and I made the first long-distance car trip of our marriage. We had been married one year and decided to drive to Dallas in our old, red Hornet to attend a conference.

We managed to get lost, which isn't too easy when you figure there's only one highway from Des Moines to Dallas. And we had all the typical mishaps, including an air conditioner that leaked water all over our feet. (At least it was cool.)

After we finally made it to "Big D," we learned we had to drive through the middle of Dallas to get to the conference site. Map in hand, gleams in our eyes, and Bibles under our arms, we headed out early for our first day.

About five miles from the auditorium, I noticed a police car in my rearview mirror. When I turned corners, it turned as well. It wasn't in hot pursuit, but it seemed to be there whenever I turned around.

Now, I don't know about you, but no matter how well I'm driving, no matter how good I try to be, when I look in my mirror and see a patrol car, I start getting a damp brow. I think God wired us with an automatic reflex on that one.

I drove to within one mile of the auditorium and came upon a huge, five-way intersection. They don't have those in Iowa. Barb had her map in hand, barking out (I mean, gently suggesting) directions, I was wondering which way to turn, the conference was about to start, and one of "Dallas's finest" was still hanging out just behind my rear bumper.

Sure enough, the red lights went on three blocks past the intersection. I pulled over, the officer got out of his car, and we began to "chat" as he looked over my driver's license.

"Sir, do you realize what you did back there in that intersection?" the policeman asked.

"Officer, I know I wasn't speeding. I've been watching you for miles in my rearview mirror."

"Mr. Rosberg [with that I looked around for my dad], you drove through a red light."

"I couldn't have. I was driving so carefully because you were right with me. I thought the last thing I would do is get pulled over."

"Where are you from, son?" (Now I was really looking for my dad.)

"We're from Iowa."

"Oh, that explains it. Please drive more carefully."

At a time like that, a mere civilian mortal comes to a crossroads. Do you defend the honor of your state, or do you graciously accept an officer's tolerance? Being the pragmatic man that I am, I did the latter. I grabbed my woman, my Bible, and my map and gratefully drove off.

I always chuckle when I remember that incident, because it created in me an aversion to red lights. I will take alternate routes, go down side streets, and run through an occasional yellow light to beat the red light if I think I can get away with it. That's how intent I can be on reaching my destination as quickly as possible. As a result, sometimes I make my problem worse and actually end up spending more time driving than I would have by going the normal way, stopping at the red light.

As I explained in the last chapter, many people come to the fork in the road in a conflict and make the wrong decision. Rather than moving forward and resolving it peacefully and biblically, they either attempt to resolve it their own way or withdraw and let it go unresolved. For many of these people, emotional red lights are the key problem. They know they need to work on the conflict, but something holds them back.

Recognizing these emotional red lights that prevent us from dealing with conflicts is another critical step in restoring broken relationships. Because it's so important, I'll spend this chapter and the next two looking at several of the more-common red lights.

RED LIGHT 1: PRIDE

Red light 1 is perhaps the most destructive and harmful of all. It's the sin we're all guilty of, pride. As the book of Proverbs tells us, "Pride goes before destruction, a haughty spirit before a fall."[1]

I sometimes sense confusion with my clients when I talk to them about pride. After all, isn't pride the stuff movie heroes are made of? John Wayne was proud, independent, self-reliant—a real man's man.

But the pride I speak of is not pride in one's work, one's family, or one's country. I refer to the type of pride that says, "I run my own life, and I don't want any interference." It's the pride that refuses to admit fault, placing all the blame for a conflict on the other person. It's the pride that sets two people in their trenches, refusing to make the first step toward peace.

"I can't do it, Dr. Rosberg. I can't take the risk of

talking to my son about our conflict. I took a stand, and I can't back off. He will never respect me or listen to me again if I do."

Those were the words of a well-intentioned but misled father. Don grew up in a home where men were men and women were women. Today the rules he learned would seem chauvinistic, but 50 years ago, that's just the way it was.

From his father, Don learned to walk tall, never look back, stand proud, and never let anybody get close. Those qualities helped him earn a six-figure income as a prominent businessman in his community. But he also developed an emotionless relationship with his four children and wife, who were starved for affection and emotional intimacy.

As his son Ryan grew up, Don pushed him hard, always letting him know of his high expectations. In an effort to please his father, Ryan attended the same college as Don, pledged the same fraternity, and majored in business. Then he went to work for Dad.

That's when the real problems began. Ryan asked Don over and over to explain why he (Don) was always "on him," riding him harder than the rest of the sales staff. Dad denied any wrongdoing—if his son were going to take over the company some day, he needed to toughen up and work hard the way he (Don) did when he was young.

The situation simmered for a few years, but

eventually the pot had to boil over. During a sales meeting, in front of all 14 staffers in the office, Ryan began suggesting some different ideas that others had given up on years ago because of Don's reluctance to change. Finally, Don hit the roof.

"Ryan, I have told you over and over that your approach in your region is not only coming up short, but it's bringing down the rest of your territory as well! If you can't improve your sales, maybe you should find some other company to pay your check. Got it?"

Ryan was so mad that he got up and walked out the door. "He hasn't been back to work since," Don explained in my office. He acknowledged he had ridden his son too hard, and he realized he shouldn't have criticized Ryan so vehemently in front of others. But he wasn't willing to resolve the conflict. "I can see why he wouldn't like what I said, but I can't back off in front of the other salespeople," he said. "If I do, I'll lose the respect of not only Ryan, but also the entire sales team."

Don's coming to me for help was a remarkable step for him, because it required the type of humility he normally didn't display. But he needed even more of it. He loved his son, and he wanted the best for him as well as for the company. But he was so fearful of his own feelings and of letting others close enough to see his faults that he ran the risk of alienating everyone.

The antithesis of pride, humility, allows one to graciously receive others. C. S. Lewis wrote in *Mere Christianity*, "If anyone would like to acquire humility, I can, I think, tell him the first step. The first step is to realize that one is proud. And a biggish step, too. At least, nothing whatever can be done before it. If you think you are not conceited, it means you are very conceited indeed." [2]

Exercising humility allows the Dons of the world to stand back and take a deep and long look inside. We see where we're losing our relationships and how to close the open loops of conflict.

It works. Don learned that when he finally went to Ryan to close the loop. It took every ounce of humility he could muster, but by doing so he began to break down the barriers that had kept him from really knowing his son.

Humility is a gift we rarely ask for, because it usually comes in the form of some difficult lessons. But it is a gift indeed.

RED LIGHT 2: GUILT

Mark's head hung so low, it looked as if he would never raise his eyes again. "I really did it this time," he said, "and I can't go back."

Mark worked as a comptroller in a manufacturing plant. He met Mary when they attended a small

Christian college. She came from a wealthy background, while Mark grew up in a working-class home and was the first in his family to attend college. They were both 43 years old and had one child in college and another in high school.

Mary enjoyed having nice things, and Mark tried to meet her materialistic desires. Though they were on a modest budget, he kept encouraging her to buy what she wanted. He wanted to provide for his wife the way other men in their circle of friends did, so he kept using credit cards and delaying payments. Then one day, he made a decision that would change the course of his life forever.

Mark discovered a $12,000 error in the company's books. As he sat at his desk reviewing the figures, he congratulated himself on a job well done. But then a new thought penetrated his thinking: *What if I didn't tell anyone about the error? Nobody else would be able to find it.*

He knew what he was contemplating was wrong, but then he thought of all the raises he had been promised but never given. *No one is looking out for me,* he thought. *And trying to keep up with Mary's spending is getting harder all the time. Maybe I can just take the money for a couple of months and then pay it back in October. No one will ever know.*

Can you see the web of rationalizations? Mark gave in to that temptation, and, not surprisingly, he never returned the money as he had planned. Now he was about to be found out by a company audit.

Mark's inability to be honest with his wife helped create the problem in the first place. But after he committed the crime, he began living with guilt. As that guilt weighed on him, it made him more moody and irritable, harder to get along with. Mary knew something was wrong but couldn't figure it out. And he avoided conflict over the family finances even further, because he didn't want to admit his crime.

Mark was filled with self-condemnation and feelings of failure as he sat in my office. "What will Mary say? How will I ever face my kids and my parents? How will I support my family? What will happen if I go to prison?"

The good news about guilt is that it can lead us to a loving relationship with God. Dr. Bruce Narramore describes one type of guilt as "constructive sorrow":

> It is the only reaction to wrongdoing that produces lasting change for the right reasons. It does not involve the use of guilt games and does not involve the feelings of self-condemnation of psychological guilt. . . .
>
> Once we have recognized the harmful effects of guilt feelings, we are free to turn

to a constructive alternative. The Bible doesn't say we are free from guilt so we can "sin it up." Instead, it says we are free from guilt so we can learn to fulfill our lives and develop inner character.[3]

Constructive sorrow leads us to repentance, a turning away from sin. The apostle Paul wrote:

> Even if I caused you sorrow by my letter, I do not regret it. Though I did regret it—I see that my letter hurt you, but only for a little while—yet now I am happy, not because you were made sorry, but because your sorrow led you to repentance. For you became sorrowful as God intended and so were not harmed in any way by us. Godly sorrow brings repentance that leads to salvation and leaves no regret, but worldly sorrow brings death.[4]

The red light of unresolved guilt can inhibit the restoration of broken relationships. When we're feeling guilty, we need to ask ourselves some direct questions: Have I violated a law of God or humanity that would lead me to feel what I'm feeling? If so, perhaps the guilt is constructive and can lead me to repentance and healing. Confronting guilt and repenting is a difficult step, but the freedom we experience is so much more refreshing than the terrible burden we feel when we don't face up to it.

RED LIGHT 3: LAZINESS

This one may surprise you, but laziness is a red light we especially like to avoid confronting. It's just plain, old-fashioned laziness—the complaint your parents used to throw at you when report cards came around; the sneer you receive from your mate when he or she passes by your chair as you watch your second football game or soap opera of the day; the shaking of your head and finger at your co-worker who regularly takes extra-long coffee and lunch breaks.

For some people, laziness is a lifestyle, and this carries over into their relationships. But how do we explain the successful, wealthy executive who is so driven to work at the office yet so lazy at home?

Many people never realize how much work a relationship takes. To them, once the chase is over, the fun is gone. They love the challenge of pursuing a new love, but they aren't willing to put in the grunt work to make that relationship last a lifetime. When conflict arises, they pull away, unplug from relationships, and plug into their fantasies. They turn on the television, pick up a book, or go out shopping. They let the world rush by them, never giving the effort to make the most important relationships of their lives really mean something.

They know they need to be more attentive to the ones they love, but they figure they'll do that "tomorrow." In his book *Will the Defense Please Rest?* Les Carter explained, "Most lazy people will admit that, when they are in a lazy mood, they tend to be very resistant to any intrusion. When logical reasoning takes hold, they may even admit that being lazy is inappropriate behavior. Yet, often they will continue in this habit because, when all things are considered, laziness is what they prefer."[5]

Laziness is an enemy of closing loops. When we refuse to work at resolving conflicts because of laziness, it deeply hurts those around us.

John and Deb have been struggling for years over John's apparent lack of interest in dealing with conflicts in their family. When John returns home from work, he immediately turns on the television. There he sits for hours on end, night after night, watching sitcoms and sporting events.

It drives Deb nuts. She grew up in an active family. They were always working in the yard, playing sports, or participating in family activities. During their courting years, John spent lots of time with Deb, and he was creative in planning special times together. But during the last few years, he has nearly removed himself from any real family activity, and it hurts Deb deeply. They have become isolated, hardened toward each other, and essentially emotionally divorced.

When you get right down to the root cause, it isn't any deep insecurity in John that keeps him from meaningful interaction. It isn't a lack of skill or time. It's simply laziness. All he wants is to forget about responsibility for a few hours. He admits it, but he's not open to change.

Such laziness can be dangerous in relationships. It indicates a carelessness, or apathy, that really bothers me. Apathetic people end up drifting from one shallow relationship to another, never willing to put the time and effort into making them work. At the end of their lives, they look back and realize they never were close to their friends, their mates, or their children, and they deeply regret what they missed.

I don't know about you, but I don't want that remorse.

RED LIGHT 4: SHAME

Annie ran from my office, tears rolling down her cheeks. Her husband, Scott, looked at me in bewilderment. "Every time we start talking about what's going on, she cries," Scott said. "I don't know how to respond."

Scott was confused. Annie felt overwhelmed. Here was a couple trying to develop their marriage in a healthy way, but a voice kept ringing in Annie's ears: the voice of her mother.

"Can't you ever clean this kitchen the way I told you to?"

"That boy touched you again, didn't he? I told you to stay away from him. That's all he wants."

"I don't know what I'm going to do with you. Just look at you! You're filthy, and Grandma is coming this afternoon. Can't I leave you alone for a minute?"

All her life, Annie had lived with those messages sent by a mother who probably had grown up in the same type of home environment. Now the messages were playing over and over in her mind.

Scott knew the impact of it, and he felt hurt for his wife. They both wanted to learn how to deal with their own conflicts over a potential career move. But each time they talked, they hit a brick wall. Annie would shut down or become overly defensive, and Scott would throw up his arms in a combination of disgust and frustration. They couldn't get past the first few minutes of discussion without blowing up. Their kids were watching and growing increasingly insecure as a third generation began to wear the pain of a shame-based family.

"I will never do it right, Scott," Annie would say. "I know I'll come up short in your eyes."

"Go without me. Look at me. I'll never be ready on time. I can't go out looking like this, Scott."

"It's no use. I am who I am. I'll never change."

These statements reflect a deep sense of inferiority stemming from a history of coming up short in the eyes of her parents and now herself. At times, these statements lead Annie to withdrawal and isolation, not wanting others to have to be exposed to her. At other times, they lead to a drivenness as she tries to measure up to an elusive set of standards that are way out of reach. A combination of humiliation, self-disgust, perfectionism, defensiveness, and a general sense of uncertainty create an explosive diet.

Shame is defined as "humiliation so painful, embarrassment so deep, and a sense of being so completely diminished that one feels he or she will disappear into a pile of ashes."[6]

People experiencing shame feel an underlying ambivalence. They want to be liked by others, but they fear letting people get too close because of their deep sense of personal inadequacy.

Secrets flourish in the shame-based home. Defensiveness prevails as a way to try to hold in the pain that is too overwhelming to face. Sometimes shame occurs in homes like Annie's, where it's passed from generation to generation, finding victims in its pathway. Other times shame finds its roots in childhood experiences, such as sexual or physical abuse, where the pain of the events is so great that the victims are unwilling or seemingly unable to communicate about them for fear of scarring the family. So they carry the secret around, praying it never surfaces to disturb the thin veneer covering their pain.

How does the red light of shame differ from the red light of guilt? Guilt deals with behavior. People feel guilty for what they did. Shame deals with the person. People feel shame for who they are. Shame cuts so much more deeply to the basis of our identity.

Sandra Wilson, in her excellent book *Released from Shame*, wrote, "Shame is a sense of being uniquely and hopelessly flawed. Shame leaves a person feeling different from and less valuable than other human beings."[7]

So how does Annie cope with the shame that binds her? By trying to be perfect in everything she does. This is a common response. People experiencing shame hope that by doing things perfectly, someone will give them the attention and approval that was so deeply missed in childhood.

A second component of shame is control. But this desire for control is not rooted in a need for power. Power isn't the issue. If it were that easy, the achievement of position, social status, or other perks would feed the craving of the shame-based person. The issue is more basic; it's safety.

Annie is so threatened by her world that she will strive for perfection so she can set the ground rules for the relationship. This allows her a sense of predictability in a world that seems dangerous, and it's part of the core reason she and Scott struggle so much in the resolution of their conflicts. Shame has so much power that it blinds Scott and pushes him away as Annie uses it to try to find boundaries that don't keep him *out* so much as they try to keep her self *in*.

Is Annie bound to the shame of her past? No. But it will take great courage and faith for her to overcome it. Pat Springle explained in his book *Codependency: A Christian Perspective*:

> Dr. Paul Tournier once compared life to a man hanging from a trapeze. The trapeze bar was the man's security, his pattern of existence, his lifestyle. Then God swung another trapeze into the man's view, and he faced a perplexing dilemma. Should he relinquish his past? Should he reach for the new bar? The moment of truth came, Dr. Tournier explained, when the man realized that to grab onto the new bar, he must release the old one. [8]

Annie and Scott learned how to let go of the "old bar" and grab onto the new one. It was painful for them to come to conclusions, because it forced an inside look at a heart that was troubled for years.

Annie needed to learn that her mother did not need to be the rule of thumb by which Annie lived her life. She came to love her mother in a new way as she released her from the powerful role she once had. Annie also needed to let go of the shame that bound her as she grabbed onto the new bar of grace God offered her.

Grace is one of two key biblical concepts a person experiencing shame needs to understand. In his second letter to the Corinthian church, the apostle Paul wrote, "But he said to me, 'My grace is sufficient for you, for my power is made perfect in weakness.' Therefore I will boast all the more gladly about my weaknesses, so that Christ's power may rest on me." [9]

It's in our very weakness that God is allowed by our prideful spirits to exercise His power in our lives.

The other key concept is *regeneration*. Shame, based on the inner core of how we see ourselves, can only be released through regeneration. We need to see ourselves as the new people God causes us to be when we place our faith in Jesus Christ.

Paul wrote to the Ephesians: "That, in reference to your former manner of life, you lay aside the old self, which is being corrupted in accordance with the lusts of deceit, and that you be renewed in the spirit of your mind, and put on the new self, which in the likeness of God has been created in righteousness and holiness of the truth." [10]

Receiving the gift of new life allows us to release to God once and for all the sins of our past. Do we forget them? Not likely. But as we understand them, we can move past them as we receive His grace and forgiveness. Annie and Scott received this type of release as their marriage healed and their kids began to see a different way of resolving conflicts.

Red lights impede us from resolving conflicts and restoring broken relationships. They simply get in the way. However, red lights don't have to stop us. Instead we can anticipate them, slow down, and heed their warnings. We can recognize their power, respond to them appropriately, and then proceed cautiously, but proceed nevertheless.

In the next chapter, we'll look at a fifth red light, one we all struggle with in one form or another.

SLAYING DRAGONS

A fifth red light keeping people from resolving
conflict may be the most formidable of all: *fear*.
All of us fear something. We all know people who
seem to handle life extremely well—until you
mention something that sparks a look of weakness and
apprehension: jet travel, snakes, heights, or the fact
that they look just like one of their parents.

What is fear? Primarily, it's a response to something we see as powerful or threatening. Fear can be
either a positive or a negative force in our lives. In the
Bible, we're instructed to fear God. The Hebrew term
yirah means "to be afraid, to stand in awe, to fear." Our
fear of God represents our deference to His power in

our lives. It is manifested in our trust. Ironically, this very trust in God protects us from having to experience the other type of fear, the one that comes as a negative response to the various events and circumstances in our lives.

In their book *Worry-Free Living*, Frank Minirth, Paul Meier, and Don Hawkins pointed out that Adam experienced a negative fear when he stopped exhibiting a healthy fear of God: "Significantly, fear is the very first emotion mentioned in Scripture. It occurs in Genesis 3:10 in Adam's statement to God, immediately following his disobedience: 'I was afraid because I was naked; and I hid myself.'" [1]

How does fear stand in the way of resolving conflict? Many people know they need to resolve certain conflicts, and often they know how to do it, but they lack the courage to confront some real or perceived threat. So they avoid dealing with the issue, deciding instead to play it safe.

Let me show you how four different types of fear prevent people from resolving conflict.

FEAR OF FAILURE

Martha is 40 years old and hasn't lived in her parents' home for nearly 20 years. Yet she still feels like a child whenever she's with her 83-year-old mother. "I'm a grown woman with kids of my own," Martha says, "and she still treats me like I need to do whatever she tells me to."

One night recently, Martha and her mother were dressing to go out for dinner. Martha walked into the living room, and her mother snapped, "Oh, you're not wearing that dress. It has buttons up the front like mine. You need to change."

Let's analyze this situation for a moment. You've probably faced similar predicaments, and you can probably guess what thoughts were raging through Martha's mind: *She has no right to tell me what to wear! Who cares if both dresses have buttons on the front—they aren't even the same color or style! I should tell her to mind her own business!*

Martha had a choice to make: Should she stand up to her mother or go change? On one hand, she was tired of these kinds of comments. On the other, whenever she tried to reason with her mother, she failed. Her mother would act hurt and say that Martha never cared for her feelings. Or she would grow angry and say something like, "You don't know anything about dressing for an occasion like this anyway. You never have!"

So rather than try to resolve a long-running problem, Martha gave in to her fear of failure. *It's not worth the hassle*, she told herself. *She's never listened in the past, and she won't listen now. She's too set in her ways.*

When we have a fear of failure, we'll go to any lengths to avoid the fear-producing stimulus, whether it be a relationship, place, or event. The fear can become so severe in relationships that communication in any form becomes a chore. We may feel as if we don't measure up to the other person's expectations, so we stay away either physically or emotionally. Wanting to avoid the pain of failure, and not having the tools or courage to face the fear head-on, we can allow conflicts to fester for years.

People who live with a fear of failure often develop a lifestyle involving a minimal amount of interaction with others. They live lives of boredom and end up dying on the vine of mediocrity. Nothing ventured, nothing lost—but also nothing gained.

FEAR OF REJECTION

Fear of rejection is the small voice that tells us, *If they really knew what you're thinking and feeling, they would laugh at you and turn away from you. They would reject you.* It's the type of fear that keeps people from explaining the true reasons for some conflicts. It's the thought that *If I really reach out, I'll be rejected again, and I can't take another rejection. So I'll crawl within myself and shut down.*

A person who experiences this type of fear may lose self-confidence to the degree that depression or anxiety could develop. The conflicts in the relationships may persist, but the pain of discussing them is so great that avoidance seems the best route to take.

One morning I counseled two different women who had the same problem: They were both abused as children, and neither had told her husband. They felt their husbands were insensitive and would not grasp how deeply they hurt.

They were determined to work out the problem themselves. But giving in to their fear of rejection was causing problems in their marriages. Polly felt she couldn't reach out to Ed because if she told him the truth, he might lose interest in her sexually. He had commented many times, after watching television shows about sexual abuse, "If I was that guy, I just couldn't stick around."

Polly didn't feel Ed was a bad husband. He provided for their family and loved their kids. But he would always become angry when discussing issues related to sexuality. He sent the message over and over, "If anything happened before I knew you, please don't tell me. I just couldn't handle knowing."

So what was Polly to do? Each time she and Ed watched a movie, read a newspaper, or even listened to a song that had to do with sexuality, she closed down, and he became anxious. She knew that complete honesty with him could mean the end of their marriage. "It just isn't worth running the risk of rejection," Polly said. "I'm stuck."

Heather had a different slant on her fear of rejection.

Her husband, Randy, worked with her brother, Fred—the same brother who had abused her. Randy and Fred not only worked together, but they also hunted and watched every imaginable sports event on television together. In short, they were best friends. And Heather was stuck right in the middle.

Fred sexually abused her four times during a two-year period. Each time she got together with her family for holidays, or even when Fred called on the phone, she would feel a strange sensation, but she never dreamed it was because of sexual abuse.

She had repressed the memory until hearing a sermon one day that jogged her memory, washing the terror of those events over her like a tidal wave. As Heather remembered the abuse, she knew she was dealing with something that needed to be resolved. Her sexual relationship with Randy had never been very healthy, and now she was beginning to realize why. And she was scared.

As Heather and I talked about the abuse, it became increasingly clear that fear controlled much of her life. She felt she was between a rock and a hard place. She didn't want to confront her brother, because she was afraid of being rejected by him and her family. She also didn't want to tell her husband, because it would ruin Randy and Fred's working relationship as well as their friendship. Finally, she didn't know if anyone would believe her even if she told them.

As a result, Heather came to the conclusion that she was trapped within her own family, holding a secret that would blow the top off the entire family if it ever surfaced.

Every day we face pressures and problems, and one of the best ways to deal with them is to talk them out with someone you love and trust. Yet both Polly and Heather held their most intimate thoughts from their husbands. They felt trapped as they experienced the red light of fear of rejection.

That fear is one of the saddest things that can happen in a marriage. Think of it: All of us look for someone who will listen to us, who is interested in us, who will see us as we are and accept us unconditionally. Often we enter into marriage feeling that way about each other. But something happens in many marriages over time, and instead of communicating love and acceptance, we begin broadcasting a judgmental attitude. Many men also harbor this fear of rejection. A husband may not discuss his sexual or emotional needs with his wife because every time he does, she seems to reject him. So he may stop making his needs known.

Then what often happens is he starts looking to meet his needs outside the marriage. This is how many affairs begin. We tend to go to where we're affirmed. If the boundaries around the marriage are not strong enough to protect it, a person may unwisely give in to the temptation of adultery.

Some people also feel that if they talk honestly about their feelings, they'll be put down: "Oh, you shouldn't even be thinking that." But they may still feel the need to express it. Honest communication greases the wheels of a healthy relationship. We don't want to be judged; we just want to be heard.

FEAR OF EMOTIONAL INTIMACY

A third type of fear that can impede the resolution of conflicts is the fear of emotional intimacy, which is different from sexual intimacy. Sexual intimacy is easy. Two bodies can meet as strangers and walk away as strangers. Emotional intimacy, on the other hand, takes work and commitment.

When we fear emotional intimacy, we "numb out," put up the walls of self-protection, and keep everybody away. We refuse to run the risk of letting anybody "in." We either blow our tops regularly so that nobody can stay close, or we avoid getting too close in the first place. Either way, we lose. And often, so do those around us.

Perhaps emotional intimacy was lacking in your home as you grew up, so you never learned how to allow other people to be close to you. If so, you may avoid dealing with conflict in order to keep the layers of self-protection intact.

That was the case with Pete. He grew up in a home where chaos reigned and emotional intimacy was a myth. His father had a ferocious temper, kicking into a rage when Pete and his brothers would least expect it. Looking for acceptance, Pete pulled away from his family and hung out with guys his parents rejected as being "from the wrong side of the tracks." His grades dropped in high school, and like so many hurting and needy kids, he began to run wild—sex, alcohol, drugs, the whole nine yards.

In his junior year of high school, Pete met Kathy, who also came from a painful home. These two love-starved kids were soon trying to replace the legitimate need for emotional intimacy with the easy answer of sexual intimacy. She got pregnant a year and a half later and considered an abortion, but she faced a dilemma. She believed her father would never forgive her for embarrassing him as her older brother had by getting his girlfriend pregnant four years before.

So Pete and Kathy decided to get married and keep the baby. As the child grew, they lived in utter confusion. Their early married years were a mixture of abuse, conflict, and emotional pain. Now in their thirties, they were trying to develop a healthy relationship. But when Kathy got too close to Pete, he would shut down and withdraw.

Conflicts intensified as they tried to learn to resolve their pain. They found it all too easy to slip back into the muck of their upbringing. Repeating the dysfunctional patterns of their own families was killing the joy in their marriage and destroying them and their son.

When I met Pete and Kathy, they were trying to deal with Pete's avoidance of Kathy. He worked long hours and hung out at the health club, but he couldn't get into the groove of regular communication with his wife. She was fed up with trying and was beginning to distance from the marriage herself. They weren't in my office for more than ten minutes when, with exasperated looks on their faces, they turned to me and said, "Gary, it's too late."

As I listened to them, it certainly appeared late, but it wasn't too late. They needed to establish healthy patterns of communication. They also needed some modeling of building a strong marriage.

As we worked on Pete's avoidance of emotional intimacy by teaching him ways to draw Kathy closer, we learned that he was afraid of getting too close. He thought that if he became too vulnerable, she would leave him. As Kathy and Pete developed a greater sense of trust, they began to respond to each other.

The walls of self-protection came down little by little as their emotional intimacy grew. Trust was built, and the lines of communication began to open up as Pete took risks to let Kathy into his life. He started to work fewer hours, and they worked out at the health club together. As their time together increased, their marriage improved.

Today, Pete and Kathy's marriage is still growing. Why? Because they recognized that his avoidance of emotional intimacy was caused by hurt he experienced as a child. Kathy was not the villain. He could trust her. He needed to give her a chance, and they needed to learn healthy communication patterns. This willingness to work—coupled with their new understanding of the dynamics of dysfunction—was the key to their steady growth.

FEAR OF SUCCESS

After reading the heading just above, you may be saying, "The fear of failure makes sense, but who's afraid of success?" In the 1940s, a psychologist by the name of Karen Horney hit on this issue. People who fear success avoid taking risks because if they risk they may succeed, and success is such an alien idea. Just when they're about to do something that will matter or change their lives, they sabotage it and pull the rug out from under themselves.

Their subconscious thoughts say, *If I succeed, I'll have to be challenged and change, and I don't know how to handle that, so I'll blow this interview or insert this rationalization into the formula to get me out of this one.* They get so close to making it in a relationship, career, or spiritual life, but in many ways they're actually so far away.

Michelle understood the fear of success. She just didn't understand why she experienced it. Her parents were killed in a car accident when she was young. Her grandparents adopted her and raised her in a typical suburban area of a midwestern city. Michelle earned reasonably good grades, participated in school activities, and tried not to give her grandparents any trouble. Her grandmother was kind but was always tentative around her grandfather, who was stern and rarely demonstrated affection.

Michelle grew up with low self-esteem. She felt as if she never excelled in anything, and she struggled with relationships with both girls and boys. She felt different from her friends who had siblings and parents of a normal age. She was thankful she had a home, but she never felt she pleased her grandparents.

After high school, Michelle attended a college near home and got a job downtown. Later, she started her career in an entry-level position, and after 12 years she had not earned much advancement. When she came to visit with me, she was frustrated and depressed.

As we got acquainted, I learned that she avoided most relationships. She would go to work each day and return each evening to her apartment, where she isolated herself. As we studied her patterns of behavior, we saw that whenever she began to develop relationships, she would somehow sabotage them. She would either become critical of the other people or distance herself from them. After a period of time, her friends would give up.

At the time we met, Michelle was going through this cycle with a friend named Amy. They had met at work and had begun having lunch together. They had a lot in common and in the early stages enjoyed each other. But as Amy learned more about Michelle, it was clear that Michelle lived a different life outside of work. Most evenings, Michelle would pull within herself and shut down. She started canceling plans she and Amy had made. Then she began to criticize Amy to other co-workers.

When Amy confronted Michelle, Michelle first denied either pulling away or making critical comments. Amy continued to initiate communication with Michelle, and when it was clear Amy was not going to back off, Michelle admitted she was pulling away from the relationship. She knew she was withdrawing and being critical of Amy, but she wasn't clear why she was doing it.

When I pointed out that it appeared she might be fearful of succeeding, she was shocked. "Why wouldn't I want to succeed?" she asked. "Everybody wants to succeed, don't they?"

I explained that while we all want to succeed, it's also true that it can be scary to give up old, familiar ways of living, even if they aren't healthy. So many people pull the rug out from under their efforts to move ahead. "Does that make any sense?" I asked.

"It sounds familiar, doesn't it?" Michelle said. "I think I want to change, Gary, but I don't know where to start. How do I do it?"

THE FINE ART OF SLAYING DRAGONS

My response to Michelle was the same as my message to you. We start by admitting that our self-defeating behaviors are just that; they're defeating our growth. We need to change the way we keep repeating the mistakes of the past.

How? By confronting the behaviors that diminish our success. And we also learn to "slay dragons." We need to slay them as if they are snorting their fear-inducing messages in our direction.

A man I saw in counseling years ago taught me how to slay dragons. Let me explain. Ray told me that when he has a fear—and he has a lot of them—he pictures a little dragon about ten feet away in the room. He may have feared failure or success. He may have even feared rejection or emotional intimacy. But he learned that the more he fed the fear with irrational thinking and worry, the more the dragon grew. The only way to stop the growth was to slay the dragon before it overpowered him.

What a word picture! A fire-breathing, smoke-snortin' dragon fed by your fears that demands to be confronted with the truth and slain! Ray's technique has not only helped many people with whom I've counseled, but it has also helped me knock off a few of my own "Snortin' B. Mortons"!

Michelle learned how to change her self-defeating behaviors by slaying some dragons and setting some realistic goals. She learned to take incremental steps to build relationships. She spent more time with new friends and, as time went on, even closed the loop with Amy and her grandparents over some issues that had remained unresolved.

As she gained some success in a few relationships and her work performance, Michelle became more confident. Her fears began to diminish, and she grew more optimistic. The fear of success *can* be whipped. But as with any fear, it means hitting the issues head-on.

The apostle Paul stated, "For when we came into Macedonia, this body of ours had no rest, but we were harassed at every turn—conflicts on the outside, fears within." [2] Conflicts on the outside, fear within. Sound familiar? For many of us, that's how we live life. We struggle through all the conflicts in our relationships and feel a dread and fear within.

Fear is mentioned hundreds of times in the Bible. We're told by an all-knowing Father to "fear not," but it still scares us to take the risk. So we empower the dragon and continue to feed it until it looms so large that we shut down or hit the bricks. However, our living God tells us to fear not and empowers us, through His Spirit, to stand boldly in the face of adversity. God promises that He will be by our side. Now, that is a true friend.

Whether we struggle with the fear of failure, rejection, intimacy, or success (or some or all of them), we can gain a true sense of encouragement by recognizing that God doesn't intend for us to exercise fear. What He does intend is for us to demonstrate faith—the belief in Someone not seen; placing our trust in Him. This faith in God allows us to slay all our dragons.

Next we look at a final red light that keeps many people from resolving conflicts, and it's a biggie.

CHAPTER 10

GIMMEE THE CLICKER

W here is that thing?" asked a frustrated dad.

"I don't have it, Dad. Maybe Mom does," fired back Sarah.

"Gary, I don't have it," said Barb. "Are you sure it isn't under the cushion on the couch? Or maybe Missy has it."

"Dad, I know where it is. It's under the afghan, over by the pie cabinet, next to my shoes," replied Missy with a bit of hesitation.

In my home, the elusive "thing" that gets tossed everywhere is the "clicker"—the remote control for the television. You probably have one, too. And whoever has the clicker can drive the entire family nuts at the push of a button. Whoever has it has the supreme power in the family, because he or she controls what's being watched on TV. Dads love to have it.

"Sarah, turn that back. I was watching that show," says Missy.

"Too bad, you aren't anymore," replies a newly self-appointed power broker.

"I'm the dad. I'll determine what we watch. Give me the clicker," says a grumpy dad.

"I was here first, Dad. Doesn't that count?" asks a daughter, realizing she's about to lose control.

"No. Not when I want to watch the football game."

Control in families is a little like the television remote control, isn't it? Whoever holds the power can change the mood of the entire family within seconds, just by "pushing a button."

"I'm going to my room. Nobody listens to me anyway. I'm tired of being around the rest of you." *Click*. Conflict.

"If I have to ask you one more time to pick up this house, I'm going to throw up." *Click*. Conflict.

"You don't care about me, do you? If you did, you would listen when I'm talking to you." *Click*. Conflict.

Do any of those comments sound familiar? An evening in my home can be progressing with little fanfare until somebody "grabs the clicker" and pushes the button that either starts a conflict or reveals the pain of his or her heart.

The desire for control is the final red light that prevents people from resolving conflict in a healthy manner. And it's a big one.

DENNY AND KAREN GRAB FOR THE CLICKER

As Denny hung up the phone, he knew the business deal he had been working on for months was going down the tubes. His sales had been off for the last two quarters, and he was getting heat from the sales manager to increase sales or run the risk of joining the unemployed. Pressure City.

There he sat in his office, feeling more demoralized than he ever thought possible. His business was getting hammered from every direction, he wasn't spending any time with his kids, and he was frustrated in his marriage. It was 6:30, and he was already late for dinner—the third time that week. It was time to head for home, if you could still call it a home.

As Denny turned off his computer, he swung his chair around to his credenza and saw the picture of his three kids. *What a memory that vacation was, even if it was six years ago. Where has the time gone?* he thought. As he held the picture in his hands, he realized it was the most recent picture he had taken of the family.

Things have been busy, he rationalized. *They understand.*

As he returned the picture to the credenza, he glanced over at a photo of his wife, Karen, and thought, *How am I ever going to describe to her how bad things are? She doesn't listen anyway. There's no way I can face her on this issue. She'll either hit the roof or call her parents when I tell her I didn't get the account. She's always running to them. I can't believe things have gotten this bad.*

Karen sat in the family room after another dinner without her husband. She had awakened before 6:00 A.M., got the kids ready for school, vacuumed the upstairs, made lunches, got dressed, and rushed to work. Following a full day in the office, she fulfilled her parental taxi duties. After getting the kids to all their activities, she got home at 6:00 P.M., prepared dinner, returned four phone calls from the answering machine, paid a few bills, fed the kids and herself, and began doing laundry. *Life in the suburbs!* she thought. *Give me Donna Reed any day!*

Karen was yanked on, pulled at, and stretched beyond her limits. She and Denny were in a cold war and had not talked—really talked—in weeks. She grew up in a home where her mother loved her dad and her dad modeled healthy relationships. *Boy, did I drop the ball!* she figured. *How did I get into this marriage, anyway?* She was full of such self-defeating thoughts.

As Karen surveyed her home, she felt totally exhausted. And in less than ten hours, she would have to get up and do it all again. She didn't know whether she should cry, scream, or leave. She was afraid to leave, but the thought was becoming more appealing each day. As she turned off the kitchen light, she said to herself, *Off for a bath and 15 minutes to myself.* So upstairs she went for a respite from the war of the worlds.

Denny got into his car and made the 25-minute drive home. As he pulled into the driveway, he noticed the kitchen light was off. *It's only 7:15,* he thought, *but they probably ate without me anyway.* His mood was beginning to shift from rejection to frustration.

Entering the house, he looked around at what appeared, in his estimation, to be the aftermath of a tornado. Shoes and a blanket were lying on the family room floor. A bowl was in the kitchen sink. To many of us, that scene would seem more the result of a gentle breeze than of a tornado, but Denny had zero tolerance for anything that was out of place. And he was getting worse. He could feel his blood pressure going up as he thought, *All I do for this family is work, and they can't even take care of things. That's just fine. See if I care.* Now his frustration was gearing up and bordering on anger.

Denny opened the refrigerator, got out some leftovers, popped them in the microwave, set the timer at two minutes, and said to himself, *I don't care how bad this place looks. I'm not going to say anything. Maybe that approach will work. Nothing else does.*

As he stood by the microwave, he started thinking,

How long does this thing take, anyway? My food isn't even heated yet! I'm getting a new microwave; this one is obsolete. Can you feel the buttons on his clicker being pushed a little harder with each thought?

As the bell rang indicating his food was "zapped" enough, Denny sat down with the newspaper to eat his dinner.

Karen heard the garage door open as she sat in her bubbles receiving the only soothing she had experienced all day. *He's home,* she thought. *Now what do I do? Do I go down and pretend everything is okay, or do I let him know how frustrated and angry I am? I'm tired of the charades and sick of his control. I know that as soon as I go downstairs, he'll either complain, demand, or ice me out.*

As Karen got ready to go down and find the answer to her self-talk, she knew Denny was going to be hot. Everything was not perfect, and with Denny it had to be perfect. *How am I going to get out of this one?* she thought. She felt out of control and knew that one way to get control of the clicker was to act surprised to see Denny home. A healthy response? No, but it was one of the games they played.

THE ENCOUNTER

As Karen walked into the kitchen, she said, "I didn't know you were home. It's only 7:15. I thought I had more time to pick up."

Ah, three shots in one, Denny thought without even looking up. Karen had just picked up the clicker.

Shot number one: *She didn't know I was home. She never does. It's been years since anybody welcomed me home to this place.* Shot number two: *It's "only" 7:15. I'm only an hour late, so give me a break! Do you know what I did today? Well, you won't hear it from me with that attitude.* And shot number three: *You would have picked up. Fat chance, Karen. You wouldn't know how to pick up correctly if the queen of England was visiting.*

"Hello, Karen," Denny said aloud. "I'm just going to eat, do some paperwork, and hit the hay. I'm beat. Where are the kids?"

"Mandy is doing homework at Meagen's, Chris is over at Brandon's, and Nicholas is over at Eric's house," she replied without even looking at him.

"Aren't they ever home? I feel like we're running a cruise ship around here," he said, his patience running thinner. *Now who had the clicker?*

Remember the old saying "If you can't stand the heat, get out of the kitchen"? That's exactly what Karen was thinking. But enough was enough. She was tired of Denny's controlling and demeaning behavior. He was tired of her controlling behavior. They were both tired of each other, and way down deep, they were also frustrated with themselves and how they were responding to their problems.

Karen decided to enter the fracas and exercise some

of her own controlling behavior. "Denny, don't start with me. [Gimmee the clicker.] No matter which way I go, you hammer at me. If I take them places and get them into activities, I'm blowing your money. If I don't, you accuse me of not getting them involved in life. I try to keep you happy, but it's no use."

"Listen to me, Karen. [Pass the clicker, and pass it now!] I work to provide for this family, and taking care of the kids is your job, just like taking care of this house is supposed to be. But you sure don't do that very well. Look at this glass; it has water spots all over it. The family room looks like a war zone, and this kitchen couldn't pass a health inspection. You go to craft classes all weekend, shop at the mall, and don't pull your weight. I've had it with you and this house!"

Now they were both exasperated and getting more angry each second. The clicker was dizzy from being tossed back and forth.

A SAD STORY, BUT TRUE

That's the sad story of a family torn apart by the red light of controlling behavior. Denny's domination was sucking the life out of their marriage. Karen's response had been to try to please him, but she was giving up on that approach because it never worked. She was grabbing the clicker and taking some of the control. They were two good people who were frustrated with a relationship that had gone from joy to neutrality to hostility.

Denny was a master controller. Karen was getting pretty good at using the clicker herself. But the two of them used different kinds of controlling behaviors. To understand the red light of control and how damaging it can be, let's take a look at their different slants on this devastating practice.

CONTROL BY ISOLATION

Denny had become isolated and wasn't sharing his feelings with Karen anymore, in sharp contrast to their dating years. He had expressed his feelings back then. But as time went on, he pulled away from his wife and put all his energy into his work.

When conflict began to brew, however, he kicked into his control cycle. He would grab the clicker and use hostility to regain command. Instead of communicating with Karen or his kids, he would bark out orders, which resulted in further alienation from his family.

You also can see in the story above how Denny would "unplug" from Karen in order to exercise control, withholding information he knew was of interest to her. Initially he rationalized he was doing it to protect her, but as time went on, he used the information as power. He reasoned, *If she can't be nice to me, I just won't tell her things. I'll show her.*

CONTROL BY UNSUCCESSFUL PLEASING AND ULTIMATE RETALIATION

Karen was also isolated. After years of reaching out to Denny and trying to keep him happy, she became increasingly frustrated and started to pull away. Her kids were getting older, and she felt no one needed her. Oh, Denny needed her to run the household and keep the plates spinning, but she didn't feel needed emotionally.

Rejection followed rejection, and ultimately the only way Karen felt she could cope was to put up walls to keep Denny out. She vacillated between trying to pull him close and getting hostile to keep him from hurting her. She was increasingly confused about how to respond to him. So she resorted to the very behavior she criticized him for: control.

Trying to please Denny hadn't worked, so she took to returning insults for insults. She developed a whole battery of weapons to get back at him. She was hurt, frustrated, and lonely, and she was fed up with his controlling behavior.

When she finally risked "talking back," she found she could also grab the clicker and exercise control. At other times, she would exercise control in more-subtle ways. This is called *passive-aggressive* behavior, which I define as "getting someone without his knowing he's getting got." We act this way when we intentionally "forget" things we were supposed to do, act in a stubborn way, or manipulate others.

THE CYCLE OF SELF-DESTRUCTION

Denny and Karen were caught in a cycle of self-destruction. A marriage that at one time was vital was now a victim of clicker abuse. The more they tried to gain control of each other, the more they contributed to the deterioration of the marriage. Their conflicts were also becoming evident to friends and family.

Their kids were busy night and day. Like most kids, they kept hectic schedules, but they had reasons beyond the typical ones. They stayed busy to avoid the stress in their home. They were exercising their own red light of control by staying out of the way. And when we talked, it was clear they wanted nothing to do with Mom and Dad. If the yelling wasn't getting to them, the absence of emotional intimacy was.

Control shouldn't be confused with *self-control*. The apostle Paul wrote, "But the fruit of the Spirit is love, joy, peace, patience, kindness, goodness, faithfulness, gentleness and self-control. Against such things there is no law." [1] Self-control is good; controlling others is damaging.

We all need to exercise self-control, but we need

to be cautious about how we use our clickers in relationships with others. Just as it's poor manners to grab the remote control from a family member when watching television, it's also inappropriate to grab the control from someone in a relationship.

THE BEAT GOES ON

Remember the old Sonny and Cher song "The Beat Goes On"? That was the theme song of Denny and Karen's home. The beat continued to go on and on, and the five family members were all leading separate lives of painful rejection and hurt. The message the kids were getting was simple: "Put up a wall, and keep your flanks guarded." They were all wounded and had no idea how to break the cycle of self-destruction.

As we conducted family counseling, I taught them about the elements of control. To deal with the potential damage from controlling behavior, they would learn to identify what they were doing and why.

Controlling behavior tends to come out of deep insecurity and manifests itself in one of two ways: (1) becoming a pleaser and avoiding the other person, or (2) becoming hostile and aggressively controlling the other individual. But there is another option. We can learn to communicate our needs directly without crossing the line of control. When I began to illustrate this point to Denny, Karen, and their kids, I used a word picture that helped them learn how to respond to each other in a healthy way.

I would like to invite you inside the four walls of my office for a bird's-eye view of how that session went. Come on in, but please keep the chatter down.

MY FOUR O'CLOCK APPOINTMENT ON WEDNESDAY: THE OLSONS

"Denny, Karen, troops. How did things go in the Olson home this past week?" As I asked that question, things got quiet within a second. *Not a great way to start the session*, I thought.

"Not real well, Gary," replied Denny as he looked at each of the three kids and Karen with one of those "I dare you to tell him the real story" looks.

"What happened?" I asked, knowing what was coming was going to make the next hour pretty interesting.

"Mom and Dad had another argument," said 6-year-old Nicholas.

"Yeah, they really blew up this time," 12-year-old Chris added.

"It wasn't *that* bad," offered 15-year-old Mandy in an attempted rescue.

"Gary, Denny and I got into a major conflict the other night," said Karen. "I think we need to talk it out, because the kids are all pretty upset. To be honest, we all need help sorting this one out."

"Were you kids at home?" I asked.

"No, we were all at friends' houses," said Mandy. "We just heard about it when we got home."

Over the next 20 minutes, the kids gave their renditions of a stressful night in the Olson home. Denny and Karen also jumped in with some honest input about a difficult conflict.

"It sounds as if Mom and Dad were pretty frustrated that night, doesn't it, you guys?" I asked as the three kids nodded. "Why don't we talk about how to deal with that frustration by using a word picture. We've used those before."

THE DOOR OF RESPONSIBILITY

Word pictures are a tremendous tool for counselors and anyone else in trying to communicate effectively. Gary Smalley and John Trent define a word picture this way: "An emotional word picture is a communication tool that uses a story or object to activate simultaneously the emotions and intellect of a person. In so doing, it causes the person to experience our words, not just hear them."[2]

At that point in the session, Nicholas chimed in, "Yeah, like the one about feeling like Chris uses my head like a basketball, always bouncing me around and shoving me?"

"That was a good word picture you came up with, Nicholas," I said. "Now let's try one that talks about how control is used in your family. Let's say I loaned you one of these books from my library here in my counseling office. If that was the case, you would be treated like anyone else who borrows a book from me—like a terrorist. I would have my secretary, Deb, fingerprint you, take your engagement ring or papers for your firstborn son —that's you, Chris—as collateral, and videotape your promise to return it within a week.

"After a couple of weeks, I would give you a call and ask you to return the book before I claim your firstborn son."

"It would be okay with me if you took Chris," said Mandy.

They all laughed at that one except Chris, who gave her the evil eye.

"I'm at home that day," I continued, "so you drive over and come up to the front door. Now, when you come up to the door, you have three options. First, you could walk right in without knocking and stroll around the house, searching for me. Second, you could lay the book on the doorstep, knock on the door, and then run away, hoping you wouldn't have to face me in person.

"The third option would be to come to the front

door, knock on it, and wait until I come to greet you. After our greeting, I would invite you in, and we would sit in the living room on those chairs no one ever sits in but that cost more than my car, have some apple cider, and shoot the breeze for an hour or so. Which one of those would you do?"

"It isn't my house. I wouldn't just walk in," said Mandy.

"It isn't polite, so of course I would knock," said Denny.

"I respect your privacy—I wouldn't just barge in on you," Karen responded.

"I'd knock and run," said Nicholas with a toothless grin.

"Well, if you did, Nicholas, I wouldn't chase you," I said. "Let me tell you why. Your responses illustrate the point of this word picture. Assume that the front door to the house represents the line of responsibility and control in a relationship." I then showed them the following diagram:

CONTROLLER	**PLEASER**
This person barges in and controls.	This person knocks at the door and runs away.

When we're controlling or allowing others to control us, I explained, we tend to approach the door with what I call black-and-white thinking. Everything is either one way or another: black or white. We have either lost the capacity to see the gray areas of life, the middle ground, or we never developed the ability to see them in the first place. We act either demanding and aggressive or avoidant. Another way of phrasing it is that we're either "controllers" or "pleasers." Let's define those terms.

Controllers bash through the door and right into another person's area of responsibility. Not only do they walk right in without being invited, but they may even break the door down in the process. Through aggression, overt manipulation, demands, or perfectionism, they lay out expectations that are too high for the other person. They feel it's their responsibility to control the situation, and they want the other person to act as they wish.

Pleasers allow others to control them. They come to the door and think, *Oh, I can't do it. I can't face him.* So they run away from responsibility. They try to be pleasers, often subjecting their needs to the desires of others. It's as if they come to the door and knock— and then run away.

Below the surface, however, pleasers aren't feeling so gracious as they appear. In fact, what they're really feeling is resentment and bitterness. There's a profound difference between being pleasing to people and being a pleaser. When we're genuinely pleasing, we're gracious and giving. When we're pleasers, our behavior looks the same, but it grows out of a passive attitude that has developed a "jump through the hoops" pattern of behavior.

Another characteristic of the pleaser is to avoid the other person. We've all done it. Someone intimidates you, so you find creative ways to ensure that your paths seldom cross. Or you adopt an attitude of indifference or passivity, setting your expectations for the relationship so low that you won't be hurt.

In Denny and Karen's marriage, he clearly was the controller, and Karen was the pleaser. But she was shifting over because of her intensifying frustration.

Both the controller and the pleaser squash relationships and leave conflicts unresolved. We put all our energy into making sure everyone marches to the beat of our drum, or we become exhausted trying to measure up to expectations (many times unstated) of others in order to win their approval. Either way, we fall into the pothole of control.

"Does that word picture make sense, folks?" I asked the Olsons as I wrapped up.

"Yeah, it's kind of like if I run up to Brandon's house and just walk in without being invited. It isn't polite, is it?" asked Chris.

"No, it isn't, Chris. You need to knock and then be asked in. When you're asked in, then you can have a good time with your friend."

"That makes sense to me, Gary," said Mandy.

"That's part of the reason we have so many conflicts at home. We keep breaking down each other's doors, don't we? It's like no one respects each other. We're either pushing on each other or running away from our problems."

"I think I'm being both a controller and a pleaser," said Karen. "Can you do both?"

"A lot of us do; I've done both," I admitted to the family. "Sometimes we go back and forth between the two perspectives. But both are problems, because we're not being honest about our feelings."

Denny quietly but directly jumped in. "Karen, kids, it's pretty clear what I'm doing, isn't it? I'm a controller, and it's taking a toll on all of you. To be honest, it's also taking its toll on me. How do we change?"

That was one of the hardest things Denny had ever done. For the first time in a long time, he said he was wrong and began to seek restoration of some broken relationships. And as he began to wrap up his thoughts to his wife and kids, I realized they were ready to take another step in the process of change. It was time for the counselor to take a risk.

"There's an option," I said, "an option that has worked for years. It has stood the test of time and is the basis for healthy relationships. It comes from a book I think you would find interesting." All five of them were caught by the hope that something could help. "The book is this one right here."

As I reached over to my desk and opened my Bible, it was clear that God had directed this session to help this family deal with a pattern of pain that was tearing them apart. "If it's okay," I said, "let me read something to you that I think will make sense. It comes from the last book of the Bible called Revelation. Jesus is talking, and He says something that I believe can help you."

A BIBLICAL RESPONSE

Then I read: "Here I am! I stand at the door and knock. If anyone hears my voice and opens the door, I will come in and eat with him, and he with me." [3]

Over the next several minutes, I showed this family a whole new level of hope that could combat their red light of controlling behavior. They listened, asked questions, caught the word picture, and acknowledged their thirst for some life-changing answers.

Remember how, in the old television series "The A Team," the colonel would say, "I love it when a plan comes together"? Well, that's what I said to myself and God as I wrapped up that session with the Olsons. I love it when a plan comes together, a plan that offers hope to those without hope and a direction to those who are lost along the way.

Just look at that verse in Revelation. It's incredible! And the Olsons could see that. "Here I am!" Jesus says. He's right at the door, knocking and waiting. Yet,

He's a gentleman. He doesn't knock it down, barge through, or act in a controlling way. He waits for you and me to open the door.

As we wrapped up the session, I told the Olsons I wanted to give them one more word picture since we did so well with the first.

"I like the story of the man driving down a country road on a foggy, fall night," I said. "He was all alone and hadn't seen any other cars for miles. Suddenly he approached a shadowy figure standing along the highway, apparently hitchhiking. As he passed, he thought he recognized him. To his amazement, it was Jesus Christ, hitchhiking right there on Highway 101."

"You mean Jesus was on a highway in our state?" asked a wide-eyed Nicholas.

"No, Nicholas," Denny said, returning to a gentleness his family remembered from long ago. "Remember, this is a word picture Gary is using."

"The man normally didn't pick up hitchhikers," I continued, "but he figured he could trust Jesus. So he screeched to a halt and then backed up to Him. He leaned over, opened the passenger door, and waited for Jesus to get in."

"What did Jesus do, Gary? Did He get in?" asked Karen.

"After a few moments, the man heard a rap at his window—on the driver's side. When he rolled down the window, Jesus leaned in and said two words.

"What do you think they were? 'My son'? No. 'You're loved'? No. He simply said, 'Move over.'"

"That's what He said, 'Move over'?" asked Mandy.

"That's what He said, Mandy. You see, Jesus didn't come to be a passenger in our lives. He didn't come to be a spare tire or a piece of luggage. He came to drive. He came to be in charge."

That four o'clock appointment opened up new doors of discussion with the Olsons. Over the next several months, they continued to confront their red lights, especially the red light of control. It was a hard process for them, but they began to heal.

Denny and Karen took long, hard looks at the destructive patterns of behavior they had established and started to build a relationship with Jesus into their lives. As the kids saw Mom and Dad learning to respond to each other, they began to feel more secure, and their controlling behaviors began to quiet. The control didn't stop completely. (I don't think it does for any of us, because we're selfish.) But they began to understand what was happening and how to confront their patterns of behavior.

ARE YOU HEARING A KNOCK AT YOUR DOOR?

For many of you reading this chapter, giving God control will mean yielding authority over many aspects of your lives. It will mean allowing Him to be in charge of other people rather than trying to exercise that responsibility yourself. For others, giving God control will mean you need to confront others whom you've allowed to control you too much.

Both groups will need to learn to respect others and their boundaries. You may need to go up to the door, express your needs, and communicate with your mate, child, friend, or parent in a respectful way without crossing over the line of control or running back to the car to escape.

The gospel is not that complicated. But inviting God into our lives also means we have to give up control, including control in relationships. And Jesus teaches us how to do that.

That's why I'm so excited about the Bible. It's so contemporary, and it works in our homes, our friendships, and our offices. It's a book about relationships, and it's as true today as when it was written.

If you're a man, be a gentleman. If you've been barging through the door of your wife's or child's "house," try knocking. Learn to express your needs and to let go of the control so your child and spouse can come to you.

If you're a woman and you're acting in a controlling manner, work at communicating in a healthy way and then letting go. Stop jumping over the line or running from the door. You may be thinking, *How do*

I do that? To help answer, I've devoted an entire chapter to communication (chap. 14).

Demanding control in a relationship undermines the resolution of conflicts. Loops remain open, hearts wounded. The appropriate resolution of conflict requires that we knock at the door and deal with the other person respectfully.

As I knock at people's doors, I try to remember that God has not placed a badge on my sweater saying "junior Holy Spirit." He already has a Holy Spirit, and He does just fine without me. I encourage you to ask yourself tough questions about where you may be trying to control others. Are you willing to take a second look at your behavior and learn to let go so the relationship can regain a sense of balance? Let's move over and let God be God. We aren't too good at the job anyway, are we?

C H A P T E R   1 1

NONNEGOTIABLE RELATIONSHIPS

"The counselor needs a counselor. Do you have a minute?" Stu Weber heard those words on the phone from a friend in the motel room next door. That friend needed someone to listen to him, someone to help him gain a clear understanding of his own pain. The friend was me. And it was Stu Weber's opportunity to be the counselor. Let me give you the background to the story.

Stu Weber is a pastor in Boring, Oregon. We have both been on the speaking team for the Family Ministry of Campus Crusade for Christ, conducting Family Life Conferences throughout the country, for the last several years. On this particular day, Stu and I were in

Minneapolis, and I needed some wisdom about a difficult counseling problem. I knew they don't come much wiser than Stu. As we headed out for a sandwich, I told him to start the clock. We were "in session," and I was now the counselee.

"Stu, I've been thrust into the middle of one of the most painful events of my life," I told him. "Barbara and I are very close to a couple who are going through an immense amount of pain. We've known these folks for almost 20 years, since we were college students, and have always admired them and thought their relationship was the type we needed to model our own after. But for the last couple of years, we've seen a tremendous amount of stress creeping into their relationship, and we've seen it tearing them apart."

"Have you talked to them about your concern?" Stu asked.

"Yes, I have. But the most frustrating thing is that I'm so close to both of them that I can't keep a sense of clarity about the issues. I think I'm too clouded by my own pain to deal with this. It's so frustrating to have the training and experience to help but to be so caught up personally that I become immobilized. I don't know what to do. I feel as if I'm going through a divorce myself. I've never felt so helpless as I do right now."

"Gary, do you feel they expect you to do something other than just care about both of them?" asked the counselor of the hour.

"I don't think so. Part of the problem is that they're so looked up to by so many people. Others around us know how close I am to them, and I think people may expect me to jump in and 'save them.' I know I can't, but I'm finding it increasingly difficult to not get dragged down with them. I feel torn between them."

Stu's response was direct, simple yet profound, and, as the proverb says, "apt as gold": "Gary, in my important relationships—with my wife, Lindy, my three sons, and my church—I've had to determine that nothing is more important than the relationship. The relationship is nonnegotiable. Anything else, other than the Bible, is open for discussion, but the relationship itself is not open for negotiation."

I sat in that deli and looked into the eyes of a man who once led troops in Vietnam as a Green Beret. Now he leads a church in a Portland suburb. And that day he led me into a clearer understanding of a problem that had been tearing my heart apart for months.

What I needed to do was to love this couple and realize that my relationship with each of them was nonnegotiable. No matter what happened, I would maintain my relationship with them. I didn't have to agree with what they were doing, I didn't have to take sides, and I sure didn't have to fix their problem. I simply needed to let both of them know that they meant more to me than the problem at hand. The issues were negotiable and up for discussion, but my commitment to each of them was not.

I just wish they had adopted the same attitude. While I remain close to each of them, they ended up splitting.

DIVORCE NOT AN OPTION

After all I've explained about the fork in the road in the last four chapters, this stage of the loop boils down to a decision: "Am I going to let this conflict go unresolved, allowing my heart to grow hard? Or am I going to move ahead by faith, despite whatever usually keeps me from closing the loop, and take steps to resolve this conflict? In other words, am I going to choose to lovingly rebuild the relationship?"

More than any other factor, your commitment to that relationship is critical. Is it negotiable? Are you willing to give it up? Or are you willing to do whatever is necessary to preserve it?

If people were honest, many would admit that getting married is like gambling—they hope it will work out, but if it doesn't, divorce is always an option. So when I take two young people through premarriage counseling, I urge them to consider their marriage an unbreakable vow. They need to commit themselves unconditionally to each other. They need to declare, "Divorce is not an option for us."

That type of commitment as the basis for relationship will not prevent us from experiencing conflict. But it will compel us to resolve those conflicts.

MY MATE IS NOT MY ENEMY

At one point during every Family Life Conference, we instruct couples to look each other in the eye and repeat a statement that we hope will burn into their memories: "My mate is not my enemy." I love that thought. So often in the midst of a conflict, two people throw darts aimed right at the heart of their mate. But the essential truth is that you're on the same team. You need to work together to restore your family to wholeness, to defeat the isolation you have experienced. When you resolve conflict, you choose to not try to win. You pull away from the easier option of avoidance or yielding, and you work to resolve.

Issues give way to the relationship. The hurt doesn't necessarily go away completely, but you choose to face the issues, express your need, listen to each other, and restore the relationship. The relationship is truly nonnegotiable and becomes vital once again.

These are not waters for the faint of heart or those who want to die on the vine of mediocrity. It takes skill and courage to open the door and to say to your mate, child, or friend, "I care."

The pain we feel after an offense can send us the

message to shut down and walk away. Or it can become the stimulus we need to reach out to someone more powerful than ourselves—someone who will always be available; someone who will "really" understand. In my life and perhaps yours, that someone is Jesus.

Experience and the Bible teach us that God sometimes has to use pain in our lives to get our attention. As C. S. Lewis put it in *The Problem of Pain*, "God whispers to us in our pleasures, speaks in our conscience, but shouts in our pains: it is His megaphone to rouse a deaf world."[1]

Once you decide your relationship is nonnegotiable, you still need the strength to take that first step toward closing the loop. That's why it's so important to recognize how God can use your pain. If you allow it to direct you to God, He will give you the strength and power to resolve the conflict.

INGREDIENTS OF RESTORED RELATIONSHIP

Yet closing the loop takes more than just skill and effort. It takes utilizing biblical principles, truths that have stood the test of time, to bring new life to a dying relationship. Specifically, it takes three ingredients that, when applied together, create a richness in the restoration of a broken relationship.

Obedience

"The reason I wrote you was to see if you would stand the test and be obedient in everything." [2]

These are powerful words: "To see if you would stand the test." Do you ever feel as if you're being tested? I sure do.

Abraham was tested when God ordered him to kill his beloved son, Isaac. I can't even imagine the pain he must have felt as he led his son to the mountaintop, knowing God was calling him to be submissive to the point of sacrificing his son. Obedience. (As we know, God ultimately allowed Isaac to live.[3])

Throughout the Gospels, we read where men left their homes, businesses, and families to follow the Christ. Peter and Andrew left their nets when Jesus said, "Come, follow me . . . and I will make you fishers of men."[4] They followed Him "at once." Immediately. They didn't turn in their notice or call a town meeting to tell everyone they were joining this man who claimed to be the Messiah. They simply dropped their nets and followed. Obedience.

Later in the same passage, James and John were mending their fishing nets with their father, Zebedee, when they were called by Jesus. The brothers left their father immediately and followed Him. Obedience.

Moses was obedient to lead the Jews. He felt totally incapable of leading, yet God told him He would lead through him. All Moses had to do was be obedient.

Just as the men and women of the Bible were called to be obedient, so are we as their twentieth-century counterparts. We're called to be obedient to close open loops and restore broken relationships. At one point Jesus said to forgive 70 times 7.[5] That's a bucket of forgiveness. Is that what we typically feel like doing? Not really. But we need to be obedient anyway to do the work of forgiveness and close the open loops.

Was the Bible given to punish us and hold us down by repressing us? No. To the contrary, it acts as a protection for us so we can be free to live holy, joyful lives. Obedience is hard for many of us as we learn to defer to Him and let Him be God. As a T-shirt I saw several years ago said, "#1 There is a God. #2 You are not Him." Is your lifestyle consistent with those facts? Or do you tend to want to live as if *you* are in control? I do at times.

The bottom line on this one is that *someone* is in control of my life—either God or me. There aren't many other choices (and none of the others is good). And I know that when I'm in control, things tend to go haywire. But when I'm seeking God's direction, obeying His desire for my life, I feel safe and protected.

Courage

"Wait for the Lord; be strong, and let your heart take courage; yes, wait for the LORD."[6]

Dorothy, the Tin Man, the Scarecrow, and Toto helped the Cowardly Lion look for his courage in *The Wizard of Oz*. Battle-weary leaders look into the eyes of the men in the foxholes and challenge them to remain courageous in the fight. Runners who "hit the wall" at mile 24 of a 26-mile marathon look into the faces of the spectators along the streets and pull on every ounce of perseverance they can muster to stay in the race.

When you're at the fork in the road, you need courage to do the right thing. If you hesitate to confront a friend about an insensitive comment because you're afraid he'll reject you, you need courage to approach him. If you're afraid to tell your spouse about a secret sin that has brought isolation into your relationship, you need courage.

God will give you and me the strength we need. Daniel exercised courage in the lions' den. Moses took courage when he led the Israelites to the Red Sea with the Egyptians hot on his trail. Noah exercised courage as he stood in the face of public ridicule and continued to build the ark.

The first chapter of the book of Joshua is another classic passage on courage. God had promised the Israelites their own land. But when they saw that the land was populated by others, they were afraid and chose not to believe God would deliver it to them. So they were banished to the wilderness for 40 years.

Just after Moses died, God spoke to Joshua and gave him this instruction and encouragement:

> Moses My servant is dead; now therefore arise, cross this Jordan, you and all this people, to the land which I am giving to them, to the sons of Israel. Every place on which the sole of your foot treads, I have given it to you, just as I spoke to Moses. . . .
>
> No man will be able to stand before you all the days of your life. Just as I have been with Moses, I will be with you; I will not fail you or forsake you. Be strong and courageous, for you shall give this people possession of the land which I swore to their fathers to give them. Only be strong and very courageous; be careful to do according to all the law which Moses My servant commanded you; do not turn from it to the right or to the left, so that you may have success wherever you go. . . .
>
> Have I not commanded you? Be strong and courageous! Do not tremble or be dismayed, for the LORD your God is with you wherever you go. [7]

I see two sources for our courage in this passage: First, we can proceed with confidence when we know

God calls us to do something. We know God wants us to resolve conflicts rather than avoid them.

Second, we can proceed with confidence when we operate according to Scripture. As we'll see in the next section of this book, the Bible is full of wisdom on how to resolve conflict. We don't have to do it on our own.

Humility

"Do nothing out of selfish ambition or vain conceit, but in humility consider others better than yourselves. Each of you should look not only to your own interests, but also to the interests of others." [8]

It takes more than obedience and courage to choose to revive a relationship and then take appropriate action. The mixture of those two ingredients without the inclusion of humility can lead to the sound of a clanging cymbal. [9] It's like making a cake with only flour and sugar. You can mix it up, but without the water, you have a dry and shapeless bowl of powder.

Obedience gives us the challenge to hang in there. Courage gives us the guts to reach out. But humility gives us the heart of a servant to bring the tenderness back into the relationship. Humility allows not only our own walls to be torn down, but also the walls of the person with whom we're in conflict.

Humility is the capacity to diminish yourself so

you can elevate the relationship. It's what Jesus exemplified when He washed the feet of the disciples.[10] It's what John the Baptist modeled when he said, "After me will come one who is more powerful than I, whose sandals I am not fit to carry. He will baptize you with the Holy Spirit."[11] It's what the prodigal son taught us when he decided to go to his father and say, "I am no longer worthy to be called your son; make me like one of your hired men."[12]

It's also what Steve Green sings in "Let the Walls Come Down":

> Let the walls come down
> Let the walls come down
> Let the walls that divide us
> And hide us come down.
> If in Christ we agree
> Let us seek unity
> Let the walls
> Let the walls come down
> Let the walls
> Let the walls come down.[13]

Humility isn't taught in classrooms but is a part of character that has to be hammered out in trials. Professional athletes don't often show it in their contract negotiations. We rarely see it on television or in the other media.

Humility tends to come when we realize in our

pain that we can respond in one of two ways, with false pride or humility, with arrogance or vulnerability.

SAFETY NETS

In our obedience, courage, and humility, we need to choose to talk things out, to close the loop. We need to be willing to work through problems, to seek out the person we have hurt or who has hurt us, and to resolve the issue that threatens the relationship.

We have to risk asking the rough question, "Can we talk?" Then we follow that question with the assurance, "I need to talk with you so we can resolve our conflict." But in the midst of our risk taking, we also need to know we're safe. That's why, during my first appointment with a couple, family, or individual, I tell them about the importance of safety nets. Let me explain.

When I take my daughters, Sarah and Missy, to a circus, my favorite act is the trapeze artists. I fantasize that I'm up there with them, but I don't know if I could climb the rope the way they do. In fact, let me be perfectly honest: I *know* I couldn't climb the rope the way they do.

When they get to the top and toss the bar out, put the chalky substance on their hands, and get ready to fly through the air with the greatest of ease, I hold my breath. The question always races through my 6-

year-old mind in this 40-some-year-old body, *Will they make it? As they swing through the sky to grab the other Flying Zambini in midair, will they slip and fall? Headfirst?*

I don't know about you, but I don't like circuses where there is no net beneath the trapeze. I would rather watch the Flying Zambinis than the Squashed Zambinis. With a net, they always look a little more daring. They're willing to take greater risks, knowing that if they fall, the net will catch them.

Taking a risk to resolve conflict is a lot like trapeze work. We're dependent on the process to get us safely to the other side. We need a "net" to catch us when we fall. It takes training, the type that requires concentration, coordination, and timing.

The net of closing the loop of conflict is our commitment to a relationship. But it's a commitment to more than one relationship. We need to be committed both to the other person and to God. We have to be willing to return to the relationship, to take the risk, so we can heal. We have to be willing to depend on the healing power of God to equip us with the necessary courage, obedience, and humility.

SURGERY OF THE HEART

Remember the story of Phil and Susan back in chapter 3? Phil had discovered Susan's affair, and Susan had asked if Phil wanted her to move out of the house. When I interrupted the story, Phil was saying to me, "I never imagined in my wildest dream— or nightmare, actually—that I would ever hear those words come out of her mouth."

Phil had several options; he had come to a fork in the road. He could have shut down, withdrawn, and started building a self-protective wall around his emotions. After the "whack on the head" he had received, that would be understandable. A second choice would have been to boot Susan out and call his attorney to start divorce proceedings.

But here's what actually happened: "I couldn't believe the words that came out of my mouth when she asked if I wanted her to leave," Phil told me. "I said, 'No, you're my wife. I want you to stay.' I told her no, Gary. How does that grab you?"

"I believe you, Phil," I answered. "Your natural response was to hang in there. You're married. The decision to stay with her is what made sense, even though you were deeply hurt."

"She began to tell me the story," he continued. "She confessed that last year she had an affair. It lasted three months. I can't describe to you in words the swell of emotion that ran through me at that moment. She was so broken as she described how much she had needed me back then, yet I was too busy for her.

"It all came back to me: how she begged me to go out with her to dinner or to the movies, but I couldn't.

I wouldn't even be lured away from my work late at night with her promises of passionate lovemaking! That wasn't even her style. How could I have been so blind? This went on for many months. She would get angry with me and tell me my priorities were all messed up. But I was on a mission and would not be swayed.

"Gary, I drove my wife from me! The most precious person I have ever known cried out for her needs to even be heard, but there was no attentive audience—at least not at home. She needed affirmation and found it elsewhere."

"Even in the midst of all that pain, you communicated," I said. "What happened then?"

"My reaction to her words came from my gut. I wrapped her closely in my arms, and we cried to God for His forgiveness for both of us. I was angry at what she did and at myself for having been so selfish and ignoring her needs. I had taken my heart away from God and my wife.

"Through that night and the next day, we held each other close and talked of the bitterness, anger, and fears we both were holding. I found myself bursting into tears at unpredictable moments, both when we were together and alone. Looking in the mirror, shaving, my eyes would redden and swell. I would grab a towel, turn on the water, and let my screams go muffled into the towel.

"My precious wife cried out how dirty she felt, and

we would cry about it together. This was an experience we had never had before—a spiritual battle in our very presence. Our God was pushing back the enemy who was telling us we could never put this marriage back together. Yet, victory came through His power."

Can you feel it? I can feel it right now, just as I did when Phil lay on the emotional surgery table in my office. There he was. Laid open. Vulnerable. Scared. Embarrassed. Hopeful. His world had ripped him wide open, and he was left with his pain.

As a counselor who has sat sometimes in his own sweat, listening to families peel away layers of self-protection and reveal their deepest pain and disappointment, I know Phil had faced a choice. He could have done what felt good and righteous and walked away from the marriage. Or he could have stuck it out and dealt with his heart's betrayal.

Phil also was able to realize his marriage wasn't just a marriage of two. It was a marriage of three: Susan, Phil, and God. At that moment—the moment Phil most needed an anchor to grab onto—he could call on the one anchor that doesn't move no matter how strong the current, the winds, or the storm. He could take hold of that anchor for dear life. Phil and Susan both chose the latter.

Why? Because they knew God had called them together. They felt their relationship was nonnegotiable. And they trusted in the living God. Phil wasn't exaggerating when he said there was a spiritual battle. There was and still is—for him and Susan, for you and me.

God gives us the strength to fight that battle. He wants us to trust Him, to believe He will never place anything in front of us that we can't handle with His help.

Jesus promised He will never leave us. We are His children. And He gives us the power to make the right decision at the fork in the road.

PART 4

CLOSING
THE LOOP

C H A P T E R   1 2

HEART PREPARATION

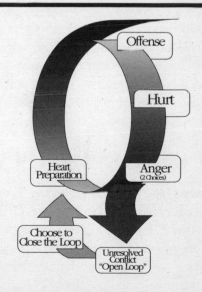

F inally we arrive at the most practical part of this book. We've stepped out by faith and committed ourselves to closing the loops in our conflicts. So what's next? What do we need to do to resolve our conflicts?

In this final section, we'll explore a five-stage process for restoring strained or broken relationships: (1) heart preparation; (2) communication; (3) loving confrontation; (4) forgiveness; and (5) rebuilding trust. We'll look at a number of practical steps we can take during each part of the process. We won't need to use every tip every time, of course, but keeping the process in mind will enable us to make great progress toward resolving our conflicts.

In this chapter, I want to talk about heart preparation. (We'll consider the remaining stages in the following chapters.) We may be sincere in our desire to resolve a conflict, but if we haven't prepared our hearts ahead of time, we may make it worse. Four steps will get our hearts ready.

STEP ONE: CLEAR OUR HEARTS

Have you ever heard the expression "I need to get away and clear my head?" I've heard it and have been known to say it. But what's often more important for me is to get away and clear my heart. At times I have an incredible need to get some distance from my daily routine and unclog the arteries feeding my heart. I don't know about you, but my arteries get jammed with misplaced priorities, fatigue, overextended ministry and counseling, and overwhelming obligations. I find that when I'm exposed to so much pain day in and day out, I need to get away and clear my heart. When I do, I begin to sense some peace returning to the old ticker.

Getting that distance is the first step in heart preparation. Sometimes it means we need to jump in the car and go to the mountains to gain a clear view from Mount Perspective. If you live in Iowa, as I do, there are no mountain ranges, so I head for the country. If you live in a large metropolitan area, it may mean going to the park to sit on a bench and let a few hours pass. I don't think it really matters where we go; what matters is that we get a little distance so we can sort out our thoughts and feelings.

At times in conflict, we often have the option of getting some time to ourselves to sort through things with God. At other times we don't have that luxury, because the resolution needs to occur sooner and it's wise to slow down and talk with the other person *now*. But if we never get any distance to allow God to search our hearts, we're setting ourselves up to lose the lifeblood that keeps the heart vibrant: a relationship with God.

The second part of clearing the heart is opening

it to what God wants to teach us. How do we do that? I don't go to my shelf of professional books. I do it through two processes: reading the Bible and praying. Pretty simple? It has worked for thousands of years, and it works today.

When I'm in the midst of a conflict, I go to the Bible to get direction on how to respond to what's happening. Often I'll take my *One Year Bible* or my *Closer Walk: New Testament* and do the reading designed for that day. That usually begins to give me the guidance I need. I've found that a consistent study of the Bible unjams my arteries and keeps my spiritual heart pumping.

The third part of heart clearing is confessing any sin we've brought into the conflict. Is there a clear violation of God's teaching that needs to be confronted *before* we go to the other person? My prayer is, like that of David, "Search me, O God, and know my heart; test me and know my anxious thoughts. See if there is any offensive way in me, and lead me in the way everlasting." [1]

If I go to the other person in anger or express emotion without first clearing my heart, I will invariably regret the results. I have done it and will again, but it's putting the cart before the horse. Reading the Bible for instruction and then confessing my sin always brings clarity to my troubled heart. It isn't an instantaneous response, but when I go to God earnestly and let go of my pride, I can begin to feel the stiff-necked part of me diminishing and the humility returning.

The fourth part in heart clearing is prayer, and I love to pray. I remember the awkwardness of prayer when I first became a Christian. I would go to Bible studies and listen to people pray out loud, and I would be praying silently at about a thousand words per minute, "God, don't let them go around the circle. What if they expect me to pray? I can't pray out loud!" Every once in a while I would get "stuck" praying out loud and would stumble through.

The more I got the hang of this thing called prayer, however, the more I realized God wasn't looking for some flowery words to impress those around the circle. He wanted one thing: authenticity. He wanted me to pray from my heart. That was all. And when I caught on to that idea, my prayer life took off. One of the greatest side benefits of being a counselor is that I'm in prayer throughout the day. The pain in other people's lives has pushed me closer and closer to God.

When I'm in conflict, my prayer is typically, "God, give me the humility to resolve this issue in a way that's honoring to You. Help me to be gracious and sensitive toward the other person's perspective. Help us to talk things through. Help us to close the loop and rekindle our love for each other." As I finish my prayer, I can usually sense the softening of my heart, and the peace that seemed so elusive begins to return to my jumbled mind and soul. That same peace prepares me for restoring the broken relationship.

Peace. What a great word! One day, about two thousand years ago, a man saw strife throughout His land and went to clear His heart. As He sat on a mountainside, His disciples came to Him, and He taught them some of the most profound truths ever recorded. In what we call the Beatitudes, Jesus gave some simple yet powerful principles to live by.

Here is one of those Beatitudes: "Blessed are the peacemakers, for they will be called sons of God." [2] Notice that Jesus didn't say, "Blessed are the trouble-makers." He also didn't praise the people who keep the fires of resentment burning. Peacemakers please God. I want to be a peacemaker.

One of the most important aspects of resolving conflict is adopting an attitude of restoration rather than strife. In my counseling, I can tell which person wants to keep an issue alive so he or she can get in one or two more shots. I can also tell if one of the people involved has humbled himself or herself and desires to move toward restoration. The former is still loading the cannon and lighting fuses, while the latter is offering olive branches with tenderness and compassion.

Have you ever been around a peacemaker? We have one in our home. Her name is Missy, and she loves peace. When Missy perceives strife in "her land," she will be the first to call for resolution by saying something like, "We need to talk this out. I want us to be a family."

When I'm angry and want to shake things up a little, the last thing on my mind is to be a peacemaker. But not Missy. She doesn't try to avoid conflicts—she just tries to help us resolve them so we can once again "be a family." A lot of wisdom is wrapped up in that little girl.

Heart preparation starts with an inside look. As we search ourselves and ask God to search us, seeking peace, we are more prepared to go to step two.

STEP TWO: LOOK FOR THE UNDERLYING CAUSES OF THE CONFLICT

After we've tuned in to God and begun to prepare spiritually for the resolution of a conflict, it's important to ask ourselves some key questions. This is a part of counseling that helps people understand what issues may be causing them significant difficulty.

In some ways, the work of a counselor can be compared to that of a detective. When people come to me, they usually want help with a particular problem they're facing. When I begin the first session, I work at developing a relationship with them. Creating security in our relationship is the first step in helping them look at the pain of their hearts. After we're starting to relate, I'll typically have them describe their problem in as much detail as possible.

If I stopped at that point and gave people my "diagnosis" and "prescription" for the problem, chances are I might not help them at all. Why? There may be many more forces at play in their situation than they realize.

To uncover those, I'll begin to ask questions about their past, their relationships with other people, and their parents. I may even need to talk with others in the family (always with their permission and typically in their presence) to gain more insight into the problem. My expectation is that the more I investigate the problem, the more patterns will emerge, and the more the real picture will start to become clear.

Recently I counseled a couple, Andrea and Rod, who were struggling in their sexual relationship. They had been married for several years but weren't satisfied with that aspect of their marriage. After several minutes, it became clear that Andrea was holding back some important information. I felt that no matter which way I directed the session, I was coming up empty-handed. Roadblocks were being erected everywhere. Rod was becoming increasingly uncomfortable as well.

"Doc, we don't feel there are any problems in our past," Rod said. "It seems that's what you're looking for. We just want to improve our sexual relationship today. You counselors are always trying to look into people's pasts for answers. Does it have to be that complicated?"

I was beginning to feel the heat. Rod was becoming increasingly defensive as Andrea was becoming more and more elusive. Something was brewing, and I had a funny feeling I was going to be the last to know.

"Andrea and Rod," I said, "when we look at the underlying causes of conflicts, the idea is not to blame but to understand. I don't ask questions to intrude but to help you get a handle on what might be the real causes of your conflicts."

"Rod, I think we need to talk to Gary about what happened before we were married," Andrea said sheepishly.

"If you feel you have to, Andrea, that's fine, but I've told you I don't think that has anything to do with why you don't like sex now," Rod answered, his voice going up a few decibels.

"Gary," Andrea began tentatively, "before we were married, Rod was sexual with another girl. I didn't know about it until our honeymoon, when he told me. I felt angry and betrayed. I also felt that what we were doing was dirty. I've been confused ever since and don't know how to let go of it. I love my husband. I want to be sexually responsive to him, but I just can't

223

forget what happened and the fact that he didn't tell me before we were married."

During the rest of that session and over the next several weeks, Rod and Andrea started to confront something he was working hard to deny: the consequences of his sin. Rod had felt compelled to confess to Andrea his premarital sexual activity. His intentions were good, but his timing was lousy. He had wanted to cleanse his conscience in order to develop a healthy relationship with his bride. She had felt betrayed (and still did), he felt exposed, and I felt we were onto some real healing.

Rod and Andrea were an excellent example of a couple whose reason for coming to a counselor was only a symptom of the real problem. Yes, they were struggling sexually, but the origin of the problem was behavior that had occurred prior to their marriage. It had left an open loop that demanded to be closed.

I'm happy to report that over time, the loop did close. Rod and Andrea listened to each other as they communicated their disappointment and hurt. He sought her forgiveness, and she learned how to respond to him in a way that built intimacy in their marriage, both emotionally and sexually.

Our pasts powerfully influence our present lives. In previous chapters, we've seen the influence of family training and the ways various differences in background, sex, and philosophy can ignite conflicts.

That's why developing an understanding of the past—
looking at the underlying causes of our conflicts—is
essential to healing.

When I'm counseling someone, I ask a series of
questions to help me discern what's really happening.
Since I'm not sitting with you asking those questions,
you need to ask them of yourself. Here are a few:

How does your family training seem to affect the
way you resolve conflict in your relationships today?

How about the family training of the person with
whom you're having conflict?

Did anything occur in your past that may be the
underlying cause of the current conflict?

Are you aware of any roots of bitterness or resentment that may be sabotaging the resolution of the
current conflict?

Is there any need to hold on to the conflict?
Could you be experiencing some control or power by
not resolving the issue? For instance, if you do resolve
the conflict, you would need to reopen the relationship, which may be a fearful prospect.

How is what seems to be going on in your life
different from what's happening in your heart? Is
there a discrepancy between what people see and
who you really are? (If so, join the club, because we
all have some degree of incongruence between the
two. But the distance between them leads to greater
discomfort.)

In one of the most profound books of recent years, *Inside Out*, Dr. Larry Crabb compares the Christian life to an iceberg and emphasizes the importance of looking below the waterline of our lives to see what's really occurring in our hearts that may be troubling us. He writes:

> No matter how together we may appear, even to ourself, buried deep within our heart is the vague sense that something is wrong, dreadfully wrong. We feel a twinge of discomfort when someone puts us on the spot, we sense a pressure to play it safe when a friend's tone becomes critical, we well up with anger when a spouse misunderstands us, we're aware of shifting conversation to a topic we can handle, we look for opportunities to modestly share some information that makes us look good, we pretend to be more spiritually minded than we actually are, we avoid subjects that put us in touch with unpleasant emotions.
>
> Just a quick glance beneath the surface of our life makes it clear that more is going on than loving God and loving others. It requires only a moment

of honest self-reflection to realize that no
matter how much we may have already
changed, we still have a long way to go.[3]

Looking below the waterline is uncomfortable,
but without an honest understanding of the underlying causes of our conflicts, the answers we find will be
superficial and short-lived.

STEP THREE: COMMIT TO KEEPING OUR RELATIONSHIPS AS TOP PRIORITY

One of the greatest saboteurs of healthy relationships is the tendency to put them on the back burner.
We've all done it. I've done it during the writing of this
book, and it has hurt. When we're stretched and trying
to live in the fast lane, sometimes the people closest to
us are the ones who get hurt the most.

My good friend and colleague Tim Kimmel, in his
best-selling book *Little House on the Freeway*, gave this
example: "A major financial magazine recently
published interviews with the '100 most successful
executives' in the country. Listen to a comment from
a man who has made the 'top 10.' 'Reaching the level
of business success that I have requires total commitment. If your family is too demanding, get a new
family. That's what I did.'"[4]

That man didn't put his relationships on the back burner—he tossed them in the trash! A commitment to keeping our relationships a top priority takes work and effort. It also takes sacrifice.

A man I have yet to meet but much admire is Bill Hybels. He's the pastor of one of the largest churches in the country, Willow Creek Community Church in South Barrington, Illinois. Every Thursday, I get a tape of his weekly sermon in the mail, pop it in my Honda's cassette player, and have church. I listen to it during the week as he ministers to me from the Bible. You know why I admire him? Because he is genuine and admits freely that he has, at times, put his relationships on the back burner. Barbara bought me his and his wife's book *Fit to Be Tied* for Christmas one year.

In the book, Hybels wrote about "crisis mode living," which he defined as "spending every moment of every day trying to figure out how to keep all your balls in the air and all your plates spinning. In crisis mode you keep running faster and faster, from project to project, deadline to deadline, quota to quota, meeting to meeting, sermon to sermon. Your RPMs keep creeping higher and higher until you hit the red line."[5]

What's the implication of crisis mode living? Relationships suffer. Energy that needs to be put into them instead goes into keeping our lives at a hectic pace. Hybels went on to say:

The problem arises when you spend too much time in crisis mode. That's when crisis mode goes from being a season of life to becoming a way of life. . . . In every other area of life, you become a miser; you hoard your energy, you engage minimally, you touch superficially, you slide along the surface, you *skim*.

First you skim relationally. Your bond with your spouse that used to be strong and intimate becomes increasingly weak and distant. You hope he or she doesn't have a serious need because you don't have energy to deal with it. You hydroplane over conflicts. You put Band-Aids on serious problems. You resort to quick fixes, and pretend things really aren't so bad. [6]

Ouch! Can you feel the pain he has experienced? I can and have. And I believe that's one of the reasons God is blessing his ministry. He knows and admits the pain caused by not keeping relationships as a top priority.

I recently counseled a man who was caught up in crisis mode living. He felt he was winning at the office but was losing at home. I explained some of the ideas in this chapter. As we looked at the reality of his busy life, he asked a great question: "If I'm to give relationships priority over my hurried schedule, what's a practical way of pulling that off? How can I find a balance between succeeding on the job and succeeding at home?"

In answer, I told him about a lesson I learned while leading a seminar several years ago. I was speaking to a group of bankers during the farm crisis of the 1980s. Banks were foreclosing on farmers throughout the country, and bankers realized they needed to improve their communication skills. That's where I came in. I contracted with the federal government and private banks to teach them how to communicate.

During one seminar, I asked a group of 75 bankers how they saw the farm crisis affecting their own families. Here they were, putting farmers out of business and being perceived as the bad guys. How did that influence them as husbands and dads? A banker from South Dakota gave a meaningful response.

"Gary, I live 20 miles from my bank," he said. "I've clocked off the halfway mark between my home and my bank and have identified a telephone pole as my marker. When I leave the bank at night, I take the first 10 miles up to that pole to think about my bank, my customers, and my job.

"But when I arrive at that pole, I switch my thinking to my family. I prepare for our time together. I mentally get ready for how to greet them and spend time with them during my evening at home. Then, when I leave for work the next morning, I spend my first 10 miles reflecting on my family. When I pass my marker, I begin to mentally prepare for the day."

Not surprisingly, that man was winning at home and at the bank. After reflecting on his wisdom, I remember thinking, *Maybe I need to move 20 miles out of town.* I often find myself walking in the door at home after work, half brain dead and not even realizing I've left the office!

One evening I entered the house in a comatose state, and Missy yelled out, "Daddy! Daddy! Daddy!"

She said "Daddy!" about 12 times, but I just kept walking. Barbara turned to Missy and said, "Honey, your daddy isn't home yet."

"Yes he is. He's right there."

"Honey, you know that. Sarah knows that. Even Katie, the dog, knows that. But your daddy doesn't know it yet."

The first 30 seconds when members of a family greet each other at the end of the day will set the pattern for the rest of the evening. That's why my parents succeeded with their custom of sitting in the family room and talking after Dad arrived home.

This is not a simple mental discipline to master. But the rewards are great. If we want to communicate with our families and avoid some unfortunate conflicts, we need to clear our minds of the baggage we carry with us and make relationships a priority.

Besides taking priority over our schedules, relationships also need to take priority over issues. Many of us set up the equation in our lives that issues are greater than relationships. When we live this way, we lose. It's imperative that we reverse that order of importance.

STEP FOUR: RESPECT PRIVACY AND ADMIT THE NEED FOR ACCOUNTABILITY

Several years ago, I realized my need for close companionship with a few men. I needed a place to just be Gary. As a counselor, I pour my life into many families every day, but that doesn't preclude my need for fellowship. In 1978, I decided to do something about it and began meeting weekly with three close friends.

During our meetings, Tim Vermillion, Jerry Foster, Mike Colby, and I do everything from Bible studies to book studies, from prayer times to joke telling. When Tuesday noon rolls around, we leave our respective businesses and head for the corner booth of an Italian restaurant.

What's said at that table stays at that table. Period. I don't even have to ask. I can be myself there. We have a physician, an insurance executive, a guy who runs his family businesses, and me. But it doesn't matter what we do—our credentials are left at the door. We're just four guys who care about, listen to, and pray for each other.

Then, in the fall of 1989, having clocked about 12,000 hours of marriage and family therapy, I realized something about the men I was counseling: Most of them had the same need I did to be around other men. Some kept making appointments, paying for time with me, not because they still needed counseling but because we had built a good relationship and they didn't want to see it end. We men often see our wives getting together with other women, but we're just beginning to realize we have a similar need.

To try to help some of the men from counseling meet their own needs, I asked my three friends if I could invite about ten other guys to a weekly study. We tried it for a few months, and it took off.

Now, every Wednesday morning, I can be found with a group of men called the CrossTrainers. These are guys from every walk of life, representing more than 40 churches, drawn from a 75-mile radius around Des Moines. I begin each meeting by giving a summary of a chapter in a contemporary Christian book. We then break into small groups and open up our hearts. We talk about what we're learning, ask each other tough questions about our growth, and hold ourselves accountable.

Our goal in the ministry is not only to "train for the cross" (i.e., grow spiritually), but also, just like athletes, to "cross train" for our different roles as Christian husbands, dads, friends, and members of our community.

One of the reasons CrossTrainers works is that we stress the importance of confidentiality, especially when a new man joins the group. As of the fall of 1991, there are more than 140 CrossTrainers in Des Moines. And God is using the group to change lives.

Confidentiality is important in all relationships, especially when we're resolving conflict. As we confront our anger and communicate with the other person, it's vital that we do so in a private and confidential way. We need to maintain the attitude that "it's just between us."

Jim came to see me recently because of a conflict with one of his brothers, Alex. As they and their other siblings planned their parents' golden wedding anniversary, they agreed they would set a budget and stick to it. Alex was placed in charge of planning the event, and he was soon faced with a decision about which musical group to hire. He decided it wouldn't hurt anyone to hire a top-notch band and assess each of the siblings an extra $125.

When Jim learned what Alex did, he was furious. He was already at the limit of what he could afford, and he knew this would not only create conflict within the family, but also with his wife, who felt they were spending too much on the celebration as it was. In his anger, Jim went to four of his siblings and built his case against Alex before even talking to Alex. Alex heard about the issue from another brother, and World War III was about to erupt.

During our session, Jim looked at me and said, "How did I get into such a mess? Now all my siblings are mad. My wife won't talk to me. What do I do now?"

Alex had committed an offense, but Jim had made it worse by going to other people rather than approaching Alex directly. Jim would have done well to heed this advice from Jesus: "If your brother sins, go and reprove him in private; if he listens to you, you have won your brother."[7]

Jesus went on to say that if the brother doesn't listen, we should bring in another person or two and confront him again. But that's only if he doesn't listen. If we go directly to the person first, we demonstrate our desire to make the relationship our top priority. And it proves we can be trusted. Confidentiality allows a relationship to grow, because it creates security for people who need to be honest and open with each other.

The other element of step four, which I alluded to briefly, is accountability. I'm accountable to my wife, Barbara. But that isn't enough. One of the wisest moves I've made has been having five men who hold me accountable. The three men I have lunch with on Tuesdays hold me accountable. My dear friend Dr. Tom Evans holds me accountable. And author and speaker Steve Farrar holds me accountable. If something bad is brewing in my life, I may get it past one or two of those guys, but chances are I won't slip it past all five.

We all need people who will ask us tough questions. Without that accountability, we can become isolated, and the chance of sin's getting a foothold in our lives increases dramatically.

In the heart-preparation stage of closing the loops in our conflicts, it's imperative that we: (1) clear our hearts; (2) look for the underlying causes of the conflict; (3) keep the relationship as priority over the issues of the conflict; and (4) maintain confidentiality and a process of accountability.

By blending these four ingredients, we lay the groundwork for effective conflict resolution that leads to the restoration of the broken relationship.

One other step needs to be taken when we're preparing our hearts for mending a relationship: dealing with our anger. In chapter 6, "The Baked Potato Syndrome," we looked at the causes of anger. In the next chapter, I'll address how we can deal with the "hot potato" of our anger in a healthy way so that it leads to restoration and not isolation.

CHAPTER 13

DEALING WITH A HOT POTATO

Remember playing hot potato as a kid? You got all the kids in a circle and tossed a ball around, getting rid of the "potato" as fast as you could. Everyone squealed with delight in anticipation of having the ball thrown to them. You developed strategies to get rid of it as fast as possible. You only lost the game if you held on to the potato too long. Why? Because you didn't want to get burned.

Anger can be good, but if it gets too hot, it can also burn, searing the heart. If it's not expressed in healthy ways, it can become such a block to effective communication that marriages are destroyed, friendships are fractured, and churches are torn apart.

In the last chapter, I described the first four steps in preparing our hearts to resolve conflicts. Now I want to address the final step.

THE HOT POTATO OF ANGER

The apostle Paul made it clear that the emotion of anger is not necessarily bad: "Be angry, and yet do not sin; do not let the sun go down on your anger, and do not give the devil an opportunity." [1]

Notice that Paul didn't say, "Don't be angry." So how can we be angry when someone has hurt us but not sin? The answer is found in learning the distinction between anger and aggression. *Anger* is an emotion, a feeling. *Aggression* is a malevolent behavior, an act of the will. Anger can be expressed in a God-honoring way. Jesus, for example, displayed righteous anger when He threw the moneychangers out of God's temple in Jerusalem. Anger can also stimulate us to resolve a conflict that has been brewing for some time.

As Dr. Archibald Hart wrote:

> My understanding of what Paul is saying here is that it is not the anger itself (as feeling) that is wrong, but that anger has the potential for leading you into sin. The point is that it is the translation or

conversion of anger feelings into aggressive and hostile acts that leads us into sin.
To feel anger, to tell someone that you
feel angry, and to talk about your anger
are both healthy and necessary. As long
as you recognize the anger as your own
and avoid hurting back the object of your
anger, you are keeping it as a feeling—
and all feelings are legitimate! What you
do with your feeling may not be, and this
is where you can fall into sin! [a]

How do we control our anger? Charles Swindoll
quotes a great American statesman, Thomas Jefferson,
who included a good answer in his "rules of living."
His rule for anger: "When angry, count ten before you
speak: If very angry, a hundred."

Author Mark Twain, about 75 years later, revised
Jefferson's words as follows: "When angry, count 4.
When very angry . . . swear." [3]

Jefferson's technique is still widely used today by
counselors, TV sitcoms, and moms and dads throughout our land. I'm afraid Twain's is also, although I can't
recommend it!

In the rest of this chapter, I'll develop a few other
suggestions that might prove more helpful. We simply
must resolve the anger in our hearts before we can
mend relationships.

DEAL WITH ANGER IN A TIMELY WAY

Earlier I quoted Paul as having said, "Do not let the sun go down on your anger." The principle to remember is that we can't let anger brew within us too long. If we do, it will turn to resentment, bitterness, or depression.

People make two common mistakes in dealing with anger. First, they allow it to boil instead of halting the conversation or argument and taking the time to calm down. When we sense we're growing angry, or if we can see anger growing in the person we're dealing with, that should be a warning sign: "Anger building! Time out!"

If this is a problem with you, you may need to slow down so you can confront your anger and the other person in a more appropriate way.

The other mistake is waiting too long to deal with anger. Many people allow the "steam" to be released from their anger and then feel it's too late to confront it because they aren't angry anymore. That's a myth. Chances are that the anger is still simmering within them, waiting for another opportunity to boil over. When Paul instructed us to "not let the sun go down" on our anger, his intent was to help us check our anger.

Be careful of extremes, however. This issue of not letting the sun go down on our anger comes up frequently in the counseling office. Many couples will stay awake late into the night trying to obey it literally.

Bob Homer, a speaker with the Family Life Conferences, tells the story of a couple who stayed up for two and a half days straight to deal with their conflict!

It's almost always a mistake to try to resolve conflicts late at night. As the evening wears on, most of us get fatigued. We need to realize that we or our mates may have heavy schedules the next day and that getting proper rest is sometimes more important than trying to resolve a conflict immediately. Often when we're still up trying to resolve things, the sun has not only gone down but is on its way up again. So the best thing to do late at night may be to agree to work at resolving the issue when we're both rested.

COOL YOUR JETS

"Here we go again. We always do it your way. I'm sick of it and you!"

"I can't believe you did that again! You really tick me off."

"I give up. You'll never change. I have to do everything around here."

Behind each of those fireballs is a frustrated and angry person. I don't know about you, but when someone comes at me with such force and accusation, I feel like saying, "Why don't you cool your jets?" In other words, "Please slow down, and let's talk about this."

It's important not to let the sun go down on our anger, but it's also important not to go flying out of the chute like a bucking bronco. When we're in the midst of a conflict, we need to slow down the process. This means checking our tongues and working through the issue with tolerance and discernment.

What gets in the way of being tolerant? For me, it's reacting before thinking. A *reaction* comes from the gut. It's automatic and at times involuntary. A *response* is thought out and more purposeful. It takes longer to come up with a response, but it's much more effective. As some wise person said, the difference between a reaction and a response is about three seconds.

In addition, it's important that we be tolerant of a mate or friend. In fact, we may be more of the problem than the other person is. So we need to be humble and willing to look inside ourselves to see where we contributed to the conflict.

I believe this is what Jesus was addressing when He said, "You hypocrite, first take the plank out of your own eye, and then you will see clearly to remove the speck from your brother's eye."[4]

The message is clear. We need to look at ourselves before we cast blame on others. We may very well be a big part of the problem. So let's slow down and check our response before lighting the fuse.

CONTROL YOUR TONGUE

As Becky stared at Randy, her eyes were almost glazed over. After a 20-minute tirade by her husband, all she could say was, "I can't hear you."

I had just witnessed a volcanic eruption. I wish I could say I was at the foot of Mount Saint Helens. But I was only in West Des Moines, Iowa, sitting in the chair I counsel from several hours per week. I sat looking at two people who at one time were fresh-faced and optimistic, hoping for a great life together. Now their relationship looked far different. There was pain in their eyes, despair in their hearts, and a futility in their communication. "I can't hear you."

I can sure hear him, I thought. *So can the people in my waiting room and in the next office.* Randy had just let his anger erupt all over his wife. His explosion led me to offer a rather unusual intervention.

"I want to describe what I just saw," I told them. "Now, this may sound a little gross, but here it goes. Randy, it's as if you just vomited all over Becky." They looked at me in shock, and I continued, "As I watched you erupt and spew anger all over your wife, Randy, I envisioned vomit flying across the room and covering her, even getting on my clothes."

"That's pretty gross, Doc," quipped an angry Randy.

"I know," I said. "That's the point. As gross as

243

that word picture is, that's how gross your communication is."

"Randy, that's why I couldn't hear you," Becky said, tears rolling down her cheeks. "When you explode like that, I can't get past my own hurt to hear what you're saying. I just see and hear you screaming, and I shut down."

Becky and Randy were the epitome of two people frustrated with their lack of skill in managing God-given emotions. Instead of shaping them, they just "let them fly." Becky went on to say that when Randy kicked into rage, she flashed back on an angry father and shut down, just as she did as a child.

Randy's problem was that he couldn't control his tongue. More than any other muscle in our bodies, the tongue has the power to do great harm. As the apostle James wrote, "So also the tongue is a small part of the body, and yet it boasts of great things. Behold, how great a forest is set aflame by such a small fire!" [5]

It's powerful. It has the capacity to heal broken relationships or to tear down other people, leaving them singed from the flames.

Dennis and Barbara Rainey, in their best-selling book *Building Your Mate's Self-Esteem*, provide another word picture of the tongue's power:

> Words are like seeds. Once planted in
> your mate's life, your words will bring

forth flowers or weeds, health or disease,
healing or poison. You carry a great
responsibility for their use. As Proverbs
18:21 says, "Death and life are in the
power of the tongue." Your words have
the power to contaminate a positive self-
image or to heal the spreading malig-
nancy of a negative one. [6]

How do we control the tongue? One way is to
slow down our communication. Often when we get
charged up with anger, we begin to get loose-
tongued, so we need to work at slowing down.
Another technique is to give the people we're
having conflict with permission to help us keep our
anger in check. If they feel we're getting hostile, they
can signal us so we can get ourselves back under
control. A third idea is to ask people, after a
confrontation, if we've offended them in any way
during the discussion. By listening to them and vali-
dating their input, we can develop healthier conflict-
resolution skills.

We would also benefit from keeping in mind the
proverb that says, "A gentle answer turns away wrath,
but a harsh word stirs up anger." [7] Gentleness and
patience, even in a conflict—or perhaps *especially* in a
conflict—can soften the delivery of our message so
that others can hear us.

WATCH OUT FOR YOUR SELF-TALK

Have you ever become so frustrated and frenzied that you started talking to yourself? My dad called it "muttering" when he heard me say something under my breath. I knew I couldn't express my thoughts out loud without experiencing severe consequences. But whether we speak audibly or not, and whether we're aware of it or not, we all engage in self-talk—conscious thought—all the time.

People who study language tell us most people speak at the rate of about 150 to 200 words per minute. Some of us can probably crank it out at almost 250 words per minute. But research indicates that our self-talk can run at the rate of about 1,300 words per minute.

This self-talk has a powerful impact on our emotional and behavioral responses. It's as if a chain reaction occurs. Here's how it works.

First comes what we in counseling call a *triggering event*. It may be something a person says, an object or a scene we see, a fragrance, a sound, or any other stimulus. When the trigger occurs, our minds start racing at 1,300 words per minute trying to interpret the message. In other words, we begin talking to ourselves as we try to make sense of the triggering event.

This automatic thought process leads to an *emotional response*. We may feel hurt, angry, fearful, frustrated, futile, depressed, contented, or joyful. These are all emotions, and they all have one thing in common: They're all results of our self-talk.

Different people may feel different emotions from the same triggering event. Our emotional response depends on our interpretation of the event. The event itself doesn't lead us to feel an emotion, but our self-talk about (or interpretation of) the event does.

What's the role of self-talk in dealing with our anger? Simply this: Some of our emotional responses to triggering events are rational, but at other times they're irrational because our self-talk is distorted. Anger may be a legitimate emotional response to a given event, or it may be inappropriate as a result of faulty self-talk.

"I can't put up with it anymore," blurted a frustrated woman as she entered my office for an appointment.

"Put up with what, Rachel?" I asked.

"My family. They're all driving me crazy."

"What happened?"

"The kids are always demanding things. I can't take care of the house, go to work, try to meet Kent's needs, and take care of the kids at the same time. I love them, but I'm a terrible mom. Plus Kent's been coming home late from work a lot lately. I—I don't think he loves me anymore."

"Rachel, you're trying to juggle several balls at once. Anyone who takes on all the roles you have will feel exasperated at times, so I can see why you're frustrated. But why do you feel you're a terrible mom?"

"Because I lose my temper and scream at them. Then I feel so guilty. I just lose control."

Rachel exemplifies the woman who tries her best to "do it all." She was juggling all the roles of a woman in a frenzied culture and was worn out. She was a wife, a mom, an employee, a friend, a daughter, and an active church member. She tried to keep balance in her life and find some time for "letting her hair down," but it makes me tired just thinking of all the roles she played. And somehow, in the midst of this hectic life, Rachel had begun to lose her self-esteem and confidence. She felt as if she was doing too many things and none of them well.

Then came the triggering event. After she had spent a long night helping her two children do homework, mediating their disputes, and putting them to bed, Rachel's husband, Kent, finally returned home from work. "Sorry I'm late," he said. "I just had to finish some memos before I could leave, and time got away from me."

Rachel erupted: "I'm tired of your coming home

late night after night! I'm tired of always having to put the kids to bed by myself and hearing them ask where you are! Do you really have to come home late, or have you started spending time with someone else?"

Shocked and hurt by Rachel's outburst, Kent stomped into the den to watch television. Then Rachel started feeling guilty. *I'm a terrible wife and mom,* she thought. *I can't take care of all these roles. I can't do anything right.*

Kent's coming home late hadn't really led to Rachel's emotional eruption. All that did was blow the lid off the days and weeks of self-talk that had left Rachel feeling inadequate, insecure, and angry. Her problem was that she never controlled that self-talk.

The truth of the matter is Rachel was not a terrible mom. Her kids hadn't banded together to make her crazy. And her husband really did love her, although he was being inconsiderate by coming home late so frequently. But by continuing to interpret events in the worst possible light, she talked herself into an emotional frenzy.

The emotion isn't the end of the chain reaction, however. The *behavioral response* is. After we feel an emotion, we do something with it: We scream, cry, kick the tire, withdraw from others, eat, drink, or whatever. Some people pull the covers over their heads and sleep for hours on end. They fidget, pace, or drum their fingers. These are all behaviors that result from our interpretation of the triggering event (self-talk) and our emotional response. So here is what the chain reaction looks like:

Triggering event→ self-talk→ emotion→ behavioral response

One of the major ways to control anger, therefore, is to control our self-talk. There are four steps to follow in doing that. First, we have to *acknowledge* that we do talk to ourselves. I do it. You do it. We all do it.

Second, we *recognize when* we're talking to ourselves.

Third, we *challenge* the self-talk to see if it's rational (supported by evidence) or irrational (not supported by evidence). Here are some questions to ask ourselves:

- What evidence is there to support how I'm feeling about this situation?
- What have I experienced lately that might be contributing to how I'm feeling about this?
- What would be the viewpoint of the person I'm angry with on this issue?
- Do the person's past actions match how I interpret this latest behavior, or do they suggest something different?
- What would be some alternative interpretations to this situation?

In some situations, we may decide that our interpretation of the situation really is the correct one. The other person really is selfish, and our anger is justified. But if we're honest with ourselves, often we'll find that we've been thinking irrationally and operating from false assumptions.

Fourth, we need to *replace* irrational self-talk with rational self-talk.

In Rachel's case, a more rational response would be: *I know the kids aren't trying to drive me crazy. I'm just tired and stressed out, and they still have needs. I just need some space. Maybe a trip to the Bahamas this afternoon would work out.* (The last statement is kicking back into the irrational, by the way.)

The more rational response toward her husband might be: *I don't believe he's coming home late on purpose. I need to tell him I'm frustrated and ask him to call if he's going to be late.*

Instead of feeling out of control, Rachel could also learn that the tendency to blurt out statements can be controlled. How? By transforming our thinking and choosing healthier responses. As I said earlier, we all blow it. But a real problem arises when we develop a pattern of expressing our anger in a hostile fashion.

I've had a great coach named Dave Boehi during the writing of this book. Dave once applied the formula I've just described in working out his anger toward a person he was working with. Unable to sleep one night, he rose from bed and began reading the Bible. Dave continues the story:

> I skimmed a few Psalms and then turned to Philippians, which always seems to have some word of comfort for me in times of anguish. I read verses six and seven in chapter four, which admonish us to pray and let our requests be known to God so His peace will guard our hearts and minds. I knew I needed that peace.
>
> Then I found myself looking at verse eight: "Finally, brethren, whatever is true, whatever is honorable, whatever is right, whatever is pure, whatever is lovely, whatever is of good repute, if there is any excellence and if anything worthy of praise, let your mind dwell on these things."
>
> Was it just a coincidence that this verse directly followed the command to pray so we'll receive God's peace? I didn't think so. I thought of the person whom I felt had failed me and decided to "let my mind dwell" on positive things by making a list of the good qualities I saw in him.
>
> I started with the strengths. I wrote of

his genuine love for people, of his commitment to his work, of the respect he's shown for me, of his steadfastness under pressure. In all I listed 27 positive qualities.

Then I began my list of weaknesses. After 20 minutes I could only come up with 3. Those weaknesses, I felt, had contributed to the problem I had with him, but somehow that list seemed paltry compared with the first.

Studying the two lists seemed to give me a more positive view of the problem. I still felt he had failed me. But, as I reflected on his character, I realized he didn't do so intentionally. He couldn't have.

I prayed for a few minutes, threw my glob of negative feelings into the fireplace, and returned to bed with peace guarding my heart and mind. [8]

Dave tuned into his self-talk, challenged his irrational thoughts, and got on top of his anger. A clean sweep. And you know what? He slept like a baby afterward. Our self-talk is part of who we are. We need to understand those messages and challenge them so that we control them instead of being controlled by them.

GIVE UP YOUR RIGHT TO REVENGE

It was fifth grade, a year that in many ways I would like to forget. There's one memory, however, that I'll never forget.

I grew up in northern Illinois, in a city called Waukegan located right on Lake Michigan. That means that during the winter, it's really cold. I remember the winds whipping off the lake and piercing our coats no matter how warmly Mom dressed us.

I attended Glen Flora Elementary School and had the knack as a little guy of getting in the middle of things. Now that I think about it, that was good training for becoming a marriage and family counselor.

One afternoon after school, I saw a group of sixth-grade boys involved in a snowball fight. Not to be outdone, I bent over, put together one of the finest iceballs that side of the Mississippi River, and checked out my prey. I identified a boy, Danny, who had been giving me problems for most of my young years, hid behind a tree, took aim, and let it fly. And fly it did. Bull's-eye! Right in the side of the head.

The whole playground full of kids came to an instant halt as all eyes turned to Danny. He let out a war whoop that I can still hear: "Rosberg, you're a dead man!" With that, all eyes turned to me as I tried to hide my joy over a direct hit with one of those fifth-grade looks that says, "I didn't do it, Larry did."

It didn't work. Too many witnesses. What happened next is a little blurry. I picked up my books to act as a shield against the bombardment of snowballs that hit me from every angle. Then I showed that dead men can still run as I shot out of the playground—but not without snow down my jacket, in my hat, and all over my books. My pride had also taken a severe beating.

When I got home, I saw my big brother, Jack, standing beside his 1945 Jeep. Jack is the kind of big brother you like to have in a situation like that. He played high-school football, had a crew cut, and later, in college, took the nickname Rotunda. That means he was a big brother not only in age, but also in size.

I was ready for a little revenge. Actually, I was ready for a lot. I had been humiliated in front of the entire playground. And then a plan entered my 11-year-old mind. "Jack, get the Jeep!" I said.

After I unfolded my story, Jack said, "Hop in. Do you know where they are?"

"Sure I know where they are. They have a snow fort at the end of the alley off Ridgeland Avenue."

As we drove, my heart was pumping, and I could tell Jack's was, too. Entering the alley, we could see Danny and the guys in their fort. It had snowed the night before, and the alley hadn't been plowed, so there were several inches of new snow. "Watch this, Gary," Jack said.

With that, my hero of a brother dropped the snow blade on his Jeep, put it in four-wheel drive, and got up a head of steam as we rolled down the alley churning up tons of snow. Danny heard the rumbling of the Jeep and raised his head just in time to see the sheer thrill in my eyes. Wham! We had gathered enough snow and force not only to cover their fort, but also to knock it over, sending five sixth-graders running for cover.

"All right!" I yelled as Jack raised the snow blade and put the Jeep into reverse. We left hoping Mom and Dad wouldn't find out but also feeling that, even if they did, it would be worth the grounding that would follow.

That day I practiced the fine art of returning an insult for an insult. This is what Peter was talking about when he wrote, "Do not repay evil with evil or insult with insult, but with blessing, because to this you were called so that you may inherit a blessing."[9]

When someone angers us, our natural tendency is to look for a way to get even. We may let fly with an insult, or we may plot a more intricate revenge as I did with Danny. The problem is that repaying an insult with an insult only fans the fire of a conflict and makes it worse.

At some point, someone has to stop the cycle and,

as Peter wrote, give a blessing instead. When we do that, relationships begin to heal. It draws people back together, softens the anger, and allows others to hear us.

Another fifth-grader by the name of Chad had just moved into a new neighborhood and was having trouble making friends. Each day his mom would see him leave for school, but instead of walking with the other kids, he would typically trail along ten feet behind them. It broke her heart, but Chad maintained a good attitude.

In early February, with Valentine's Day approaching, Chad asked his mom to take him to the store to buy materials so he could make valentines for each child in his class. So she took him to the drugstore to get construction paper, glue, crayons, and tape. She was afraid her young, sensitive son was setting himself up for rejection, but she helped him work for days making the valentines.

On Valentine's Day, Chad's mom greeted him after school with his favorite peanut butter cookies and a glass of cold milk. He looked pretty upbeat, but she was concerned because he came in empty-handed. "Chad, how was the party?" she asked.

"Great, Mom," he said as he snarfed down a cookie.

"Did you give the kids the cards?"

"I sure did, Mom!" he answered, a milk moustache covering his upper lip.

"How did it go?"

"It was neat, Mom. I didn't forget a single one. Not a one. They all know I love them." [10]

Would Chad have been justified in not giving a single valentine because of the rejection he experienced in that neighborhood? I'll bet most of us would answer yes. But Chad demonstrated a maturity way beyond his young years by so graciously returning a blessing for an insult. I don't know what happened after that, but I wouldn't be surprised if some of those other kids had milk and cookies after school with their own moms and maybe realized Chad wasn't such a bad guy after all.

When we're in the midst of a conflict and we've been wronged, we have a choice. Do we repay an insult with an insult? Or do we repay it with a blessing?

The choice is whether we want to continue stoking the fire of anger or move toward dousing the flames. Until someone stops repaying insults with insults, the cycle will continue.

"Not a one. Not a single one." I remember making a somewhat similar statement as Jack and I drove home in the Jeep that winter afternoon. It went something like this: "Hey Jack, I don't think one guy got out of there without getting covered with snow. Not a single one."

The next day, however, I learned that the war hadn't ended. My initial insult (the iceball), which was repaid with their insult (their snowballs), which was repaid with my insult (the wrecking of their snow fort), was repaid with the entire sixth-grade boys' insult the next day during recess. I got killed with snowballs.

So much to learn.

We need to learn how to deal with hot potatoes. We all have them. Some of you reading this book don't get angry very often. Some of you, on the other hand, are angry most of the time. Anger can be dealt with in a healthy way, but it takes commitment.

In the next chapter, we'll move beyond the heart preparation stage and address the importance of just how well we communicate.

ELEVATOR TALK

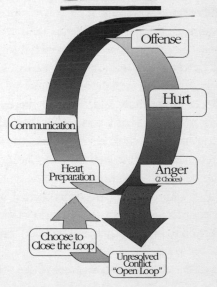

Offense

Hurt

Communication

Heart
Preparation

Anger
(2 Choices)

Choose to
Close the Loop

Unresolved
Conflict
"Open Loop"

We were at the halfway point of another Family Life Conference. It was Saturday afternoon, and Bob Horner and I had just dismissed 400 couples for an hour-long couples' project. Some would talk, and others would listen. Several would check the local team's football score, and some would sleep, but few would affect us like the couple we met on the elevator that afternoon.

When that couple stepped onto the elevator, they did a curious thing. They broke the rules. You know the rules of elevator etiquette: When you ride an elevator, you're supposed to face the door and look down at your shoes or up at the lights indicating what floor you're on. If you speak at all, you're supposed to talk about something trivial, like the weather.

Well, this couple did a most amazing thing. They stepped onto the elevator and stood facing us. Then the husband looked straight at Bob and me with a sincere look and simply said, "This conference has saved our marriage. Thank you." With that, Bob and I, looking like two parakeets on a pole, turned our heads in perfect unison toward the wife. She didn't say anything but gave an enthusiastic nod.

The elevator bell rang, the doors opened, and our close encounter was history. After the doors shut, Bob and I turned to one another, and he said, "So much for elevator talk."

Elevators aren't known as places where you have

deep conversation. Genuine communication, however, provides depth and insight into the heart of another person.

Unfortunately, many couples find themselves stuck in elevator talk. Their communication rarely runs deep. In survey after survey, couples rate this as a major problem in their relationship.

Communication is typically the first issue people raise in my counseling office. I remember one wife who said, "He tuned me out years ago. He just doesn't listen to me or hear me. He's so preoccupied with work, TV sports, and his stock portfolio."

Her husband retorted, "I tell you when I'm coming home late."

Here were two people, living in the same household, but the husband might as well have been deaf for all he was hearing and understanding from his wife. It had been years since they had talked of the intricacies of their lives, the things necessary to weave a closely knit relationship.

After heart preparation, the next stage of closing the loop in love is communication. So in this chapter, I'll discuss a variety of communication principles. Some will help your relationship every day and will even help you prevent future conflicts. Others will be helpful in the context of the next chapter, in which I'll provide some more-specific principles to follow in resolving specific conflicts.

TAKING OUR TEMPERATURE

One unforgettable Sunday afternoon in 1983, I received a message from the mouth of my five-year-old daughter, Sarah, that sent this young father into a tizzy.

It was a beautiful spring day, the kind made for bike riding and sunshine on your face. But not for this dad. You see, I was on a mission.

It was early May, and I had just completed my course work, comprehensive examinations, and dissertation for my doctoral degree in counseling. My graduation party was planned for 20 days from that day, and my family and I were exhausted from the work that had gone into earning "that degree."

Only one hurdle remained: the oral defense. Every doctoral student goes through it. The eager and sweaty student stands before peers and professors and defends his or her original research in the face of questions and critiques. If you can get past this event, you are welcomed into the fraternity of doctorhood.

I had two weeks to prepare for my defense. So on that Sunday afternoon, I sat in my favorite chair studying the important concept of *psychological androgyny*. It doesn't seem too important today, but it sure was then.

Sarah came swooping into the living room with a piece of poster board and a nifty five-year-old grin. "You want to see my picture of the family, Daddy?" she chirped.

"Not now, honey, Daddy is studying," I replied without even looking up from my book.

"I know, you're preparing for your oral defense," she responded respectfully. Sarah was the only five-year-old in the neighborhood who knew what an oral defense was, I can assure you.

"That's right, Sarah, come back later," I mumbled.

About four minutes later, Sarah returned and said, "Daddy, it's later, isn't it? Do you want to see the picture I drew of our family?"

"Sarah, Daddy is really busy. I really would like it if you would come back later. I don't want to tell you again, honey." I went back to studying as she stomped off, pounding her Strawberry Shortcake tennis shoes into the shag carpet.

Moments later, she returned. With all the assertiveness a five-year-old could muster, she belted out her final request: "Do you want to see my picture or don't you?"

Now I was steamed. "No, I don't, Sarah. Now please leave this room."

Well, she huffed and puffed, and with steam flowing from her ears, she left. As I returned to my important studies, it began to dawn on the great family counselor just how badly I was acting. So as I sat in the chair, I called out, "Sarah, please come back here."

You know how resilient kids can be. With that she came running in, squealing like the three little pigs we like to read about, and showed Daddy her masterpiece.

There was a picture of our house on 38th Street in Des Moines, with all the trees and the birds in the air. There was the sun wearing sunglasses. In front of the house was a group of people. On the top of the picture was the caption "Our Family Best."

"Here's Mommy. Isn't she pretty?" said Sarah with a gleam in her eye.

"Yes, she is pretty, Sarah. Just like you," I replied. There was Barbara: long, blonde hair, standing in front of the house, smiling and waving with her stick-figure hand.

"And here I am, Daddy."

Yep, that was Sarah all right. A smiling face with a few teeth missing, standing right next to her mom. To be candid with you, I was delighted to see she was smiling. When I see kids in counseling and have them draw pictures of their families, I always focus on the expressions on their faces to see what's going on in their little hearts.

"Here is Middy," said Sarah as she pointed to her sister's place in the family picture.

"Middy" was actually Missy, two years old at the time. Sarah couldn't quite draw a baby in a cradle, so she drew a stick figure of Missy lying in the street with her arms outstretched. We laughed as we looked at the picture of our family.

"And here is Katie, Daddy," she said. Katie was our

Irish setter pup that terrorized the neighborhood. Sure enough, there was Katie leaping around the front yard.

"And here are the trees, the squirrels, and the birdies."

"Honey, this is a great picture," I said. "Let's hang it up in the dining room so that every night at dinner, we can look at it and see our family." After a whopper of a hug, she jumped from my lap and was off to dress one of her Cabbage Patch dolls.

What a feeling of satisfaction! You've experienced it if you're a parent. It's one of those quality moments you love to hold onto but that tend to be as fleeting as beautiful spring days.

Well, back to the studies, doctor, I thought. Doctoral students say things like that to themselves to keep their heads in the game during the homestretch. But after about five minutes of studying, something dawned on me. You may have already guessed it. Something was missing from Sarah's picture.

"Sarah, come back here and get on Daddy's lap with your picture again," I called. "I need to ask you something."

She crawled on up, big brown eyes and all, and looked lovingly at her daddy. I had no idea she was about to teach me one of the most important lessons of my life.

"Do you want me to tell you all about my picture again, Daddy?" she said.

"No, honey. I just have a question. Here is Mommy. There you are, Sarah. And here is Missy, and we even have Katie romping in the yard. But something bothers me about your picture."

"What, Daddy?"

"Where is your daddy, Sarah?"

The next six words were spoken matter-of-factly. They weren't meant as an announcement, a complaint, or a revelation. But Sarah's reply penetrated me like no other message I've heard before or since.

"Oh, you are at the library," she said.

Ouch! I remember the stab in my heart. I can feel the pain almost as sharply today as I did years ago when we had that little conversation. What a memory!

I began to realize that my working full-time and finishing up a four-year doctoral program were taking a greater toll on my family than I had realized or at least been willing to admit. I knew it certainly was hurting my performance as a husband and father. Barbara was parenting our girls virtually single-handedly.

I wish I could say I was sophisticated enough to make big changes at the time. But I wasn't. Here I was, preparing to start a Christian counseling ministry, and I was on the verge of losing my own family.

A few months later, though, I reflected on that darkest moment in my parenting career and realized something needed to change. We started a new custom in the Rosberg home called "taking our temperature." Just as a physician will use a thermometer to check body temperature, we needed periodically to take our relationship temperature.

Here's how it works: Every four to six weeks, I take each member of my family out on a date. During our time together, I always ask two questions. First I ask, "How am I doing as a husband or father?"

Then it's feedback time, and usually they're honest. Oh, sometimes they say, "You're a great daddy." But other times one of my girls will say something like, "You know, Dad, you're gone a lot. I'm glad you're helping other families, but I miss you."

It doesn't impress children that you go all around the country to fancy hotels and conference centers and speak to people. Kids just know that their daddy isn't at the dinner table at night.

The second question is, "What do you need from me?" Sometimes, of course, Sarah and Missy say "more allowance." But usually not. Typically my family will say they need more time with me as their husband and dad. At other times, I've been asked to be more patient. I remember one time being asked not to yell. Another time the request was just for more hugs.

"Taking our temperature" doesn't cost anything, but it pays big dividends. Sometimes we do it while skateboarding, bike riding, or eating a pizza. Other times Barbara and I will do it while on a walk, after a date night, or during those darker times when I see

I'm not doing such a hot job as a husband.

And it really paid off when one of my children followed me into my bedroom after a long day of work, tugged on my suit coat, and said, "Daddy, we need to take our temperature."

As I looked down, I saw seven-year-old Missy looking up at me with that sweet little face. She got my attention, big time. The next Saturday was spent one on one with little Missy as we played all day. Her comment at the end of the day was another of those quality moments that appear out of nowhere and get lost almost as quickly, except in the memory bank of your heart: "Daddy, I wish this day would never end."

By the way, here's a copy of a family portrait that Missy drew for me when she was five or six.

I was back in the picture, and I was there to stay! This picture hangs in my office across from the chair that I counsel families from all day long. I look at it often as I reflect on the message I'm giving to families. The message is that there is hope. Families can be restored. Dads can return home. Children can forgive. Communication is important.

Taking our temperature is the foundational component to communication in our family. It's more than talking. It's more than listening. It's the sharing of our thoughts, our feelings, our needs. It is truly whole communication. And it defeats sending messages that fall on deaf ears. It can be risky, but without the risk there is no opportunity for growth.

"BILL, WE NEED TO FIND YOU A GOOD MAN TO MARRY"

When Bill and Arlene came to see me, they said they had hit an impasse in their relationship. After 11 years of marriage, she felt isolated and alone. He had courted her well enough in the early days of the marriage, but for the last few years their time together had dwindled to a few dinners per week, church every other week, and a few grunts while watching television.

They had lost their enthusiasm for each other. They were both busy in their careers and found most of their encouragement in friendships and work. She was ready to turn her husband in for a new model because of his perpetual lack of willingness to communicate with and listen to her.

As we began to unravel the sources of their conflicts, it was clear that they had a fundamental problem: Arlene treated Bill as if he were another woman, and Bill expected Arlene to communicate with him as if she were a man. In fact, I suggested to Bill that we could go out and find him a good man to marry. That got his attention.

Studies have indicated that "the average woman speaks roughly 25,000 words a day, while the average man speaks only 12,500." [1] The implication for Bill and Arlene was simple: Bill used up about 12,250 of his daily words at work, and when he went home, he didn't care to talk much. But Arlene, who also used about 12,000 words at work each day, was just warmed up by the time she reached home. He wanted to rest his mind; she wanted to talk. Is it any wonder they had conflicts?

So how do we handle this difference? A simple awareness that the difference exists is a great start. Then we need to ask ourselves, "What can I do to meet my mate's need for communication?"

We also need to conserve energy for communication at home. We literally need to save some of our word power for our families. This is especially important for men to remember. If they make meeting the needs of their wives a priority, they might even find they have a greater capacity for talking than they realize!

CIRCUS ACTS

You wouldn't try to take a nap or read a book in the middle of a three-ring circus, would you? Then why do people choose similar settings to attempt heart-to-heart communication?

You're sitting at home, reading the newspaper in the family room, with the dog barking and the television blaring in the background. The kids are running in and out. And that's when your mate says, "Honey, we need to talk."

You're beat after a long day at work and taking care of kids. You're lying in bed, about to fall asleep, when you hear those dreaded words: "We haven't talked much lately—I hardly know what's going on in your life."

What do these situations have to do with communication? They both illustrate the importance of setting and timing.

Let me tell you about a dear friend of mine. His name is Tom Barrett, and he works in Washington, D.C., with the Christian Embassy of Campus Crusade for Christ. In addition to ministering to members of Congress, he's a fine counselor. In fact, if I needed a professional counselor, he's one of two men I would seek counsel from. So with that kind of respect, when Tom says something, I listen.

Tom and I were talking one day about communication when he said something significant: "All healthy relationships are a function of schedule and skill. Even though the skills of communication are important, we must also be able to schedule the time it takes to grease the wheels of effective communication. This entails establishing and putting aside the time and determining the setting."

When I conduct marital and family counseling, I ask families or couples about where and when they communicate. This question often results in a blank expression and a question like, "What do you mean?"

Communication is a process that allows two or more people in a relationship to express their hearts to each other. It not only entails expression, but also a commitment to listening and understanding. When the speaking and listening occur, a sense of emotional intimacy is established that allows the relationship to blossom.

To do this effectively, we need to make communication a priority. And one of the best ways I know to do that is to plan a time and setting for it to take place.

My parents modeled this principle beautifully.

Each weekday evening, my dad arrived home from work at about 5:30. The four kids would run to greet him, and then we would return to watching "Gilligan's Island," riding bikes, or doing homework. Meanwhile, Mom and Dad would sit in our family room for about an hour and talk. If we were there, it was because we were in deep weeds. What did they talk about? The business. The children. Their relationship.

We kids knew we weren't invited, and believe me, we didn't want to be there. But at times I would go into the kitchen and watch them through the doorway. They didn't know I was watching, but the computer chips in my memory bank were racing. I recall some pretty serious times when they were dealing with the family business and the problems they were experiencing. Other times I remember laughter or true emotional intimacy. But they always talked.

And you know what? It made me feel secure. They didn't learn this skill at a marital conference or in a book. Somehow they just knew it helped their relationship. It has also helped mine.

My encouragement to you is that whether you're resolving a conflict or just taking part in consistent communication, it's wise to develop a pattern of daily interaction. This will not only help to avert some conflict, but it will also put the process in place for times of significant communication.

THIRD AND LONG

I love a good football game. There's nothing like a cool fall day, plenty of sun, and 75,000 fans packing a college football stadium. And communication is a bit like football. (I know some of you are rolling your eyes, wondering how I'm going to tie the two topics together. Please stay with me.)

I see three different components in a complete message: thoughts, feelings, and needs. Thoughts are a little like the first down in a series of plays. The quarterback huddles with the team and tells his squad what play he wants to run. Then he breaks the huddle to send them to the line. They know what to do. They've been told what he's thinking.

This is also the first component of communication. To send a complete message, we must identify in our own minds what play we want to carry out. What message do we desire to send? We need to identify the objective and subjective data. This includes our perceptions, ideas, values, and biases. It deals with what we think about what we're talking about. It sounds like this:

"I've been thinking about how to respond to this issue with my parents. It seems to me that we need to talk with them to confront this conflict."

"I've been struggling with your responses to me recently."

"This is a difficult issue to talk about, but I see our financial situation from a different position, and I disagree with the decisions you've made."

Each of these statements contains the thoughts of the person sending it. They're statements that can be clarified by the listener through questions or restatements.

Feelings are the second down of the series. We're deeper into the other team's territory and need to take a greater risk to gain yardage. Feelings are emotions like fear, pride, joy, sadness, frustration, betrayal, rejection, anger, anxiety, anticipation, contentment, depression, and so on. This is the down where many of us men seem to lose our way.

"I feel we should think about this issue" is not a feeling. It's a thought.

"I feel as if you never talk" is also a thought rather than a feeling, because it's a statement about your interpretation of another person's behavior.

When we truly express our feelings, we become more vulnerable. It means we dig deeper and reveal our hearts in a way that can lead to a greater understanding of our mates, friends, children, or parents.

"I feel hurt."

"I feel abandoned and alone."

"I feel angry with you."

Those are feeling statements. When they follow

the expression of our thoughts, they can pack a powerful message.

"I know you're trying the best you can in our marriage. It seems you want to reach out, but at times I feel so betrayed."

"I've thought about what you said, Sally. I agree that we have to resolve this conflict for our relationship to heal. I've felt anxious and angry."

Those statements reflect a combination of thoughts and feelings, but the two are very different from each other. It's the same thing as going from the first to the second down. Both plays can yield yardage, either gained or lost, but they're different plays.

The third down is expressing our need. The quarterback returns to the huddle and tells the team it's third and inches. We've made good progress on the first two downs, but we need to get another first down or we'll have to punt the ball away.

Expressing our need can push us over the line for the first down. Failing to express it can stop our progress fast. It's during this third down that a team can really shine.

In communication, the person revealing his or her heart, seeking to be understood, needs to say what he or she needs the other person to do.

"I need you to listen to me."

"I need some time to sort through this issue."

"I need more information so I can understand your hurt."

I think. I feel. I need. These are the three key components of one side of communication. The other side is *listening*.

HARRIET TAKES WALTER FOR A RIDE

Harriet and Walter were a delightful elderly couple going on 60 years of marriage. They also had recently encountered one of the complications of aging: Walter couldn't pass his driver's license test. Whenever they needed to go somewhere, Harriet now had to drive.

Walter was a talker, and Harriet was having trouble adjusting to his incessant chatter as she took over the wheel. She found that she could put up with him, however, by just acting as if she were listening—nodding and tuning in here and there so she wouldn't miss everything he said.

One afternoon, Harriet and Walter went for a ride, and Walter carried on, barely taking a breath. When Harriet made a left turn, the passenger door opened, and Walter fell out of the car and started rolling down the street! Harriet, meanwhile, drove on, not realizing what had happened.

Fortunately, two police officers parked nearby

watched this entire event unfold. One signaled that he would help the elderly gentleman, while his partner took off after Harriet. Six blocks later, with siren blaring and lights flashing, the officer finally pulled Harriet over. Nervously she rolled down her window and fumbled for her driver's license. "Officer, was I speeding?" she asked.

"No, ma'am, you weren't speeding, but when you turned that corner a few blocks back, your passenger door opened and your husband rolled out of the car!"

To which Harriet replied, "Thank goodness! I thought I had gone deaf!"

We chuckle at this story, but unfortunately, Harriet and Walter represent a lot of couples and the lack of effective listening in our families. Most people begin tuning each other out long before they reach old age.

When I was young, I tried to set the national record for talking. Nothing is different today from then except the years slow me down a bit. As a lad, I remember my father's telling me, "Gary, the good Lord gave you two ears and one mouth for a purpose—so you would listen twice as much as you talk." Good point, Dad.

The Bible says, "My dear brothers, take note of this: Everyone should be quick to listen, slow to speak and slow to become angry, for man's anger does not bring about the righteous life that God desires."[2] That says it well, doesn't it? Quick to listen, slow to speak, and slow to become angry.

If we're quick to listen, we'll be more concerned with understanding another person and less concerned with expressing what we think or feel. Oftentimes, all we need to do to resolve a conflict is to truly listen to the other person—we'll understand the situation better, we'll be better able to make a decision about the conflict, and the other person will be happy that we took the time to listen.

Instead, however, many people are more concerned with winning the argument or expressing their opinion than with understanding the situation. I was a good example of this a few years ago as I flew home from a speaking engagement. We had just lifted off when I heard this *bang* and smelled something burning. I looked across the aisle and read the lips of a businessman saying to himself, "Oh no!"

The captain came on the intercom to say, "We are obviously experiencing problems, so we're turning this plane around to land." After that, I watched some of the most amazing handling of a 747 I had ever seen. He turned that thing around, and as we landed—safely, by the way—we could see the emergency gear hitting the field.

As we entered the terminal (I wish they'd call it something else), the passengers broke into three distinct groups. A whole contingent headed for the bar, either to celebrate life or to sooth their frazzled nerves. A second group started arguing and demanding new tickets so they could catch another plane. The rest of us were more quiet and just thankful to be alive.

I ended up having to fly to Houston and then to O'Hare Airport in Chicago, but it was after midnight when I arrived. Since I couldn't fly to Des Moines until later in the morning, I went to the airline's customer service area and asked for a room in a hotel across the street. What happened next is a scene I will never forget.

"Dr. Rosberg, we don't have a room for you, nor are we obligated to get you a room," said the representative. "I can call a hotel for you, but you need to pay for it yourself."

I couldn't believe my ears—so I turned them off and engaged my mouth. "Do you mean to tell me you won't get me a room? First you almost kill me in that airplane. Then you route me to Houston and now Chicago in the middle of the night. I'm missing a day in the office, and now you don't have a room?"

"That's right, sir." She wasn't about to back off, and to be honest, neither was I. I'm generally an easygoing kind of guy. But way down deep, beneath all the capacity to listen and empathize, lies a lion that can roar with the best of them.

"Ma'am, do you have your ears on?" I said. "I *demand* a room, and I demand it now." Then I leaned across the counter, within 18 inches of her face, and locked stares with her. She matched my stare for almost a minute.

"Okay, Dr. Rosberg," she finally conceded. "I'll get a room for you. But the Hilton is full. A limo will be waiting for you outside in ten minutes to transport you to your hotel."

"Thank you." I was a gentleman, so I still needed to say that. As I got in the backseat of the limo, I thought, *I won. Sometimes you just have to stand up and get a little aggressive, or people will stomp all over you.*

Well, I *thought* I had won. What I didn't realize was that the limo was taking me to a dumpy little hotel half an hour from the airport. It's probably reserved for ornery customers.

Did I listen in this situation? No. Was I about to listen? No. The only thing I had on my mind was getting my point across and winning the battle. Did I win? No!

I learned a lesson that night. When I get into conflict, demanding my way won't resolve the issue. Even if I think I've won, it may be just a short-term celebration.

As my dad said, "Gary, the good Lord gave you two ears . . ." I know, Dad. I just forgot.

DRESSING THE CHRISTMAS TREE

Earlier in my marriage, I sometimes couldn't figure out why Barbara and I would hit a wall in our communication. We were both reasonably well educated and well-intentioned, but sometimes we just couldn't understand each other.

After eight or nine years of marriage, something occurred to me. When Barbara would tell me a story or inform me about her day, she would include all sorts of details and information that I found superfluous to the meat of the story. Let's say she went to a Bible study and out to lunch with some friends. That night, she would describe what people were wearing, what they had to eat, and what music was playing in the background.

Remember what I said about self-talk in the last chapter? As Barbara would talk, my self-talk was generating more and more messages like "Come on, Barb, get on with it" or "And then what happened?" You see, I didn't care about those details. I usually didn't remember what I ate for lunch, let alone what other people were wearing.

After years of frustration, it finally dawned on me that Barbara and I just had different styles of communicating. While she was talking and enjoying the process, I was searching for the punch line. I just wanted to find the solution.

Journalists call this process the "inverted pyramid." When they write news stories, they give you the main point in the first paragraph: "Tornado claims hundreds of lives." "Pentagon steps up war effort." "Famous actor dies." Then the subsequent paragraphs give additional information. That's my kind of conversation—straight and to the point. And that's the way most of us men are.

Many women, on the other hand, prefer the novelist's approach. They slowly unfold the plot, giving all kinds of details, and often come to the point at the end of the story.

Barbara and I have learned to communicate by understanding that difference. Now when we have our evening discussions, she gives me the "bullets" of information, which satisfies my need to know up front what we're talking about, and then continues with additional information. On the other hand, when I tell her something, I give her all sorts of information, weaving in as many secondary issues as I can muster, and then deliver the punch line. We both feel fulfilled with this type of communication.

If we're dealing with a conflict, we use the same approach.

"Gary," she'll say, "I need to talk to you about the way you barked at the girls this morning."

I can handle that message. I know the agenda and will typically respond, "Tell me what you're concerned about, Barb." With that we start to communicate and resolve the issue.

If I were to approach Barb with that direct approach, I would run the risk of wounding her, so I'm more apt to start by setting the stage. "Barbara, I need to talk with you about something that's been bothering me." That statement will alert her that I need to talk, but it matches her personality and communication style more effectively.

I call it "dressing the tree." It's like trimming a Christmas tree. Many people start at the bottom with the ornaments and the lights, and then, when the tree is almost done, they place the angel on the top of the tree. That's how Barbara communicates, but not me. I like to put the angel on the top and then trim the tree downward.

Neither is right or wrong. They're just different styles. The key is to identify how our mates communicate and then communicate in that fashion to meet their needs.

"ARE YOU TRYING TO TELL ME SOMETHING?"

"Ruth, I don't think I want to go to your mother's today for dinner. I have a lot of work to do around the yard."

If Ruth takes that comment at face value, it looks

pretty good. It's true that Brent has yard work to do. It's also true that if he goes to his mother-in-law's house, he won't get the yard done. But Ruth has a sense that something else is being said nonverbally. Do you think she's right? Let's put this in context.

Historically, when Ruth's family gets together for Sunday dinners, a few things happen. Her dad jumps all over her mom. Her mom complains that her husband never turns off the sports on TV. They both gripe about not seeing the grandkids enough. When Brent and Ruth leave, they're both frustrated. Ruth is caught in the middle, feeling defensive about her parents yet wanting to agree with Brent. She understands his lack of enthusiasm for "blowing a Sunday afternoon" when the only time he has for yard work is after church.

Go back to Brent's statement: "Ruth, I don't think I want to go to your mother's today for dinner. I have a lot of work to do around the yard." Is it true? Yes. But is it the whole story? Probably not, and both Brent and Ruth know it. Brent is actually avoiding going to his in-laws' but is not stating it directly, and this frustrates Ruth.

You've been there: Someone sends you a message that looks good on the surface, but you have this strong sensation that there's something going on he's not admitting. And you sit back and wonder, *Is he trying to tell me something?*

Often two different messages are being sent simultaneously: the spoken message and the unspoken. Which one do we usually believe? That's right, the unspoken message. We often try to say something without saying it directly, and it gets lost in our verbiage. So a key principle in communication and resolving conflicts is to seek to understand the true underlying need of the other person. Is she saying one thing but trying to send a more important message? What really is the underlying issue?

Ruth is at a crossroads. She can "backdoor" Brent and sweet-talk him, "take a shot" at him and be aggressive, or seek the truth in a fair and assertive manner. Here are three possible statements she can choose from:

1. "You know, Brent, if you go over there for dinner just this one time, I'll never ask you again." That's the backdoor approach, which would lead Brent to think, *Fat chance, Ruth.*

2. "Sure, Brent, we always do what you want to do. The world revolves around you, King Tut." This is the aggressive approach. It would produce a full-blown conflict that would probably keep them from getting the yard work done *or* going to dinner at her parents' home.

3. "Brent, I know you have yard work to do. I appreciate the way you take care of the yard. I also have a need to spend time with my

parents. Do you think you're avoiding them because of the conflicts in their home?" That's the fair and assertive approach.

By responding with the third option, Ruth would be doing three things. First, she would be affirming Brent for taking care of their yard. Second, she would be expressing her need to spend time with her parents. Third, she would be challenging Brent about whether he was saying what he was really thinking.

Fortunately, Ruth chose the third approach. Then Brent faced a dilemma. Would he stick to his mixed message that Ruth knew was misleading, or would he answer her directly so that his spoken and unspoken messages matched?

"Ruth, you're right," he said. "I do avoid going over to your parents'. When I'm there, I'm uncomfortable." Bingo, Brent. He was honest with this response, and as soon as he was, Ruth became less defensive. They were communicating effectively and came to a resolution.

Here's how they handled it: They decided to go to dinner, but for only two hours instead of the usual four. They also talked honestly with her parents. It was difficult to approach them, but they took the risk, and it went fairly well. Her dad was defensive when they started out, but as they talked and affirmed their love for her parents, her dad responded better. Ruth's mom was relieved, because she also knew they were trying to tell her something, but she was avoiding it as well.

People will often appreciate our willingness to dig a little deeper and help them articulate something that's going on below the surface. Relationships will also be enhanced by digging a little deeper, and they'll be more honest and healthy, too. They'll also be defensive sometimes, because speaking directly creates anxiety. But directness can help resolve conflict and avoid the building of additional conflict.

Let me now summarize the seven techniques for improving communication that this chapter has covered:

1. Take your temperature regularly, seeking answers to the following two questions:
   a. How am I doing in our relationship?
   b. What do you need from me?
2. Recognize the differences between men and women. Although they're somewhat stereotypical, they tend to hold true for most relationships. An understanding of our different communication needs can lead to significant growth in relationships between men and women.
3. Recognize that all healthy relationships are a function of schedule and skill. If we need to put aside additional time to improve our relationships, let's make the sacrifice to do so. If we

need to improve our skills of conflict resolution and communication, we can commit to do so by reading additional books on these topics, attending a Family Life Conference, or seeing a qualified counselor who works from a biblical perspective.

4. Practice communicating with whole messages, including thoughts, feelings, and needs. Keep in mind that anything short of whole messages will run the risk of sabotaging the relationship.

5. Commit to active listening with the other person. Tune into the message, and "keep your ears on."

6. Develop an understanding of the differences in communication styles between people who prefer the three-volume novel rendition to a synopsis of the story. We're different in the ways we communicate—not good or bad, just different. We need to understand the other person's approach and stretch ourselves to see things the way he or she does to develop empathy.

7. Look at the unspoken as well as the spoken message. Realize we may need to dig a little deeper to get at the real meaning of the message.

By practicing these seven techniques, we can improve our communication skills and enhance our relationships.

Elevator talk is superficial and easy. Real communication takes work. It isn't passive, especially in the midst of conflict. Real communication means we need to have someone seeking to understand as well as someone seeking to be understood. It means emotional intimacy needs to occur as we empathize with our friend, child, parent, or mate.

Resolving conflicts occurs more readily when there's a commitment to communication and the relationship as a whole. But what do we do about the specific problem? We'll cover that next as we consider how to conduct a loving confrontation.

C H A P T E R   1 5

LOVING CONFRONTATION

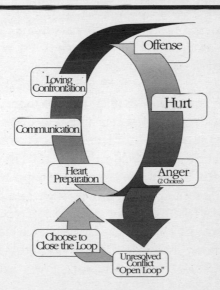

Get outta here." That's not exactly the most professional thing to say to a couple in a counseling session, but those were the words that came out of my mouth one November morning.

"We have never had a conflict, Dr. Rosberg," said a young man named Dave. He and Marcy had been dating for two years and were going to be married just after Thanksgiving. As Dave said those words, I looked over at Marcy, and sure enough, she nodded in agreement.

"No, let me rephrase the question," I tried. "When you're having a conflict, how do you handle it? Do you blow up or isolate from each other? One of the most important parts of our premarriage counseling is to help equip you for dealing with the conflicts in your relationship." Then I thought, *Okay, now I've explained myself better.*

"Doctor, we don't fight or disagree," Dave said. "We've never had a conflict, have we, honey?" He spoke with one of those cute little looks that only an engaged guy could give. Marcy squished up her face, giving him a little squeeze of the arm, and I thought I was in the Twilight Zone. After their response, they both looked at me, waiting for the next question.

Now, I was trained not to display a lot of reaction to statements. I have listened to people tell me some of the most incredible stories you could imagine. Almost 20,000 hours of counseling gives a counselor a truckload of experiences to draw upon. But when Dave and Marcy turned to me, they caught my jaw dropping on the floor.

"You mean you've never had a disagreement? Never a fight? You've never been ticked with each other?" I thought about going to borrow a stethoscope from one of my medical doctor friends to see if their hearts were still pumping.

"Never, Gary."

"Well, I'll be. This is a first," I said as I tried to gather my composure. "Let's go on to the next section on my outline. One of the adjustments couples need to make in their marriage is to determine how to spend holidays, balancing the need for each person to spend time with his or her own family. Thanksgiving is coming up in a couple of weeks. Where will you, as a couple, be spending the holiday?"

What happened in the next five seconds is one of the most memorable experiences of my counseling career. I had no sooner got the question out of my mouth when Dave and Marcy said in perfect unison, "My parents' house." As they said it, they turned to each other with their jaws dropping a few inches and one of those "Uh-oh" looks on their faces.

I looked at both of them, clapped my hands once, and said, "All right! We have a conflict!"

I laugh about that story today, but at the time I was a little unnerved. They worked it through, and I had the opportunity to sit in with them as the bubble was perforated just a bit. By the way, they're doing well today in their marriage, and we all three laugh about that experience.

Conflicts come. Some of you reading this are thinking, *Boy, do they!* I have them, you have them, we all have them. So how do we deal with them? In this chapter, I want to offer some concrete ideas on how to deal with the conflicts in our lives through loving confrontation. And there's no better place to start than by learning to take the fire out of conflict.

DISARMING CONFLICT

Here's a phrase that will disarm our conflicts and set the stage for what follows: "Let's pray together first."

Prayer has an interesting impact on the resolution of a conflict. It takes an issue between two people who have chosen sides, often against each other, and welcomes into the relationship a third person—Jesus.

Here we are, all loaded up for the fight, with an arsenal of weapons just waiting to be called to the front lines for the attack, and the other person says, "Let's pray together first." Talk about taking the wind out of your sails! It not only takes the fire out of a situation, but it also allows the people in the relationship to humble themselves.

Listen to the apostle Paul: "Devote yourselves to

prayer, being watchful and thankful."[1] There are three important thoughts in that one sentence.

"Devote yourselves to prayer." Amazing things happen when we bring prayer into a confrontation. God starts to bring restoration to our conflicts. He is glorified, and we begin to experience healing.

"Being watchful." That means holding our tongues rather than shooting down anyone in our path. It means being more cautious and teachable.

"And thankful." When we're thankful to God, we humble ourselves and recognize not only the gifts, but the gift giver Himself, Jesus.

When I first thought about how to introduce the steps involved in conflict resolution, I realized there's no better place to start than with our own hearts. If we go to resolve a conflict and our pride is leading the way, we're in for a long night. Is prayer what I feel like doing in that situation? No way. I want to howl like a wolf. But the very howling that comes so naturally will only perpetuate the problem. The only way I find I can reduce that pride is to humble myself before God and approach the conflict in prayer.

I not only try to pray by myself, but if I'm going to resolve an issue in my family or with a friend, I will also try to pray with the other person. "Lord, this is a tough one," I'll pray. "I'm angry right now, and I want to demand or act out. Please soften my heart and my approach to this person. Be in the center of our discussion so that we will not sin in our anger and frustration. Help us to resolve our problem and come together in this conflict."

Such prayer will not only lead to resolutions that are pleasing to God, but it will also probably shorten the length of the discussions. As He is allowed access into our lives, our pride is diminished and our hearts are softened.

TIMING IS EVERYTHING

Timing is important in setting up a successful business, conveying an important message to someone, and resolving a conflict. Yet it's amazing how often people violate this principle. Rather than choosing the right time, circumstances, and setting for resolving a conflict, they leap into the fray when they feel like it and end up making the conflict much worse.

Consider Bob and Margie. The common mistake they make is to try to resolve conflict just before going to bed at night. It happens all the time in their home: Their anger is triggered, they avoid each other for a while in the evening as the pressure builds, and then they decide to "have it out" after the ten o'clock news.

I know another couple who tried to resolve a conflict on their way to work. This was a kind of hit-and-run approach. They tried to work it out quickly and get it over with before a long day at work. But they didn't have time to really deal with the issue, and they had to halt their conversation midstream.

Or take Brenda, a busy and, at times, harried homemaker. She's an orderly person, the type who likes to work from a to-do list each day and clean up a mess as soon as it's made. Her daughter Megan, however, didn't share her passion for orderliness. For weeks Brenda harped on Megan to keep her room clean, and finally she came to the end of the proverbial rope. Three minutes before Megan was to leave for school, Brenda called a family meeting to deal with the disaster area on the second floor. She wanted to tackle the problem *now*.

The problem needed to be addressed, but the timing was all wrong. Megan was under pressure to get to school and was not in the mood to discuss the condition of her room. Tempers flared, emotions ran sky high, and a loop was opened even wider.

Here are some hints for choosing the right time and setting for dealing with a conflict: First, *choose a time when you won't be hurried*, when you can really communicate. Make it a time when you're both rested, when you won't have any outside distractions, and when your emotions will have cooled down.

If you're a parent with small children, finding the right time and setting to discuss a conflict with your mate may be difficult. You probably ought to do it after the kids are put to bed—but you might be pretty tired yourself by that time. You may need to schedule a date or just a special, out-of-the-ordinary time when the two of you can be alone.

Second, *be sensitive to the pressures on the other person.* Is he or she preoccupied with other things? Is your child preparing for an exam or your mate getting ready to leave for a meeting? When I'm ready to deal with a conflict, I want to do it right now—not in an hour, not tomorrow, but now. If the other person isn't ready, however, I should hold off.

Third, *ask permission from the other person to take the time to deal with a conflict.* This is a custom we keep in the Rosberg home. If Missy and I need to talk about an issue but she's doing homework or even playing with a friend, I need to be sensitive to that and ask her if it's a good time to talk. The other part of the custom is that if the other person doesn't feel it's a good time, he or she can't just say no but needs to offer an alternate time.

Fourth, *take care in choosing the setting for resolving a conflict.* Is it a place where we can talk privately? Is it out of earshot from the kids? I'm not suggesting we mislead our children so that they think a relationship can be free of conflict. What I am suggesting is that adult communication be handled between adults, not in front of the kids. No matter how secure a family is, children can be frightened when they see their parents experiencing conflict.

Barbara and I were closing a loop one night when our daughters came into the room. We asked them to leave because Mommy and Daddy were working out a conflict.

After the discussion, Sarah came into the kitchen and asked, "Are you going to get a divorce?"

"What?" I said.

"Are you and Mommy going to get a divorce? When I hear you argue, I get scared."

My initial thought was, *What business do I have writing a book about resolving conflict when my own kids would express that type of fear?* Then I thought about her statement and realized my daughters are growing up in a culture where divorce occurs in about half of all marriages, and they're not insulated from that fear. No matter how secure I try to make them, I still need to recognize the incredible sense of powerlessness they feel when Barbara and I are having a conflict.

I took Sarah and Missy aside and said, "I want to promise you girls something. No matter how frustrated I may become, no matter what kind of conflict your mom and I have, no matter what happens, I will never leave your mother. I promise you I will always love your mother. I will never divorce her."

With that statement, two wide and relieved grins came over their faces, and they felt secure again.

We must be willing to teach our children that resolving conflict is part of any relationship. Even in a society that throws relationships away, our family and your family can resist the pressures and stick together. At the same time, though, we need to watch how much we do and say in front of our kids.

"SARAH, WATCH OUT! RUN!"

The warning "Sarah, watch out! Run!" was about all I could get out of my mouth that hot July day in 1981. Sarah, three years old at the time, and I were playing quietly on the front porch of our neighbor's house, trying to make it through a sticky Iowa summer day. I remember looking at her, thinking what a swell kid God had given to me to steward for a time.

As she was walking along the front porch, she approached the mailbox at the front door. As most three-year-olds do, Sarah was expressing her curiosity and banging the mailbox lid up and down, making a racket. On about the tenth slam, suddenly I heard a buzzing that came out of nowhere. It reached a crescendo that sounded like a chain saw ripping through an old oak. I turned to Sarah and saw an angry swarm of bees surrounding her. "Sarah," I yelled, "watch out! Run!"

I ran toward Sarah and the bees, waving my arms like helicopter propellers. The bees went after both of us, stinging us all over. I will never forget Sarah's hysterical cry, Barb's shrieking, and the panic that overtook the three of us. We ran to the car and headed for the emergency room of a local hospital to have scores of stingers removed from us.

Many attempts at resolving conflict unfold in the same fashion. Two people are trying to deal with a problem, and one of them opens his mouth and lets out a whole string of issues dating back to the beginning of the relationship. The other person is completely overwhelmed.

Barney and Val are a case in point. "Barney, you never take me anywhere," said an exasperated Val.

"I never take you anywhere, huh?" replied a frustrated Barney. "Well, if you would have cleaned the kitchen, I wouldn't have been late picking up Amy at gymnastics."

"Clean the kitchen? Your dad even helps your mom with the dishes. You haven't picked up a dish towel in five years."

Get the idea? Val would express a complaint, and Barney would respond with his own. She would start to respond to Barney's statement and then bring up an entirely new issue.

This type of conflict resolution can kill a relationship. Concentrating on just one issue at a time allows us to get some focus and keep a sense of boundary around the conflict, allowing resolution rather than annihilation.

Barbara and I have learned a great way to deal with "swarming bees." When we hit on a second topic during the heat of battle, whoever recognizes it first will say, "It seems we now have two issues on the table. Let's deal with the first one and then go back to the other, okay?"

As Barney and Val learned, it's also important to allow one person to talk at a time, without interruption, while the other tunes in for the intended message. Two people can't talk at the same time and still be heard.

MISSY'S FIERCE DAY AT SCHOOL

Here's a note that eight-year-old Missy brought home one day from school:

> by Melissa Anne Rosberg
> called Missy's fierce day at school
> jan. 2 1989
>
> Dear Mrs. Wilson,
> It all started two months ago.
> I can't remember how but this has been going on for along time. It is Billy [the names have been changed to protect the guilty—I mean, innocent]. He hurts me every day.
> But now Ben has ganged up with him. I'm crying at night almost every night. Billy every day at the lunch room stomps on my foot that really hurts and I'm not kidding.

I do very bad want to be his friend.

I'm trying so hard to make friends with Billy and Ben. All I know is that I really only have 3 friends in my class and that is Chris, he cheers me up when I am sad. Heather L., she's always no matter what my friend. Meagan she is very very nice to me. But I've always wanted to be Billy's friend and Ben's.

But then this really bothered me when Billy and Ben said that my mom was mean and that is when I was home sick for her. When school started Billy was very very nice to me. I don't know why he doesn't like me. Mrs. Wilson I know you do understand because you probably know that I'm not making all this up.

Mrs. Wilson I need a hug sometimes because I miss my mommy and daddy so much. I promise I cry every night. And I want to ask you permission that maybe sometime any day this week that just me and you could have a talk at the back table. I have never had a better teacher in the world.

Your Student
  Missy
  THE END

What a great letter, especially the last sentence! Missy will probably be the next author in the Rosberg family.

She certainly had a "fierce day" at school, didn't she? Yet she followed one of the best guidelines in dealing with her conflict and anger: She expressed it, but gently. What she (and her dad, by the way) wanted to do was to go up and bust old Billy and Ben in the chops. But being the fine, upstanding father I am, I resisted my temptation and encouraged her to handle it. And she did.

A wise man once wrote, "There is one who speaks rashly like the thrusts of a sword, but the tongue of the wise brings healing."[2] Missy was wise. Dad would have been rash. She got her hug and received understanding from her teacher. It's difficult to argue with someone who doesn't climb into the mudslinging with us. When we speak gently, we are heard.

IT'S NOT POLITE TO POINT

One way to approach a conflict gently is to use *I* statements rather than *You* statements. To show what I mean, let's look at a few lines that don't cut the mustard when we're trying to deal with conflict:

"Why did you think that?"

"You shouldn't feel that way."

"You're feeling too strongly about this issue."

"That's not how you should look at it."

"You're never going to get rid of this problem."

"Why are you always doing that?"

Those are all *You* statements, and if our tendency is to try to win in conflicts, we probably use lots of them. But such statements are like pointing a finger in the other person's face. Feel good? Not to me. Yet we often, without realizing it, tell others what they should think or feel and make exaggerated accusations.

How does it feel when someone says, "You're feeling too strongly about this issue"? It usually makes us feel even more strongly, doesn't it? We can't help the way we feel. If anyone tells us we shouldn't feel that way, it only makes us angry.

I often see men use this technique against their wives: "She needs to come back down to earth. Women are always too emotional." But I doubt men are less emotional; they're just more accustomed to concealing it.

Another tactic, exaggerated accusations, will only fuel a conflict. We need to avoid the words *never* and *always*. They're guaranteed to anger the other person and cause him or her to focus on the exaggeration instead of the problem.

Let's say a husband is not doing a good job of balancing the family checkbook and has lately bounced a couple of checks. If the wife says, "You always overwrite on our checkbook," he can avoid the problem and put the focus on the exaggeration instead: "What do you mean 'always'? That's not fair!"

This is where *I* messages can help: "I get frustrated when we overdraw our checking account. We need to stay within our balance. How can I help with this?"

That message illustrates two principles for making good *I* statements: Express your feelings, and express your need. Here are some other examples:

"I'm really feeling upset by this situation, and I need to talk it out with you."

"I know we disagree, but I need you to listen to my perspective."

"I have a problem with you that needs to be resolved. Let's take some time tonight, away from the kids, to work through this conflict."

By shifting the approach from "you" to "I," we avoid making the other person the focus of the conflict and are better able to deal with the issues.

"GIVE ME THAT PILLOW"

Another technique Barbara and I have used is to depersonalize our conflicts. One of the most frequent mistakes we made, especially in the early years of our marriage, was to be accusatory with each other. And even after the conflict was over and things had cooled down, we often felt we had added fuel to the fire because of that approach.

One day, in the midst of a conflict in our living room, I was feeling exasperated and wanted badly to blame Barbara for what was wrong. But what I really wanted to say was that I was frustrated with one of her behaviors. Then the phrase "My mate is not my enemy" (see chap. 11) rang in my head as I was trying to make my point. I looked over at the sofa, picked up a pillow, threw it on the floor, and said, "Barbara, that pillow represents our problem. You are not the problem. I am not the problem [I was hoping]. That pillow is the problem. You are not my enemy. We are on the same team. Let's work together to talk about 'it,' the issue."

She looked at me, and it was as if a lightbulb went on for both of us: We needed to depersonalize the issues so we could team up to talk about our problems rather than hammer away at each other's sensitive spirits. In my office, this one technique has done more to help couples deal with problems than I can tell you. We spend a lot of time throwing pillows on the floor. It works. Try it!

MR. FIX-IT

I'm not exactly your most adept handyman. I remember when I took 13-year-old Sarah out to buy a new bike. As we looked at one particular model, the salesman tried to explain how to take the front wheel off. He did it easily and then said, "Okay, Gary, you got how to do it?"

Sarah rolled her eyes, knowing her father is a giant amoeba at repairs, as I said, "Mike, you know me. I'm a counselor, not a mechanic."

When it comes to conflict, however, I'm like many other men—I'm looking for a solution to the problem, while my wife is often just looking for a chance to tell me what she's feeling.

Most of us men haven't quite figured out that often, when a woman is expressing her frustration, she may not want an answer to the problem. She may just need someone to listen to her. As Kevin Miller wrote in an article called "Are Men Bad Listeners?":

> A husband's inexplicable inattention, therefore, may stem from his idea that discussing something (possible translation: having to discuss something) means there's a problem with it. Otherwise, why would his wife say, "We have to talk about this"? And who wants to admit there's a problem with his marriage, his kids or his ability to provide for his family?[3]

So what's a man to do? One word: Ask. Simply ask his partner what she needs from him. This works not only in marriage, but also with parents, kids, friends, and co-workers. Perhaps they need someone to help them generate solutions, or maybe just options. At other times, they may need someone to stick up for them. Sometimes they just need someone to keep his mouth shut and listen, then give a hug. And at other times, they need someone to empathize with their hurt.

SO WHAT DO WE DO NOW?

Some conflicts never reach the stage of decision making because the acts of communicating and listening seem to resolve them. But with others, a decision needs to be made.

"Gary, I think you're overcommitting again," Barbara said to me one time. "So many people want a piece of you, and sometimes there isn't much left over for us at home." I can still feel the sting—no, the sledgehammer—of that comment. And she was right. I needed to hear it. I had overcommitted to counseling appointments and speaking engagements, and the two were on a collision path with my home life. I was so busy helping others and feeding my own need to minister that I was getting off track again, just as I had in my doctoral program. The warning light was blinking, but I hadn't been looking at it.

We talked. I listened to Barbara's frustration. As

much as she supports me in my ministry, she also is the most effective person I know at expressing her honest needs. She listened to me voice my frustration, too, with not being able to do everything I felt called to do. We prayed and sought God's direction. We talked about whether I was always responding to God's calling or if "my own calling" got mixed up in there somewhere. We validated each other's hurts and frustration. But we also needed to take an extra step; we needed to make some changes in my schedule. We weighed options and reached a mutually satisfying decision.

When I come to the decision-making stage, the first question I try to ask myself is "What does the Bible say about this situation? Is there a clear admonition we need to obey?" How's that for getting to the heart of the matter?

The first question *isn't* "How do you feel about it?" It isn't "What do other people think you should do?" Nor is it "What do you, in your wisdom, suggest?" Those are all good questions, but they're secondary to what God has to say. We need always to place the Bible over other variables in resolving conflicts.

If the Bible does not give a clear admonition, we need to seek God's wisdom about the decision. I have a few tips that have worked as I've tried to solve conflicts and help others do the same.

First, it's good to stay open to different options.

Business people know about options. They build them into their strategies. It's always wise to have an option built into a contract to give us some leeway for growth.

When dealing with a conflict, it's important to avoid tunnel vision—thinking our way is the only way. We can get so locked into our way that we fail to recognize or appreciate the options the other person may be offering for the resolution of the issues.

After generating different options, we can try one out. It doesn't have to be cast in stone. The best approach is to try one option but remain open to changing our minds later if that option doesn't prove to be the best.

Barbara and I generated some options about cutting back on my counseling schedule. As my speaking schedule increased, it was clear I needed to diminish the number of counseling appointments I was taking. I couldn't increase both.

Second, we need to be open to not doing it our way. How do you think another person would react if you said something like, "You know, I think your idea is just as good as mine, if not better. Why don't we try doing it your way?" If the person tends toward being control-oriented, no other statement would cause more shock!

Although that would be a great way to resolve conflict, it rarely happens that way. Instead, we instinctively want to resolve things according to what we think is best.

One of the most important aspects of resolving conflict is to elevate the other person, helping him or her to see that he or she is more important than the issue at hand. That's essentially what Paul meant when he wrote, "Therefore encourage one another and build each other up, just as in fact you are doing."[4]

Paul hit it on the head. We're to build others up and give them encouragement, elevating them just as we would desire they do for us. That may mean swallowing our pride and not being in control.

My encouragement is that we take a head-on approach to dealing with the conflicts in our relationships. This honest, direct, and caring style will bring the combination of our thoughts, feelings, and needs to the decision-making part of the process known as resolution. As that occurs, we're ripe for the next stage of relationship mending. This stage is probably the most difficult for many, yet it brings the greatest amount of healing. It's the process of forgiveness, and it brings us closer to God than anything else we can do.

CHAPTER 16

A LESSON IN FORGIVENESS

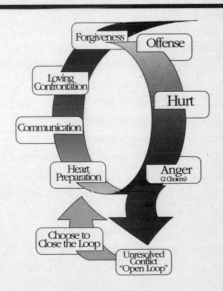

Forgiveness

Offense

Loving
Confrontation

Hurt

Communication

Heart
Preparation

Anger
(2 Choices)

Choose to
Close the Loop

Unresolved
Conflict
"Open Loop"

It was a sunny December morning. Five inches of fresh snow blanketed the ground. As we walked to our car after church, an idea hit me. "Barb, kids," I said, "when we get home, you need to dress warm, because I have a special treat in mind for all of us."

All the way home I was baited, begged, and pleaded with to give in and reveal the big secret to my three girls. They really tried to get it out of me, but I stuck to my guns.

When we arrived home, my instructions were simply to dress up nice and warm and meet me outside. As I led the troops into the front yard, with our 12-year-old Irish setter, Katie, in step, I found the perfect spot.

"Okay, this is it!" I declared.

" This is what?" they chimed.

" This is the spot for our first-ever snowman." I thought this was about the coolest idea (no pun intended) I had come up with in years.

" That's what we're going to do?" they asked. "We thought we were going somewhere."

"We don't need to go anywhere to have the fun we're going to have. Watch this." I bent over and began to roll a snowball that would, within minutes, become the base of our first snowman.

As I rolled the ball around the yard, Barb and the girls began to get into it. Grins appeared from ears to ears. As we progressed, the snowman started to take shape. He was the best-looking snowman I've seen in years—unique yet stately, all five and a half feet of him. He had charcoal eyes, a carrot nose, rocks for his mouth, stick arms, and a red-and-white-striped hat.

"He needs a name, girls," I said when we finished. "What do you think?"

"How about Frosty?" squealed Missy.

"Frosty it is!" I answered.

With Frosty in shape, we decided to roll around the yard making snow angels. It was a great afternoon, and we didn't even have to go to Disneyland. Missy hugged Frosty throughout the day and prayed he would "stay with our family forever." At one point, Barb and I caught each other's glances as we realized Missy would not let go of her new friend easily.

That evening, we decided to drive around looking at Christmas lights. As we were about to leave, Missy voiced her fear that Scott, a neighborhood boy, might knock Frosty down. It seems the neighborhood kids had talked of such dastardly acts over the last few weeks, and Missy was looking pretty insecure. As we pulled away from the house, I discreetly glanced in my rearview mirror for any of the guys who might be lying in wait for the kill. Seeing none, I thought, *No problem. We'll only be gone for 30 minutes or so. Frosty will be okay.*

Upon our return, however, our worst fears were

realized. Frosty lay in pieces throughout the yard. His head was crushed, his carrot nose broken, his hat gone, and one charcoal eye missing. Missy wept. Barb and I took one look at each other and knew who the culprit was—Scott.

As if on automatic pilot, we headed across the street to Scott's house for a little chat. Predictably, he denied the cowardly act and had a whopper of an alibi: "I've been in the house all afternoon working on a paper."

"Sure, Scott," I replied, giving him my best glare. "We know you did it. I can't believe you would hurt an innocent little girl! She's crushed."

Recognizing he wasn't going to "fess up," we went home to put Frosty back together. Soon I heard footsteps coming across the snow. I turned around and saw Scott in tow behind his dad, Nick.

"Do you have something to say to my son, Gary?" Nick bellowed. "Because if you do, you can start with me."

"Nick, look at this snowman," I replied. "It was destroyed. They're just little girls, Nick. It looks as if Scott and the boys got out of hand, wouldn't you say?"

"No, I wouldn't, because Scott has been in the house with me all day, working on a paper for school. There's no way he could have done it. Now you and I have a problem."

"He's been in all day?" I asked with a little less enthusiasm than I had before.

"Yeah. In the future, if you have a problem, try coming to me. Don't *ever* blame my son for something again unless you know you're right."

Nick and Scott turned on their heels and started walking home, while I turned to Barb and the girls. Missy stared down, Sarah looked as if she were going to throw up, and Barb gave me one of those "Uh-oh" looks.

"Missy," I asked, "did Scott tell you he would tear the snowman down, or did you just *think* he might?"

"Well, Dad, he didn't actually *say* he would."

"Missy, let me get this straight. Scott didn't say he was going to tear Frosty down. You just thought he might do it. Why?"

"Because he's always doing stuff to us," she replied. "But I don't think he did this one, did he?"

I led the family into the house so we could talk about this new family crisis called "How to alienate the neighbors in 30 seconds or less." I realized we also needed to walk back over and talk to Nick and Scott.

"I'm not going over there."

"Dad, you go. You're the father."

"Can I stay home? I feel sick."

Those were the three responses I got. (I'm not telling which one was offered by Barb.)

319

"No," I replied, "we're *all* going to go. I'll call Scott and his dad and ask them to meet with us. But before I do, I think we need to talk about what we're learning from this."

Boy, had we learned a lot already! We recognized we had falsely accused Scott and made unfounded assumptions. I personally learned that tears, the very ones flowing all around the room, could lead to healing. They were tears of hurt and humility, as well as of fear of facing our neighbors. I also learned that families need to bind together during tough times like this.

Finally, I called Nick. "Could we please come over and talk with you and your son?" I asked.

"Gary, there's nothing I want to talk to you about."

"Nick, I'll do the talking. Please, just come to the front door and give me a couple of minutes. It's important that my entire family talk with you and your son."

"Okay" was all he said as he slammed the phone down on the receiver.

As we bundled ourselves up again, we prayed. Oh, how we prayed! With incredible trepidation, we tromped across the street, our hearts pounding as they seemed to rise up to our throats. We rang the doorbell, and Scott and Nick came to the door.

"Nick, Scott, I and my family have offended you," I said, my voice wavering. "We don't ever want to offend someone like I did both of you, and we're very sorry. Will you please forgive us?"

The next three minutes stick in my memory as one of those power-packed experiences that help to change lives. Nick, obviously surprised, was the next to speak. "I'm sorry, too, for getting so mad, Gary. I was pretty hot. Scott had been inside all day, so I knew he hadn't torn down your snowman, Missy. It's okay. Let's just forget it."

Soon a repentant Missy was weeping and hugging her teenage neighbor as Scott said, "Missy, it's okay. I know how you feel. By the way, Missy, I think I know who did it."

"Never mind, Scott," I threw in. "I think we've had enough emotion for one day."

There on that front porch, under a dim door light, stood six neighbors, all slapping shoulders and nodding in agreement that it had been a rough day. My family was reconciled with our neighbors as they graciously forgave us.

When we returned home, we had our second family meeting. It was another first for the Rosbergs—two family meetings in one day. We sat on the family room floor in a circle and stated what we had learned: That when you humble yourself, people's hearts soften. That when you wrong your neighbor, it's worth the risk to ask for forgiveness. That accusations need much prayer before they ever leave our lips. That angry words need to be checked before being blurted out.

And there was one more lesson as we held hands in prayer: Snowmen, just like the children who build them, only last for a brief time. We need to hold on to our kids and our snowmen very loosely and to be good stewards of them, because they aren't really ours at all. They belong to the Father.

Missy wrapped up the evening with one last comment: "There will only be one Frosty in our memory, and he was the best snowman ever."

I think you're right, Missy.

Forgiveness. Restoration. Repentance. Reconciliation. All those lessons were wrapped up in three balls of snow on that cold Sunday in Iowa. The experience showed all of us the importance of forgiveness in restoring a broken relationship.

Remember the movie *Love Story*? When Ali MacGraw looked into Ryan O'Neal's eyes and said, "Love means never having to say you're sorry," we all oohed and ahhed and thought, *Hey, man, that's heavy!* Well, today I hear those words and think, *Hey, that's wrong!*

To me, forgiveness is the key step in choosing to resolve conflict and closing the loop in a relationship. Without it, we're trapped by our anger. Without it, we can't know reconciliation of two hearts that once again are tender toward each other.

HAPPY FATHER'S DAY

A few years ago, a mother brought her 14-year-old daughter to see me. Six years before, the father had left the mother, saying he had found someone else. See if you can discern the problem as you read a Father's Day letter the girl wrote to her dad.

Dear Dad,

Happy Father's Day. Well, better late than never, wouldn't you say, Dad? I want you to know I regret not being with you today. It being Father's Day and all. But I guess Jimmy and Janet will have to help you have a good Father's Day by giving you their love, and that's just as good. They are your kids now. They are lucky.

It is just another day for me, Dad. I don't have anyone to play the role of father for me. Somehow I feel like I should be happy to just know I have a dad, but it doesn't quite cut it. I probably should be thankful you are alive, but to me my dad is dead. It is the only way I can make any sense of my life. My life ended the day you left Mom. Things are a lot different, Dad. At least for me and Billy [her brother].

323

*You probably think I don't love you. I do,
but it is a different type of love. Not the kind
that a daughter would have for a dad who
raised her. You never went through the
tough times together with me and gave me
love and advice when I needed it. You
weren't there and aren't there now, Dad.
Instead, you are just like another man,
because you are really someone else's dad.
Jimmy and Janet have you for a dad now.
It is hard for me to face up to the fact that
you are just physically my dad. You are not
the man who played the role of my father. I
don't have a man in my family to do that.
In fact, I would bet that there are days that
you don't even think about me and Billy
and Mom.*

*I don't mean to sound like an ungrateful
daughter 'cause I am glad that you are happy
and that things are working out. Yet I can't
help but think how things could've been
better, but my life was made from the decision you made to leave my mom. I am sorry
you did it, and I am suffering for it along with
Mom and Billy.*

*I realize I am not the first and certainly not
the last to go through this, yet I am a person,
and I hurt. I know you went through life in*

a split home, and I know things were rough, so you know what I am going through. If you loved me enough, you would have spared me from having to go through what you did. I realize that when you got the divorce you weren't thinking of me at all, 'cause all you wanted was to get away from me. Maybe Mom isn't such a rose all the time to live with, but she is the most wonderful person in the world, and I know she loved me 'cause she kept me and supported me. She didn't run off.

I hope you treat your other kids with all the love that is meant for us, because they deserve it, and if we can't have it, then all the more for them to have a happy and loving father. The past can't be changed, so all we can do is go on from here.

Sincerely,

Jessica

Can you feel the pain this adolescent girl was going through? At the same time Jessica was trying to grow into the woman God created her to be, she was also trying to pick up the broken pieces of her life, to make sense of it all. She was hurt, angry, and on the road to a state of bitterness that could spoil her personality and her outlook on life.

An open loop? I would call it a gaping hole. Offense layered upon offense. The security blanket had been ripped from Jessica's hands when her parents allowed the chasm of conflict to grow wider and wider, sending them scurrying to their corners in isolation.

Her father did respond to Jessica's letter. About three months later, he sent a card with one line on it, "Jessica, sorry, Dad." And as this young woman read the letter, she was thrown into another boiling pot of confusion: Should she forgive him?

"Gary, he said he was sorry," she told me. "I have to forgive him, don't I? I'm a Christian. But I want to hurt him and never see him again. What do I do?"

Good questions, Jessica. She represents the dilemma many of us face as we look at the open loops in our lives. We're offended, we experience years of pain and rejection, and then finally we hear a shallow, empty "I'm sorry." We never sense that the person truly understands the pain he has put us through, yet now we feel obligated to forgive. And we feel guilty for not wanting to do so.

That was Jessica's dilemma. Could she forgive? *Should* she forgive? Was her dad offering her a repentant heart committed to reconciliation, or was he just trying to get off the hook? Let's take a look at forgiveness and what it really is.

FORGIVENESS IS CHOOSING TO RELEASE THE OFFENDER

Have you ever held on so tightly to something that the very idea of releasing your grip sent a chill through your body? A friend of mine, Dan, experienced that sensation one afternoon as he and his girlfriend, Joan, participated in a sport that I find confusing—*rappelling*. Who in their right mind would leap off a cliff with only a rope to keep them from falling hundreds of feet? Not me. When I watch people rappelling, I can hear my mom saying, "I suppose if one of your friends told you to jump off a cliff, you would do that, too!"

On that particular afternoon, Joan and Dan decided to give it a shot. Dan's best friend, Bart, had rappelled for years and was to be their guide. They climbed the mountain early that morning, and after they got to the peak, Bart put the apparatus on, secured the rope, and went over the side. Joan and Dan watched over the edge as Bart bounced down the side of the mountain. The rope alternately hummed through his hands and screeched when he applied the brake, leaving himself hanging hundreds of feet in the air. What a thrill!

When Bart reached the bottom, it was Joan's turn. But as she turned her back to the valley below and prepared to kick off the side of the mountain, she looked Dan in the eye and said two words: "I can't."

Joan clutched Dan's arm so hard that she cut off the circulation. He replied, "Yes you can. Just remember what Bart taught us. Take it a little at a time. You can do it."

"Dan, please don't make me. I can't," she pleaded as she continued to leave what appeared to be permanent marks in Dan's forearm.

Dan looked her straight in the eye and gave her the message she needed to hear: "I believe in you. You can do it. Let go."

Almost before Dan's words left his lips, she let go, kicked back, and began to sail through the air, squealing like a schoolgirl. As Dan looked over the edge, he sat back and whispered to himself, "I knew she could do it."

Dan had responded to Joan in just the right manner, and his approach was also freeing for those of us who have been wounded: a balance of belief in the person, a hearty dose of encouragement, and the instruction to let go.

How about you? Whose arm are you digging into with such intensity that you're leaving scars? What offense are you holding onto so tightly? Is it a hurt you've carried for years from a parent? Perhaps it's a grudge you're still carrying toward old friends who betrayed you? We hold on tightly to our hurts, grudges, and losses, even when we know deep down that we don't have any power over them.

Yet our instruction from God is the same instruction Dan gave to Joan. She had to let go of him and trust the rope. We need to let go of our pain and trust God. You're not in control, and neither am I. He is. As soon as we learn that truth, we're free to let go and rely on Him.

A major step in the process of forgiveness is releasing the person who hurt us, giving up the control of revenge and retribution—canceling the debt owed us, if you will—and allowing God to work in the person's heart.

Forgiveness really does set the offender free. It also sets *us* free. Jesus gave us a poignant example of this in the parable of the unmerciful servant. [1] He had just answered Peter's question about how many times Peter should forgive his brother for offending him by saying, "I tell you, not seven times, but seventy-seven times." In other words, continuously. You see, the number of times we forgive isn't as important as our attitude. Jesus is calling us to be forgiving people.

Following His response to Peter, Jesus told the story that shows in startling terms what canceling a debt really means. He described a servant who owed "ten thousand talents" to the king. In today's economy, that would be millions of dollars. Yet the king forgave this considerable debt. A hardened heart, however, prevented the servant from showing the same forgive-ness to a fellow servant who owed him the equivalent of a few dollars. He threw the man into prison until the debt could be repaid.

When the king learned of the action taken by the man he had released from his debt, he had the unfor-giving servant thrown into prison as well. Jesus concluded, "This is how my heavenly Father will treat each of you unless you forgive your brother from your heart."

FORGIVENESS IS VALIDATING THE OFFENSE

Jerry had been counseling with me for a few months when he said, "Gary, if I forgive him, it will be as if I'm saying to him, 'You really didn't hurt me as badly as you did.' I can't do that. If I take him off the hook, he'll hurt me again."

That was Jerry's dilemma as he dealt with the fact that he had been wounded by his dad's critical spirit. Jerry never seemed to measure up; he felt he always paid for the conflicts between his mom and dad. He did the best he could to please his dad, but it was never enough.

Jerry's dad would kick into rages and take out his anger on Jerry. The other three kids recognized Jerry was the family scapegoat, but they always thought it was because he was the oldest. After helping Jerry understand the pain of the relationship with his father, we learned that when his dad looked at Jerry, he saw the spitting image of his own mother. When he started to simmer and reach a full boil, Jerry got burned.

Now Jerry was facing the pain of his heart, and he was confused about how to resolve it. "I'm just beginning to realize the hurt I feel," he told me. "I don't want to let go of it and have him think it really wasn't a big deal, because it was."

Dwight Carlson, in his book *Overcoming Hurts and Anger*, wrote:

> Forgiveness means that we actively choose to give up our grudge despite the severity of the injustice done to us. It does not mean that we have to say or feel, "That didn't hurt me" or, "It didn't really matter." Some things may hurt very much, and we must not deny that fact, but after fully recognizing the hurt, we should choose to forgive. [2]

Jerry was on the path of learning what Carlson said so aptly. Forgiveness means we actively choose to let go of the offense, but it doesn't mean we invalidate it. It happened. It's history. It's real. Forgiveness says,

"I know what you've done, and it really hurt. But in full view of this reality, I choose to forgive you. I do this because of the example and power of Christ, and because I want our relationship to be healed."

When we validate our hurt and realize we don't have to deny the offense, we are free to forgive. But this means looking inside and facing our pain. Our tendency is to pull away and deny it happened, hoping it will go away. At other times, we may rationalize the offender's behavior. Jerry tended to try to rescue his dad from the responsibility he carried. When Jerry began to recognize he could confront his own hurts and honestly face them, he was on the path to healing. It's often painful to admit our hurts, but it's the first step to restoring relationships.

FORGIVENESS IS GIVING UP RESENTMENT

"Dr. Rosberg, I'm not the kind of person who holds grudges. Really, I'm not."

You may wonder why this woman added the second sentence. It was because her first sentence didn't fit with everything else I could see in her attitude. She conveyed such a tarnished perspective on her boyfriend that her statement didn't ring true.

Grudges. Bad feelings. We've all had them. Even though we try and try to put aside the problems, there are times when we just can't shake that monster of resentment, and it roars in our ears: "Get back at him!" "Don't ever let her forget what she did to you!" "Don't get back into that relationship—he'll just burn you again!"

But forgiveness means giving up resentment and our right to revenge.

I can't think of a better example of giving up resentment than Joseph in the Old Testament. Genesis 37—50 tells how he was sold into slavery by his own brothers. God used that act of evil for His own good, however, and eventually placed Joseph in a position of power in Egypt.

His brothers later traveled to Egypt, looking for food. They came to Joseph, not knowing who he was. At that point, Joseph could have returned their wrongdoing with his own. But what did he do? He forgave them. They didn't deserve it, but he decided to forgo resentment and restore his family's broken relationships.

Resentment feeds anger and keeps the loop open. It impairs our sense of understanding, undermines the healing of our hearts, and destroys the working of a gracious God in our lives.

I'm not saying forgiveness is easy. Forgiveness isn't about ease; it's about releasing the iron grip that resentment builds in us. It means that through the power of a God who models giving up what was His (His Son,

Jesus), we learn to let go. As resentment is released, layers of self-protection can be peeled away one at a time, allowing the emotional intimacy that leads to the closing of the loop.

FORGIVENESS SETS A PRISONER FREE

"When you release the wrongdoer from the wrong, you cut a malignant tumor out of your inner life. You set a prisoner free, but you discover that the real prisoner was yourself."[3]

I like that statement by Lewis Smedes because it sums up a key benefit of forgiveness. When we forgive someone, we cast off bondage of our own.

A man with a well-known family name is one of the most amazing examples of forgiveness in action. His name is Adolph (Ad) Coors IV, and he has known the burning rage of hatred. But today he knows the healing of a relationship with his heavenly Father through grace. A few years ago, Barbara and I joined several other couples in a week-long seminar held in the Colorado mountains. That's where we first met Ad and B. J. (his wife) and heard Ad's story.

Ad grew up on a ranch in Golden, Colorado, in a family known worldwide for one thing: beer. But when you get to know Ad, you forget his last name and remember him for something else: integrity.

In 1960, his life was ripped apart by the kidnapping and murder of his father. Ad wrote of that experience:

> Dad had been trapped into thinking that this man was a stranded motorist, broken down by the side of the road. When he got out of his car to help him, a tremendous struggle apparently ensued. Finally, my father's body was stuffed in the trunk of the other car, and we never saw him again. Life runs out sooner than we think! My dream world came apart at the seams. [4]

Ad thought about following in his father's footsteps and becoming president of the brewery. But as he struggled through his pain and the bitterness that gripped his mother, his fascination with the fast track diminished. He joined the Marines instead.

While serving there, Ad tried to fill the void in his life by weightlifting and studying martial arts. He went from 195 pounds to 272 pounds. "On the outside, I was rough and tough. But each time that I battled someone who tried to cross me, a confused, frustrated soul screamed out, 'Please, somebody recognize what is really happening to me on the inside!'" [5]

He later went to college and got into investments, hoping money would ease his aching heart. But when the market soured, Ad once again came up empty-handed. He returned to the family business seeking employment, but he wasn't placed on the executive track. Instead, he was hired to conduct tours. Later, his responsibilities included scrubbing the fermenting tanks. He started from the bottom and put in long hours, often working the graveyard shift to provide for his wife and kids.

Early one morning, as he returned home after working all night, he fell asleep at the wheel and had a serious accident. He didn't regain full consciousness for six days, and it took him two years to recover fully.

During that time, Ad began to ask tough questions about who he really was. Soon after that, a Christian friend confronted him with the truth of the Bible. A short time later, Ad prayed a simple prayer of faith and received Jesus as his Savior.

Did Ad Coors realize God's forgiveness? Yes. But during the next couple of years, he realized he still had some unfinished business. He had to resolve his bitterness toward the man who had kidnapped and murdered his father.

Ad decided to visit the Colorado State Penitentiary to meet with that man. When the man refused to see him, Ad wrote him a letter. In it he wrote of the hatred he had carried for him for more than 15 years. And then he did an amazing thing: Ad asked the inmate for forgiveness and told the man that he had forgiven him!

Incredible? Yes. Why did Ad forgive his father's murderer? Out of obedience to God. Was it natural? No, to the contrary, it was supernatural. But when Ad released his dad's murderer, he himself became free. Forgiveness really does release both the offender and the offended.

FORGIVENESS IS AN ACT OF GRACE

Remember the parable of the prodigal son in chapter 2? Its primary truth is that forgiveness is an act of grace, of unmerited love. We can't work for it. We can't jump through the right hoops to earn it. We can't perfect our performance so that we deserve it. Grace is simply unearned. The Bible instructs us to be "kind and compassionate to one another, forgiving each other, just as in Christ God forgave you."[6] Or as F. F. Bruce wrote, "The free grace of the Father's forgiving love is the pattern for his children in their forgiveness of one another."[7]

How are we reconciled to God? Do we earn His forgiveness? Did Jesus die on the cross because we did something to merit such a sacrifice? No, God forgives us out of His grace. It's unearned.

We don't offer forgiveness with any conditions. We don't offer it because we feel like it. We simply offer it as God does.

The Bible states, "For we do not have a high priest who is unable to sympathize with our weaknesses, but we have one who has been tempted in every way, just as we are—yet was without sin. Let us then approach the throne of grace with confidence, so that we may receive mercy and find grace to help us in our time of need."[8]

What great encouragement those words are to me! God can sympathize because although He was and is God, He became a man and shared my weakness. He knows my heart, and He knew that His becoming a human being would give me the model to follow.

Jesus was both man and God. But what was the difference between Him and us? When He was tempted, He didn't sin. I do sin. I offend people and am offended by them. Yet He modeled the way to restore my broken relationships: forgiveness through grace.

FORGIVENESS GIVES US SECOND CHANCES

Philip Yancey wrote some profound words about forgiveness in *Christianity Today* magazine:

> Forgiveness breaks the cycle. It does not settle all questions of blame and justice

and fairness: to the contrary, often it
evades those questions. But it does allow
relationships to start over. In that way,
said Solzhenitsyn, we differ from all
animals. It is not our capacity to think
that makes us different, but our capacity
to repent, and to forgive. Only humans
can perform that most unnatural act,
and by doing so only they can develop
relationships that transcend the relentless law of nature.[9]

That's the supernatural power of forgiveness.
Through it God allows us to start over and relationships to grow even deeper and more meaningful than
before.

Arnie and his wife, Brenda, sought counseling to
deal with an open loop between him and his mother.
He had not had any contact with his family for more
than five years, except for an annual business meeting
to discuss the family trust.

Much of the conflict stemmed from severe problems between Arnie and his sister, Phyllis. Phyllis had
never accepted Arnie. He was born five years after her
and was favored by their paternal grandfather. As a
result, Phyllis developed major problems with her self-
esteem and self-confidence.

Arnie, on the other hand, often felt his mother

regarded him as a dummy and not as smart as his sister. He never felt he measured up to his mother's expectations. The stress between Arnie and his mom increased. As a result, the family split over a serious disagreement in which Arnie became angry and took it out on his mother by severing the relationship.

During the course of our counseling, Arnie described his pain. He hid it well, but whenever he slowed down enough to take a real look at himself, he felt emotions he had denied all his life: hurt, anger, resentment, and even regret. Although he and his mother had both contributed to the conflict, I recommended that Arnie consider taking the first step toward reconciliation.

His mom had been placed in a nursing home only weeks before our initial visit, and Arnie realized time was running through his fingers like sand. But he felt he was doing what he needed to do: sit back and wait for her to initiate resolution of the conflict—even if it meant he would never see his mother again.

Meanwhile, Arnie's daughter, Melissa, was 14 and feeling the loss of the relationship with her grandmother. In a letter I received from Arnie and his wife, they wrote, "We both agreed that Melissa should be allowed to call or go visit her grandmother, because life is so short, and we both see that it's important that our daughter never be denied the right to see or communicate with her own grandmother."

Arnie was deeply concerned that Melissa could resent him for years to come if his mother died and Melissa never had the chance to see her again. So one spring afternoon, Arnie agreed to drive Brenda and Melissa to the nursing home. But he refused to go in himself.

When he returned to pick them up, Melissa stuck her head in the car window, tears rolling down her cheeks, and simply said, "Dad, please see her."

Arnie had lived through years of resentment and hurt, but he had never prepared himself for the look in his daughter's eyes that afternoon. Reluctantly, he got out of the car and told Brenda and Melissa to wait outside—he'd be back in ten minutes, tops.

As he walked down the hallway of the nursing home, Arnie glanced into several rooms. Seeing the deep loneliness in the eyes of forgotten person after forgotten person, he realized his own sense of loneliness for his mother. He wasn't certain if he was lonely for what they had together or for what he had missed, but he knew he was aching for a renewed relationship.

"Mom" was all Arnie said as he walked into the room.

"Hello, Arnie. I didn't think you were going to come in."

"Mom, I need to talk to you—really talk, I mean, not just chat."

With that opening, Arnie started to explain his

341

years of hurt and disappointment. His mother responded with her own hurts. But something was different for both of them. Instead of just talking, they were also listening, really listening, wanting to understand. Forty-five minutes went by. Brenda and Melissa sat in the car and prayed, not knowing what was happening inside. Then Arnie stepped out into the brightness of the afternoon sun. Brenda and Melissa searched his eyes for a sign of what had occurred in the room, and as he entered the car, they knew that all had been healed. A loop had been closed.

Arnie thanked Melissa and said he thought things would be better in the future. "I asked my mother to forgive me, and she did. You know what else? I forgave her. I really forgave her." As he described the meeting, Melissa and Brenda wept tears of gratitude to a God who heals broken relationships. Melissa saw a dad whose heart had softened. She also saw a mist in his eyes that she had rarely seen before. She was proud of her dad. And she was thankful for a family that took a risk to receive a second chance.

Second chances really do happen. Forgiveness can occur, even in some of the most difficult situations when it just doesn't seem possible. But we need to take action and seek out the person who has offended us or whom we have offended.

Several months ago, I received an update on Arnie and his family. Brenda wrote to say:

It's a good thing they talked and forgave each other, Gary, because a few months after their visit, his mom was diagnosed with a brain tumor. As I thought about this situation, I am so grateful that the Lord moved in the heart of my husband to "go the extra mile," because now they can be assured that his motive was pure and that we took the time to go see her before learning of her brain tumor. Please encourage others who have a relationship that needs mending to do it before it's too late.

Brenda was so right: We don't know God's timing for us. What we do know is that He is the author of second chances. Go the extra mile. Search out the person you need to be reconciled with. Take the risk.

We've looked in this chapter at the foundations of forgiveness. But to fully understand this vital subject, we also have to deal with the myths that are perpetuated about forgiveness. We'll turn to those next.

CHAPTER 17

THE MYTHS OF FORGIVENESS

One rule of effective propaganda is that if you repeat a lie often enough, people will start to believe it. Because they hear it so much, they assume it must be true. Unfortunately, a few lies about forgiveness—myths, if you will—have taken root in the popular consciousness of our society. People believe them because they hear them so often. And if we're to take the vital step of forgiving those who have hurt us, we have to clear those lies out of our way and get to the truth behind them. Let's see if any of them ring a bell with you.

MYTH 1: "IF I FORGIVE, I ALSO HAVE TO FORGET."

How many times have you heard this statement: "I know I haven't forgiven because I haven't forgotten what he did to me"? The idea that forgiving equals forgetting is a myth. As Lewis Smedes wrote in his popular book *Forgive and Forget*:

> When we forgive someone, we do not forget the hurtful act, as if forgetting came along with the forgiveness package, the way strings come with a violin. Begin with basics. If you forget, you will not forgive at all. You can never forgive people for things you have forgotten about. You need to forgive precisely because you have not forgotten what someone did; your memory keeps the pain alive long after the actual hurt has stopped. Remembering is your storage of pain. It is why you need to be healed in the first place.[1]

I don't think God intends for us to forget the pain of our lives. To the contrary, we're to remember it so that we can value the lessons we learned. Remembering also helps us to keep from repeating the mistakes.

A woman named Jill came to me for counseling. She made a statement counselors hear frequently: "Gary, I can't forget what he did to me. It plays over and over in my head." She went on to explain how her husband had offended her repeatedly. He was gone from their home 15 to 18 hours per day, either working or playing golf. When he was home, he was emotionally absent or hostile. He alienated the children and shut down emotionally with her. They had not sat and talked for months. She felt trapped and was becoming embittered.

"But the Bible says God forgives and forgets," she said as she stared out my office window hopelessly.

"That's true," I replied. "But you're not God. You're Jill." As we talked, we reviewed the verse in the Bible that says, "For I will forgive their wickedness and will remember their sins no more."² God has the power to forget, but we don't. As Jill started to learn that forgiving is different from forgetting, she gained hope that she could resolve the pain of her heart.

How do we resolve such pain? First, the very admission that we don't have to forget begins the process. Then we can ask God to ease our adjustment to the pain. This takes us off the hook of trying to make ourselves forget something that has wounded us profoundly.

Our pain also eases as we try to experience some joyful interactions with the person who hurt us. God can generate fresh memories, and our hearts can then renew the relationship threatened by the offenses.

If the offender is not present or isn't willing to participate in building new memories, our activities with others can develop new memories not associated with the painful situation. Such involvement can help shift our focus from ruminating on the difficult times we've gone through. It's also important to grow in our relationship with Jesus, seeking Him for instruction and comfort.

Asking ourselves these questions can help: What is He teaching me through these difficult times? Am I finding the balance between dealing with my painful memories and seeking positive interaction with others?

Will we forget over time? Probably not the major hurts of our lives. But time and communication, soaked with prayer and God's grace, will soften our memories.

MYTH 2: "FORGIVING HIM IS IMPOSSIBLE. I'D LIKE TO SEE YOU DO IT."

Can you feel the sting of a comment like the one above? I can, and I did. Those words came from a person just like you or me, and she was wounded. Her comment reflects another myth about forgiveness: that it is sometimes impossible. We've all endured situations so painful that we wonder if we can let go of the offense and forgive the offender.

I encounter this myth most often in my counseling office when we deal with the issue of sexual abuse. I rarely see kids who are currently being abused or have been abused. Instead, I see the adult survivors of sexual abuse and incest. From them I've learned that if there's an offense where forgiveness seems impossible, this is it. Robbing the innocence of children and exploiting young people to meet the desires of mentally unhealthy adults is terrifying at best. And it happens all the time.

Such abuse results in a lack of trust, misconceptions about a child's own sexuality, and distortions of healthy relationships. A victim is left confused and angry. Often in my early appointments with such a person, he or she (most of them are women) will bring up the issue of forgiveness. Sometimes she will angrily declare, "I suppose you'll tell me I have to forgive him." She may also say, "I will *never* forgive him. I don't care what you say."

At that point, discussing forgiveness is useless, because the person is feeling too much pain. So I'll typically answer by gently saying, "It does seem impossible to think of forgiveness, doesn't it? Let's just seek to understand what has happened and leave the issue of forgiveness alone for now."

Note that my statement is not a denial of forgiveness, nor is it a suggestion that forgiveness is not vital.

But at that point, when a person is crumbling emotionally, offering her a pat answer would cheapen the miraculous gift of forgiveness God has given us.

But adult survivors of sexual abuse aren't the only ones who sense that forgiveness is impossible. Whenever there's a deep wound, the idea of forgiving the offender seems improbable at best. Why? We fear that if we forgive, we'll end up denying the offense ever happened. Further, the hurt is so pronounced that we have trouble getting past it.

Forgiveness is *not* impossible, however—it never is. Even when we don't *feel* like it, we can *choose* to offer it anyway, drawing on strength from God. In counseling, I've found that I need to listen to, affirm, and embrace people's pain to help them recognize they're not in that situation alone. Once they begin to realize I'm on their team, that I'm not going to cheapen their pain with quick and easy "religious" answers, I can gently lead them through the loop and show them how to resolve the conflict. When they're ready, I've found that talking about what the Bible says about forgiveness becomes a lifeline that helps them find healing.

MYTH 3: "I JUST DON'T FEEL LIKE FORGIVING."

When I've been offended, I often don't feel like forgiving the offender. But you know what? Forgiveness really isn't about feelings. It's a choice, an act of the will. It's volitional. If I wait until I feel like forgiving, I'm actually choosing to feed the monster of resentment and bitterness.

I need to acknowledge my feelings of hurt and anger, express them, and then choose to begin the process of forgiving the person or seeking his or her forgiveness.

While the choice to forgive supersedes our feelings, it doesn't deny them. It embraces them and allows us to express them through effective communication, then resolve the conflict by entering the process of forgiveness. Even when we don't feel like forgiving, we need to ask God for strength to enter the process. He will direct us if we honestly seek Him.

MYTH 4: "I SHOULDN'T GRANT FORGIVENESS UNLESS THE OTHER PERSON IS WILLING TO RESPOND."

I'm often asked, "What if the other person won't communicate and doesn't want to close the loop? Am I stuck?" The life of Ad Coors, which I discussed in the last chapter, is a poignant example of a man who desired to close a loop with someone who was not interested in responding. Ad's situation represents many who are reading this book. And as in his case, the answer is that we are only responsible for ourselves. We can't control the other person.

The apostle Paul wrote, "If it is possible, as far as it depends on you, live at peace with everyone."[3] Ad desired to be at peace with his father's murderer. We are responsible to try to close the loop as well, but we can't control the response of the other person.

Should we still try to communicate? I believe so. It would be easy for many of us, with the profound hurts we've endured, to use the other person's resistance as a rationalization to not try to close the loop. But while the other person's lack of willingness makes the resolution more difficult, we can still forge on, making our intentions clear. We can also seek forgiveness from God regardless of the other person's response. This is where God's grace can be experienced, allowing us to rest in the knowledge that He forgives us.

There's another issue to consider here as well: Is the person really unwilling to respond, or are we just assuming that? In many situations, especially in family disputes where neither side is talking to the other, the opposing parties desperately want to resolve the conflict, but nobody is willing to take the first step. "I'm willing to stop this feud at any time," goes the common refrain, "but he's not. When he is, he'll come to me, and we'll work it out." I've seen people go for years in this state, never realizing the conflict could end if one was humble enough to approach the other and start the process.

MYTH 5: "FORGIVENESS MEANS ACTING AS IF NOTHING HAPPENED."

The myth that forgiveness means acting as if nothing happened comes up when people are working through deep pain or are sick and tired of a pattern of behavior they think will never change. It comes up in statements like these:

"I've forgiven Frank hundreds of times over the years for his critical attitude and controlling behavior. But he never seems to change, and I'm getting tired of it."

"Every time I find that Sue has spent too much on clothes, I confront her on it, and she cries and swears she won't do it again. So I forgive her, and two weeks later she does it again. I don't trust her anymore."

"My son, John, has been stealing money from my wallet for several months. When I caught him doing it once, he admitted he was wrong and asked for my forgiveness, and I gave it. But then he did it again the next week. I've always believed that forgiveness gives you a new start on life, and that's what I tell my children. But John is taking advantage of that. He knows Mom will forgive him, so he can always have his slate wiped clean."

Forgiveness does not mean nothing happened. On the contrary, granting forgiveness requires us to confront the reality that something *did* happen. It's a fact. Frank *has* been critical over and over. Sue *does* continue to overspend. John *has* repeatedly stolen from his mother's wallet.

Sometimes the truth hurts. To forgive does not mean we enter into a sense of denial about the nature of the offense or its impact on us. When we fall into this trap, we contribute to the patterns that destroy relationships. Instead, we need to confront the issue, deal with our emotions, communicate effectively, and then seek and grant forgiveness.

Another problem is that people assume that when they forgive someone, they should also trust the person. But forgiveness and trust are two different concepts. Forgiveness is a gift, freely bestowed. Trust needs to be earned. We may forgive someone for a series of offenses, yet it may take years to trust that person again.

In many cases, rebuilding trust is such an important part of choosing to close the loop that I've devoted my last chapter to it.

MYTH 6: "I HAVE TO FORGIVE IMMEDIATELY."

Listen to Anna as she described an incident with her husband:

"My husband—now I'm not criticizing him, you know—but he believes that forgiveness must happen right now, as soon as the offense occurs.

"One night I was having conflict with my sister-in-law, Kelly, and was feeling some anger in my heart. I was getting ready to go to sleep, and as we were lying in bed, with the lights out, my husband asked me if something was wrong. I told him no, not really, I was just hurt and angry at Kelly for what she had said about me to their mother.

"With that, my husband threw on the light switch and told me to get out of bed . . . now! I was so frightened."

"Sure you were. What did you do?" I asked.

"Well, I did what he told me to do. I got out of bed and looked at him. He was so demanding. He then told me that I could not go to bed with any anger in my heart. He made me kneel at the foot of the bed and pray and forgive his sister before I went to sleep. I was so confused because I knew I hadn't forgiven her, but we were up until 3:00 A.M. fussing about it.

"Is that right, Dr. Rosberg? Do I have to forgive a

person immediately? I was so hurt and then got more confused the more he yelled."

Anna's story is a painful example of another myth about forgiveness—that it must be granted immediately. Often this myth is mistakenly based on Paul's teaching that says, "Do not let the sun go down on your anger." [4]

I've heard stories of couples who have stayed up all night trying to resolve a conflict because they honestly thought the Bible commanded them to do so. Often they end up too tired to deal with the problem effectively, and the conflict worsens. The irony is that if people applied the verse literally, they would realize there's nothing magical about postponing sleep.

I don't believe that Bible verse is a formula for the amount of time it should take to grant forgiveness. The Bible does instruct us to restore broken relationships and makes it clear that we should not let anger fester in our hearts. Forgiveness, however, is an act of the will, and it may take some time to come to the point where we're able to grant it.

How do we know when we're ready? Lewis Smedes suggests that "you know it because you find yourself wishing them well." [5] When we think of the offending party, instead of wishing calamity upon him or her, we bless the person. If the offense was minor, the forgiveness process may take less time. But if the offense was major, we need to be prepared for a long process. The only error we make is in refusing to enter the process.

Think about how the Christian culture deals with this issue of forgiveness. Often when a pastor presents a sermon on the subject, he emphasizes the command to forgive, and 20 minutes into the talk he asks everyone to bow in prayer and forgive those who have offended them. Or he instructs the congregation to think of those they may have hurt and then approach them to ask for forgiveness.

The problem is that this can lead to what I call "cheap forgiveness." We've all seen it happen. People apply the formula, but they never ask for forgiveness out of a genuine sense of sorrow.

Here's a typical scenario: Cousin Carla is at your house for Thanksgiving, and she remarks, "I can't believe how clean this house is! I've never seen it like this before!"

Her remark hurts and angers you. *Carla knows I usually keep a clean house*, you think. *She doesn't have kids of her own, so she can't understand what it's like. Besides, usually she shows up uninvited, and she always seems to show up at the end of the day, before I've had time to clean the baby's mess. I wonder what shape her house would be in if I showed up out of the blue like she does?*

You think of the other insensitive things Carla has said over the years and the disagreements you've had about how much to spend on Christmas presents for the family. You remember the family vacation when she made you feel guilty for not having the money to eat at restaurants every night like everyone else.

All these thoughts flash through your mind in about two seconds, and you let Carla have it: "Are you telling me my house is usually filthy? Well, next—"

"Oh, sorry, forgive me," Carla breaks in, and then she leaves the room to talk with another relative. You're left still fuming, still stuck in your anger.

A couple of hours later, the family members are starting to head home, leaving you with a pile of dishes. Just before Carla walks out the door, you yell, "If you really want to see a clean house, how about helping me wash the dishes?"

"Hey," Carla replies, "I said I was sorry. If you aren't able to forgive me, don't blame me. It's your problem now, not mine." She slams the door behind her, and you're left even angrier than before.

Now let me ask you: Do you have a responsibility before God to forgive Carla? Yes. Do you need to do it immediately? No, because you aren't ready. Carla's apology was so quick and superficial that you never had the time to work through your natural emotions. She never indicated she understood how she hurt you. And then, feeling off the hook because she had asked for forgiveness, she made you feel as if you were not obeying God because you hadn't forgiven her yet.

Look at the loop again.

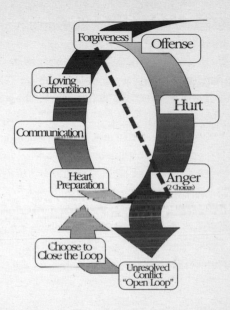

What Carla did was to leap too soon to the act of asking for forgiveness. If you follow the steps of closing the loop, you'll see that when a person zooms past the conflict-resolution stage and goes directly from the offense to forgiveness, you're left with the same emotions of hurt and anger. This shortcut impedes the resolution of broken relationships. Conflict settlement needs to follow a process, and it often takes time.

That's why Anna felt so much commotion in her heart. She knew she was called to forgive, yet her husband's demand that she do it immediately invalidated her emotional response to the offense and impeded her need of communicating directly with him about the offense.

One key to the process is knowing how to ask for and grant forgiveness. If we do it right, we'll move beyond cheap forgiveness. In the next chapter, I'll explain how to do it.

CHAPTER 18

WHOLE FORGIVENESS

A couple of years ago, I had the privilege of speaking at a Family Life Conference with a couple named Jim and Renee Keller. In speaking to the audience, Jim said something I have never heard before or since about a pattern of communication he and Renee have used since the first day of their marriage.

Jim told the audience that before they got married, he realized that both he and Renee were a little headstrong. Accordingly, he knew they needed a plan for dealing with conflict. So he promised her that whenever they had conflict, he would initiate the resolution of it and the process of forgiveness—no matter who was responsible for the problem.

I sat in the back row of that auditorium and waited for the punch line. But he had already given it. I was in awe.

Later that afternoon, I took Renee aside and said, "Okay, Renee, this is just between the two of us. You've been married well over a dozen years; how many times has he violated that promise?"

"Never, Gary," she replied with a smile and a twinkle in her eye. "He has initiated forgiveness every time."

"You're kidding!" I barked. "That's unbelievable!"

"No, Gary, that's Jim." Score one for Renee—and one for Jim.

Now let me ask: Do you think Renee deserves Jim's sacrificial approach to resolving conflicts? There were times when Jim felt he was 100 percent right and Renee was 100 percent wrong. Yet he would still take the leadership and move the relationship toward forgiveness and reconciliation.

Why? Because he's leading his home in a way that keeps any coals of resentment from bursting into flame. Jim Keller is a peacemaker. He understands "whole forgiveness." As we'll see, whole forgiveness takes two people (one seeking forgiveness and one granting it) and a combination of components.

SEEKING FORGIVENESS

Glenn had just about had it. Every time he tried to get his son to do something around the house, it took an act of Congress. He thought he was a pretty good dad. Josh had everything he wanted: a good bike, a stereo, and plenty of privileges—certainly more than Glenn had when he was a kid. But it seemed like a one-way street. Glenn gave and gave, and Josh never did much in return. Glenn was getting fed up with the pattern.

One night, after a particularly stressful week at the plant, Glenn came home and discovered Josh's bike lying in the yard. Glenn stormed into the house and screamed, "Where's Josh?"

Josh's sister, Mandy, ran from the family room to tell Josh he had better get downstairs fast, because Dad was on the warpath again.

When Glenn caught up with Josh, they were both out of control. "How many times have I told you not to leave that bike in the yard?" Glenn yelled. Whenever Josh tried to speak, Glenn cut him off.

What Glenn didn't know was that Josh had been home sick in bed all day. He hadn't even been out on his bike. And when Glenn heard this from Mandy, his red face turned from rage to embarrassment.

Glenn threw his hands in the air, went back to the garage, got in the car, and took a long drive. After about 30 minutes of wandering around, he began to cool down. He pulled over to the side of the road, looked in the rearview mirror, and asked himself a tough question: *What has become of me? I don't even ask questions anymore, I just accuse. I've alienated myself from my family, my friends, and even myself. Something is wrong, and I need to correct it.*

With that insight, Glenn sat in the car and prayed that God would soften his heart and restore the relationship between him and his son. He was reminded of the Bible verse that reads, "And he will restore the hearts of the fathers to their children, and the hearts of the children to their fathers, lest I come and smite the land with a curse." [1]

When Glenn returned to the house, he saw that Josh's bedroom light was on. He parked the car, went in the back door, and simply told Mandy and his wife, "Give me a few minutes alone with Josh, please. I need this right now."

Element #1: "I am wrong."

Glenn knocked on his son's bedroom door. "Josh, it's me, Dad," he said. "Can I please talk with you for a few minutes?"

"Dad, I really don't feel like talking," Josh replied.

"You don't have to, Josh. Just listen to me, son. Please."

"Okay. Come on in."

"Josh, I took a drive after our argument and did some serious thinking. You see, I've been so out of touch with the entire family that my tension has given way to a simmering anger. Things that used to just bug me are now ripping me apart."

"Dad, you seem mad all the time. I wish our family could be the way it used to be. I don't ever see you. You're either at the office, watching TV, or working in the yard. I don't want to hurt your feelings, but I just want us to be a family."

"I hear you, son." Glenn was listening to Josh for the first time in a long time. It was as if he needed someone else to pop the bubble of rationalizations that had created a gap between him and his family. "Quite honestly, Josh, I feel like I'm doing a lousy job as a husband and dad. I need to make some changes, and I want to start with you right now. Son, what I did earlier tonight was wrong. I came in the door accusing and yelling, and it was wrong."

Josh was surprised by his dad's comments; he had never heard his dad admit to being wrong. But Glenn was demonstrating the first element of whole forgiveness, the admission of wrongdoing. He wasn't trying to compensate for it, he wasn't rationalizing his behavior, he wasn't pulling rank on a 13-year-old kid. Instead, he was facing up to his own responsibility and admitting he was wrong, with a capital W. Such an admission of wrongful behavior starts the process of whole forgiveness in motion.

It isn't enough to say, "Okay, if you think I did something wrong, let's talk about it." Nor is it appropriate to say, "I don't think I did anything that was such a big deal, but since you think I did, let's talk." We need to confront the wrongdoing: "I am wrong." "What I did to you is wrong." "I have done wrong and need to talk to you about what I did to offend you."

Element #2: "I'm sorry."

As Glenn continued talking to his son, he said, "Josh, what I did to you was wrong, and I'm sorry I did it. I feel bad not only that I yelled at you, but also that I've developed an attitude of harshness with the entire family."

How often have you sought forgiveness and said "I was wrong," thinking that would take care of the problem? Perhaps the offended person appeared confused, leading you to think, *Well, I said I was wrong. Shouldn't that be enough?*

Just admitting our wrong behavior, however, doesn't cut it. We need to express our sorrow. The combination of these two elements leads people to sense the sincerity in our hearts. By expressing our sorrow, we can develop empathy for the other person. It builds bridges and helps to restore relationships.

Paul understood the expression of sorrow as he wrote:

I now rejoice, not that you were made sorrowful, but that you were made sorrowful to the point of repentance; for you were made sorrowful according to the will of God, in order that you might not suffer loss in anything through us. For the sorrow that is according to the will of God produces a repentance without regret, leading to salvation; but the sorrow of the world produces death. [2]

As Paul said, if we're made sorrowful to the point of repentance, it's a healthy expression of our emotions that leads to healing in our relationships with the other person and with God. It also leads to empathy and a true sense of restoration.

Seeking to communicate with empathy allows the other person to feel heard. *Empathy* means "seeing the issue from the other person's perspective." It's like the old admonition to "walk a mile in the other person's shoes." Empathy diminishes the resistance between two hurt people, allowing communication to open up and self-protection to be quieted.

Element #3: "I don't ever want to hurt you this badly again."

"Josh, I know I hurt you," Glenn continued. "I could see the pain in your eyes as I laid into you. Son,

I don't ever want to hurt you that badly again."

Glenn expressed two things with that statement: First, he acknowledged he had hurt his son. This is so important to those we offend—they need to know we feel just a bit of what we put them through.

Second, he expressed repentance by indicating he didn't want to hurt Josh again in the same way. Admitting our wrongful behavior and expressing our sorrow without indicating a desire to change leaves the forgiveness incomplete. Our repentance tells others we desire to turn from our hurtful ways.

True repentance necessitates a change of heart and mind. It goes beyond an "I'm sorry" to a turning away from our sin as we seek forgiveness. It's more than an apology, which can be granted on the surface of a cold and hardened heart. Forgiveness without repentance is shallow and disturbing to the offended. It cheapens the act of forgiveness. But repentance suggests that a healing begins to take place.

Those who receive forgiveness from God are also released from the guilt they carry. As God forgives, He also softens our hearts, and we become more responsive to the work of the Holy Spirit. As our hearts change, our attitudes also change, and we seek restoration of broken relationships. That's why forgiveness and repentance go hand in glove.

Think back to the prodigal son in chapter 2. His repentant heart allowed him to really heal the relationship with his father. His brokenness, which could only be healed by a reconciliation with a dad who loved him, really led to the closing of the loop in their relationship. When we truly have repentant hearts, we're able to seek out the other person and pursue restoration.

Element #4:
"Will you forgive me?"

Now it was time for Glenn to add the final touch to whole forgiveness: "Josh, will you forgive me?"

That request is the ultimate in humility. It means laying yourself at the feet of another person. I tell clients that if they ever want to punish another person, they should refuse a request for forgiveness. People are never more vulnerable than when they're making that request.

"Will you forgive me?" brings the process of whole forgiveness to a crescendo. It is intimacy at its best.

If we leave any of the four elements out of our request for forgiveness, we run the risk of leaving the conflict unresolved. Too often, Christians leap to the final element and ask for forgiveness without acknowledging any understanding, remorse, or repentance. This is, again, "cheap forgiveness," and it leaves the person whose forgiveness we're seeking feeling torn. Only with the combination of all four elements do we hit a grand slam with forgiveness.

GRANTING FORGIVENESS

The person granting forgiveness has two functions: to grant the forgiveness *graciously* and to grant it *specifically*.

Element #5: *"I want to forgive you and to close the loop on this issue."*

When Josh granted his dad forgiveness, he did so by exercising the grace God models for us. "Dad, I've never seen you so open. I'm sorry, too. Of course I forgive you. We're all hurting. I just want us to get along."

Rather than going for the jugular and attacking his transparent father, Josh was gracious. He let go of the offense and received his dad. He could have returned an insult for an insult, but instead he returned a blessing. [3]

When we speak graciously to those seeking forgiveness, we exhibit God's love for them. We give them something undeserved. Our forgiveness is free; it can't be earned or bargained for. It can't be taken back or returned. It's a gift without strings attached.

As forgiveness is given, both the giver and the receiver experience emotional relief. The pressure is off, the pain begins to subside, and healing starts.

Some of us will give the gift of forgiveness with a slap on the back, essentially saying, "Hey, no problem.

We all mess up." Others will do it with a whisper as we send the message gently and intimately. We may look into the other person's eyes in one of those rare moments of closeness, or we may cast our eyes down in humility.

God doesn't care much about our posture and tone of voice. He does care about the sincerity of our hearts. And when we're gracious, others know it instinctively. It's real—authentic and supernatural. And by granting forgiveness graciously, we begin the work of reconstructing the broken relationship.

Element #6: "I forgive you for_____."

In addition to granting forgiveness graciously, we need to be specific: "Dad, I forgive you not only for yelling tonight, but also for the anger that's been building."

Being specific informs the other person of how complete the forgiveness is. It doesn't leave the offense hanging in the air but clarifies the question running through the seeker's mind: *Did she forgive me for all the issues I asked about or only for one of them?*

ONE MORE COMPONENT

Finally, there's one more element of forgiveness that doesn't have to occur but that, when it does, brings the finishing touch to the process of whole forgiveness. I'm talking about *reconciliation*. Can we have forgiveness without reconciliation? Yes, I believe so, but it's incomplete. Can we forgive another but not reconcile the relationship? Yes, but then we miss the joy of the restoration.

As Dr. David Stoop wrote, "Forgiveness is unilateral. It is something we can do all by ourselves. Reconciliation requires the participation of another person. We cannot 'make it happen,' no matter how hard we try."[4]

"Gary, no matter what happens to our marriage now, I know I can forgive him." These words came from Samantha, a woman at a Family Life Conference. The situation she and her husband, Wayne, faced was not much different from hundreds of cases I've counseled. They had two kids and had been married nine years. But they had drifted apart, and he had started spending time outside the church with a woman from their Bible study. Samantha constantly asked if anything was going on between the two of them, but he always insisted nothing was.

As time went on, however, the relationship went from an emotional affair to a full-blown sexual affair. Both couples separated, and four adults and six kids were affected by the selfishness of two adults.

At the end of the conference, having been presented with God's blueprint for healthy marriages, this couple sat and talked with me. The two of them couldn't have been more different from each other. Samantha looked free and relieved, as if a heavy weight had been lifted from her shoulders. Wayne, on the other hand, appeared unable to extract himself from the mess he had created. Even with all the information on how to restore their marriage, he was not willing to leave his affair.

We talked about their marriage for the next hour. I gave them every ounce of energy I had left after a long weekend, but my words bounced off Wayne like a rubber ball off a concrete wall. Just as we were about to leave, Samantha turned to him and made the statement you read at the beginning of this section: "Gary, no matter what happens to our marriage now, I know I can forgive him."

"Even if he doesn't come home, Samantha?" I asked gently.

"Even if he doesn't come home," she replied with tears rolling down her checks.

Wayne was sorry for what he had done. And Samantha, somehow, was able to forgive him. She was still deeply hurt and fearful about the future, but she had learned that if she withheld forgiveness, he would not only wreck her family, but he would also destroy her personally.

Samantha was a rare woman, for she was able to give Jesus control of her life rather than Wayne. She had captured the truth that God would not come up short, and she knew she could trust Him, even though her trust in Wayne had been destroyed. You see, Samantha didn't forgive Wayne because of who he was and what he did or didn't do. She forgave Wayne because of who Jesus is and what He did.

Unfortunately, Samantha wasn't able to reconcile with Wayne. She was willing; he was not. Reconciliation can only occur when both parties want it and are willing to work it through—to confront the offense, the hurt and anger, and then choose to communicate.

If one of the people involved is unwilling, true reconciliation won't occur. It may look like reconciliation as the two people reopen the lines of communication, but something will be missing: genuine forgiveness. And that lack will be a gaping hole in the foundation of the relationship.

Samantha learned to accept something that is painfully difficult for all of us. She was not in control, and reconciliation was out of her hands. But she knew forgiveness *was* within her control. Such one-sided forgiveness is the only way some of us can ever close loops with people who are either unwilling or no longer living. And by forgiving, Samantha was no longer trapped by Wayne. She was free.

A man I counseled a few years ago had been emotionally wounded by his daughter during her adolescence. She rebelled against the family and left to lead a life of drug abuse and sexual promiscuity. In his frustration, the father shut off all communication with her, hoping it would bring her home. Instead, however, his isolation solidified the break. Neither was willing to give in.

Sixteen months after she left home, the girl was killed in a car accident. You can imagine the guilt her father experienced. As I helped him through the grieving process, we got to the point of forgiveness, and he stated, "She can never forgive me, Gary. She's dead. How can I ever close this issue?"

Over the next several months, we worked together to resolve his loss by helping him forgive his daughter for her rebellion and forgive himself for shutting her out. He also sought God's forgiveness. It took time—he's *still* healing from his loss—but he now realizes he is forgiven. Was he able to reconcile the relationship with his daughter? No, that was impossible. But he was able to be forgiven.

One step remains in the process of choosing to close the loop. I used to think forgiveness was the final step, but I've since learned there's another. I've hinted at this final step already, and in the next chapter I'll explain it more clearly.

C H A P T E R   1 9

FROM RUBBLE TO RESTORATION

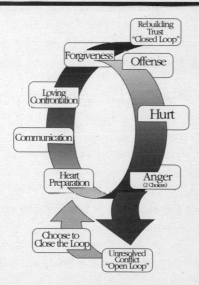

A s Tina Baker pulled into the driveway an hour early, she was surprised to see her husband, Roger, home. He usually didn't return from work before 6:00 P.M.

What she didn't know was that Roger had been coming home before 6:00 P.M. for several weeks. He had been sitting on a secret he had needed to tell his wife about for months, but he couldn't figure out how to tell her. When she pulled into the driveway early that night, he knew it was finally time to open Pandora's box.

"Tina, there's something I need to talk with you about," he said.

"What, Roger? Did something happen to my mother?"

"No, it isn't your mother—it's me. Tina, I've been lying to you again. I lost my job."

"You what?" Tina was caught completely off guard. "When? How did it happen?"

"I lost it a long time ago. In August."

"August! What do you mean? You get up every day and go to work! This is nuts! Where have you been going every day?"

"I just leave. Some days I look for work. Other days I just hang out. I go downtown and walk around. I just can't face it."

"Roger, you mean you've been lying to me for two months? How have we paid the bills?"

"Yes, Tina, I've lied. It's wrong. I know that. I don't know what to say other than that I've blown it. The bills are paid. But that's why there's one other thing I need to tell you."

"Not another woman! If you tell me there's another woman—I can't handle that."

"Tina, that isn't it. I mortgaged the house."

"What do you mean?"

"I mortgaged the house, and I've spent the money. I spent $25,000."

"On what?"

"I kept most of the bills paid, but the rest of the money is just gone." As Roger continued to confess his string of lies, he began to weep. They were the tears of a man with a heavy heart, but also the tears of a man who had finally started the cleansing process.

Tina, meanwhile, was so stunned and angry that she could hardly think. This had been going on for months, and she didn't know about it? All that money, gone. How many times had he lied to her in the past? Was he lying now? She knew he needed her love and forgiveness, but how could she ever trust him again?

As Roger and Tina continued to talk over the next few hours, they were able to make significant progress in restoring their relationship. Tina was committed to Roger—she abhorred divorce. With Roger more transparent than she had ever seen him, for the first time she began to understand his pain and private struggles. And he understood more than ever before just how much his treachery was hurting her.

After months of consistent communication and working through their conflicts, Roger received forgiveness from Tina. She had no problem with that issue. But both of them knew the act of forgiveness had not closed the loop. Too much had happened; he had hurt her too many times. Something had to change if Roger was ever going to regain Tina's trust and fully restore their relationship.

The final phase of closing the loop is rebuilding trust. In some conflicts, this stage is not necessary. But for many of the deepest wounds of the heart, it's essential.

When someone hurts us repeatedly, we may be willing to forgive that person. But that doesn't mean the relationship is completely healed, that we can go on as if nothing happened. For true restoration to occur, that person must be willing to work to regain our trust and to rebuild the relationship over a period of time.

A CITY IN RUINS

Almost 2,400 years ago, the city of Jerusalem lay in ruins. King Nebuchadnezzar of Babylon had ordered his army to plunder and destroy it, tearing down its protective wall and enslaving the Jews who lived there. [1]

The biblical book of Nehemiah tells the stirring story of a man who dreamed of rebuilding the city. Let me describe Nehemiah's life to help you understand the impact he has had on our history, as well as the model his story offers for closing loops. Nehemiah served as the cupbearer to King Artaxerxes of Persia. (Persia had conquered Babylon and taken over all its territories.) A cupbearer was the right-hand man to the king. His job included tasting the wine before the king drank it to make certain it wasn't poisoned. This allowed the cupbearer to develop an intimate relationship with the king he served, giving him an informal type of power. Nehemiah enjoyed that kind of relationship with Artaxerxes.

But Nehemiah wasn't only a cupbearer. More importantly, he was a man of God and of prayer.

In the beginning of the book of Nehemiah, we discover that Nehemiah learned there was great distress in Jerusalem. His brother Hanani and some men from that area came and told him about some Jews who had escaped and survived the captivity in Jerusalem. Nehemiah was told that "those who survived the exile and are back in the province are in great trouble and disgrace. The wall of Jerusalem is broken down, and its gates have been burned with fire." [2]

In that time, the wall around a city was vital for protection against enemies. The primary goal of an invading army was to destroy or breach that wall. Rebuilding the city of Jerusalem, beginning with its wall, became Nehemiah's passion.

In the same way, a relationship between two people needs a wall of protection around it to keep it healthy and secure. This wall is built by faith in God and by developing disciplines and habits that strengthen commitment and trust. When a loop has been opened and people are wounded, the wall of protection begins to crumble. Repeated offenses tear down that wall just like the battering rams of an invading army. Hearts are plundered, security is undermined, and people are torn from their homes.

As Roger and Tina learned, those walls need to be rebuilt. And as I read Nehemiah's story, I see a process Nehemiah went through in rebuilding Jerusalem's wall that's the same process a couple should follow in rebuilding the wall of trust around their own "city." With that in mind, let's look at how Nehemiah went about his task.

STEP 1: WEEP AND SEEK GOD.

Nehemiah was greatly troubled by the news he heard. He held a position of power in Persia. He had a direct line to the king. What should he do?

Notice that his first response was *not* to ask for a meeting with the king. He didn't jump in and say, "No problem. I'll get my people with your people and set up a restoration commission for Jerusalem." Instead, he responded like a man who had been wounded: "I sat down and wept. For some days I mourned and fasted and prayed before the God of heaven."[3]

Roger responded to his situation in a similar way. He wept tears of anguish for his sin and tears of relief over a secret held too long.

"Tina, I want to change," he said. "I *need* to change. I want to work on our marriage. I need you. I know I can't ask you to trust me. I'm just asking for a chance to try."

STEP 2: PRAY.

Next Nehemiah admitted his own sins and asked God to give him favor with Artaxerxes. [4] Nehemiah knew in his heart, as he prayed, that he could help to restore the wall around Jerusalem.

Think about it for a moment. When our walls are coming down all around us, what do we do? Here are some options. We run in fear. Maybe we deny it's happening. Or perhaps we get angry. I've done all three. But look at what Nehemiah did. After expressing the pain of his heart, he prayed.

As the second chapter of Nehemiah reveals, his prayer wasn't a quick one, either—no four-second, "Thanks for the grub, God. Let's eat." Nehemiah prayed earnestly. In fact, he prayed for four months before he sought to bring the king's attention to his concern.

As another verse says, "The effective prayer of a righteous man can accomplish much."[5] When we're attempting to rebuild a relationship, we need to pray earnestly that God's will be done. Then we need to trust Him as He works His will in our lives. And you know what? He will.

Roger prayed, "God, I have hurt Tina. I've wounded her deeply and have sinned against her and You. I'm sorry. Please forgive me. Please give her the grace to forgive me as well. I know it will take time, lots of time. Give me the strength to rebuild this relationship, the patience to reconstruct her trust in me. If it's Your will, and I believe it is, work through us to restore this broken relationship."

STEP 3: COMMUNICATE NEEDS HONESTLY.

One day, as Nehemiah was serving King Artaxerxes his wine, the king noticed that Nehemiah was "sad."[6] This gave Nehemiah the opportunity to explain his feelings about his homeland's lying in ruin.

The king, who must have valued his relationship with Nehemiah, could sense the hurt in his servant's heart and asked, "What is it you want?"

Nehemiah responded by asking for the opportunity to go to Jerusalem and rebuild the wall. Straight and to the point. But if you read the passage, before he made the request, he did this: "Then I prayed to the God of heaven, and I answered the king." [7] He didn't jump the gun and spit out his request.

Here was the king of Persia, asking what he wanted. The timing was perfect for Nehemiah to "go for the gold," but this man of God didn't forget who the real King was. He prayed and relied on God for the strength to confront Artaxerxes with the boldness he needed to make the request.

The king's response was simply, "How much time do you need?"

Nehemiah gave him a specific time of leave that he believed he needed to complete the task. Then he took the issue one more step. He asked for materials for part of the rebuilding project.

Why do you think the king granted his request? Because Nehemiah did such a terrific job of asking and using his influence? No, Nehemiah himself explained, "And because the gracious hand of my God was upon me, the king granted my requests." [8] Even as he scored a grand slam, Nehemiah gave God the glory. He got the okay, the letters of protection he needed to travel, materials for part of the rebuilding process, and even a military escort for the journey.

When Roger prayed for guidance in the restoration of his marriage, God answered his request. But Roger also had to make his needs known to Tina. He had to ask not only for her forgiveness, but also for her help in rebuilding the relationship and in holding him accountable not to lie anymore.

We can't always make the changes we need to make on our own. Nor should we. We need God's help, as well as that of family and friends.

STEP 4: TRAVEL TO JERUSALEM.

As Nehemiah set off on that journey of hundreds of miles, I wonder what went through his mind. He probably had no idea of the extent of the devastation he would encounter. I also wonder if he realized the degree of resistance that lay before him and the tremendous work ahead needed to restore the city wall. He certainly had many days to think about how great the task would be, and, being human, he must have fought through hours of doubts.

His job was little different from yours, mine, or Roger and Tina's. As we sit back and anticipate the work of restoring broken relationships, we probably ask some of the same questions he asked himself: Is it really worth it? What if it can't be done?

The same God who led Nehemiah on that mission is willing to lead you and me. The key is whether we're willing to trust Him and say, "God, I'm willing to be willing. I will work to restore this relationship no matter how hard it is or how long it takes. But I need You to go before me. I'm not going unless You lead the way."

STEP 5: SURVEY THE DAMAGE.

After three days in Jerusalem, Nehemiah went out at night to evaluate the damage done to the wall. The rubble was so great that he couldn't even pass on his mount. It must have been overwhelming.

Curiously, Nehemiah surveyed the damage alone, without telling anybody. He started his mission quietly and prayerfully.

When we start to close a loop, we also need to do it without fanfare. We need to go prayerfully and quietly so that we can minimize the attention of others, allowing God to work in two hearts as the restoration process occurs.

Roger and Tina likewise needed to evaluate the extent of the destruction to their relationship. "Roger, I don't know how to respond to you," Tina said. "You've kept things from me before, but this is the worst ever. I don't know whether I feel more betrayed by your lying about where you've been every day or by the second mortgage. Both make me angry. How am I ever going to trust you again?"

"Tina, you're right," Roger replied. "I haven't been honest with you. I just know I had to tell you the truth. It was eating me up inside. I also know that now that I feel better, you feel worse. I hurt you either way I go, don't I?"

"Yes, you do. But I need to know the truth."

As relieved as Roger felt after finally telling the truth, he was overwhelmed at the extent of the damage to their marriage. Just as Nehemiah looked around and surveyed a huge pile of blocks and burned wood, Roger and Tina were left with a pile of "stones" themselves. Roger still had no job, and his self-confidence was at an all-time low. That made it hard for him to believe he could ever find a good job, much less build a successful career. Through his frivolous and uncontrolled spending, he had put their finances in serious jeopardy. They were in danger of losing everything they had.

In addition, Roger had built a habit of deceit that he didn't know how to break. He felt powerless to change his life. And Tina felt hurt, betrayed, and angry. She loved her husband, but she wondered if he would ever change.

Yes, they had major damage.

STEP 6: CHALLENGE THE PEOPLE.

As Nehemiah's drama unfolded, he went to the people:

> Then I said to them, "You see the trouble
> we are in: Jerusalem lies in ruins, and its

gates have been burned with fire. Come,
let us rebuild the wall of Jerusalem, and
we will no longer be in disgrace." I also
told them about the gracious hand of my
God upon me and what the king had
said to me. They replied, "Let us start
rebuilding." So they began this good
work. [9]

In his challenge, Nehemiah appealed first to the
degree of pain the people felt. They knew they were
in disgrace, and rebuilding the wall was their chance
to start a new life. In addition, Nehemiah told them
"about the gracious hand of my God upon me and
what the king had said to me." He thereby showed
them that God was with the project and had proved
it by giving the plan favor with Artaxerxes.

So the work began, and it's obvious that
Nehemiah had a building plan from which to operate.
In fact, many of the people were assigned to work on
the wall in front of their own homes. What better
motivation could Nehemiah have provided?

Both of these points—trusting God to make the
rebuilding possible and devising a plan to work from—
are critical in the process of reconstructing trust. In
many of the situations for which rebuilding trust is
necessary, the people involved may be helpless to
change their lives by their own power. Perhaps they've

tried repeatedly and failed. They need to devise a solid plan but make sure they always trust God to make it possible.

When Roger went to Tina, he knew what he had done to her and to their relationship. He was willing to rebuild the relationship, but he needed to make her willing to try as well.

"Tina, our relationship has been ripped apart by strife and conflict. I've lost your trust, and I accept that. I don't deserve to have your trust.

"The boundary protecting our relationship has been torn down. But I know we can rebuild it. Other couples have done it, and we can, too. The first thing I have to realize is that I can't change on my own. I need to make my relationship with God a priority and let Him work in my life. I know it will take time, but I also know God can do anything.

"I want us to work out a specific plan for what we can do. I'm willing to get the counseling I need, to rebuild my career, and to learn how to handle finances correctly. We probably need to see a counselor together as well.

"Please work with me, and let's restore our home."

In our society, when people undergo the type of pain Roger and Tina experienced, they usually toss in the towel. They have no hope that such huge problems can be solved, and they aren't willing to put in the time and effort to rebuild the relationship. But just as the people in Jerusalem replied by crying, "Let us start rebuilding," so I've seen many people like Tina respond to their mates by saying, "Yes, we can do it. Let's start rebuilding. It can happen. It won't be easy, but we can do it."

STEP 7: BEGIN WORK.

Chapters three and four of Nehemiah describe the actual building of the wall. Nehemiah wrote, "So we rebuilt the wall till all of it reached half its height, for the people worked with all their heart." [10] Sounds like good, old-fashioned perseverance to me. How about us? When we're rebuilding a broken relationship, do we work with all our heart?

There's almost a honeymoon effect in the rebuilding of relationships. At first we may doubt the possibility of healing, but then we choose to forgive and rebuild, and the healing begins. But we often fail to realize how much energy and time it takes to complete the rebuilding. People like Roger frequently leap with all their energy into the first few days or weeks of rebuilding trust. But then their enthusiasm wanes, and they often slide back into their old habit patterns.

One big difference between Nehemiah's rebuilding of the wall and our attempts at rebuilding trust is the amount of time involved. While the wall was rebuilt in a miraculous 52 days, it may take much longer to rebuild a relationship.

The element of time plays two roles in the rebuilding process. First, it takes time to heal the pain—often months and even years. Many times people tell us, "You'll get over it eventually. It just takes time." And that's true to a degree.

Second, however, we also need time to add some positive experiences to a relationship that's accustomed to pain. As two people spend time nurturing the relationship and storing up positive memories, the healing process is encouraged. So when rebuilding trust, time is of the essence.

Roger did follow through on counseling. He committed himself to the process and began to see great results. He realized he was fearful of not measuring up to his own expectations, so he had developed a pattern of covering up his failures. He learned to communicate honestly with Tina, even his shortcomings.

As she stuck with him during the tough times, he started to trust her more and became more willing to risk being emotionally intimate with her. As Tina saw him opening up, she began to trust him more. They were on the road to healing.

Was it a perfect process of steady growth? No. Just like all of us, they struggled, often with a lot of pain. But the safety net of their commitment allowed them to continue to take risks, and their relationship became stronger and stronger.

Another element that contributes to the honeymoon effect in rebuilding trust is the cost involved. As Nehemiah continued to reconstruct the wall, the people grumbled about the lack of food, the loss of their lands, and their financial losses. And it was all true. They did encounter serious loss in order to rebuild the wall.

Restoring broken relationships can also cost us a lot. Look what it cost Tina and Roger. It cost them their pride. They faced months or even years of leanness as they worked their way out of the financial mess Roger had put them in. It cost them their sense of security as they took risks to open their hearts to each other.

There's a cost to any rebuilding.

STEP 8: TRUST GOD THROUGH THE INEVITABLE RESISTANCE AND CRITICISM.

Nehemiah faced resistance continually throughout the project. His main enemies were Sanballat the Horonite and Tobiah the Ammonite:

> When Sanballat heard that we were rebuilding the wall, he became angry

and was greatly incensed. He ridiculed the Jews, and in the presence of his associates and the army of Samaria, he said, "What are those feeble Jews doing? Will they restore their wall? Will they offer sacrifices? Will they finish in a day? Can they bring the stones back to life from those heaps of rubble—burned as they are?" Tobiah the Ammonite, who was at his side, said, "What they are building—if even a fox climbed up on it, he would break down their wall of stones!" [11]

Those enemies devised all kinds of plots against Nehemiah. They tried to stir the people against him, planting doubts in their minds. They conspired to harm him. They accused him of scheming to become a king and lead the Jews in revolt. They even hired a prophet to try to intimidate him. In each case, Nehemiah prayed to God for guidance and asked Him to lead the way. These words of his were typical: "Hear us, O our God, for we are despised. Turn their insults back on their own heads." [12]

The last thing Satan wants is for us to be reconciled with someone else. He loves to put isolation and distrust into a relationship and drive people apart. When we seek to restore a relationship, the enemy gets busy and starts to throw doubts at us from within and arrows of attack from the outside.

Just when we're about to try to restore a relationship, somebody says: "It will never work. Your marriage is too far gone. It's good that you forgave him, but you'll never be able to trust him again."

Some people have all their friends and family on their team as they seek to mend relationships. But that's often not the case. Very likely someone else— a friend, child, lover, or parent—will put up strong resistance.

These people usually have their own reasons for trying to keep us from reconciling. Perhaps they encouraged the problem in the first place and don't want to admit their interference. Perhaps they enjoy the extra attention we're giving them as we talk about our problems, and they know they'll experience a sense of loss if we reconcile. Maybe they never thought the relationship would work in the first place, and they want to be proved correct.

Who *does* want us to close loops? God. Forgiveness and restoration of broken relationships are always His desire. That's why, when we use other people as our rule of measurement for our own behavior, we often become frustrated.

Roger and Tina experienced some resistance as they began to rebuild their relationship. Tina continually battled a voice inside that said, *You're not going to trust him again, are you? He'll never change. You're nuts!*

Her parents had given up on Roger long ago. "Tina, your husband is too far gone," her father said. "Your mother and I would never have done this to each other. Kick him out. He's a disgrace to our family." (Remember the voices in chap. 4?)

A friend who was recently divorced also had her doubts. "I know exactly what you're going through, Tina, but I just don't understand why you think a man like Roger can ever change. My ex-husband told me again and again that he would stop drinking, and it only got worse and worse." (Another voice.)

As time goes by, those messages can sow the seeds of profound doubt. When I'm helping a couple get back on track in their marriage, I warn them that they may experience this. It invariably occurs, for example, just when we get the husband going in the right direction and encourage him to take the risk to work on the relationship. Then the wife gets discouraged and begins to pull away. The kids, the parents, and the friends throw up their arms and say, "I knew it would never work." And guys like me lean back in our counseling chairs, look at the clock, and say, "Okay, God, we've got 19 minutes to score a touchdown. Give me the right words to help them restore hope."

The Jews experienced this type of doubt. Nehemiah wrote, "Meanwhile, the people in Judah said, 'The strength of the laborers is giving out, and there is so much rubble that we cannot rebuild the wall.'" [13] They were wearing down under attacks from every angle.

Then Nehemiah had the people do an amazing thing:

> From that day on, half of my men did the work, while the other half were equipped with spears, shields, bows and armor. The officers posted themselves behind all the people of Judah who were building the wall. Those who carried materials did their work with one hand and held a weapon in the other, and each of the builders wore his sword at his side as he worked. [14]

What an incredible response! No throwing in the towel for this wall builder. He instructed the people to work with one hand and to guard their homes with the other. They were a vulnerable people, and so are we.

The truth of the Bible is so relevant to us today. When we're restoring a relationship, we need to work with one hand to get the job done. We need to persevere when the times get tough. We need to confront our doubts, realize they're not from God, and pray as we work at rebuilding.

But with the other hand, we need to be on guard and watchful. As friendships, marriages, and families are being restored, we need to be on alert to protect them from future attacks. Letting down doesn't finish the job, just as forgiveness doesn't close the loop. The wall still needs to be rebuilt. Trust still needs to be reestablished as the wall gets solidified brick by brick.

Tina and Roger experienced the need to be on guard. There were times in their rebuilding process when he was tempted to lie again. From time to time, he found himself rationalizing why he wouldn't have to tell her things. But then he would be reminded that it was time to trust God again. Time to face his pattern of deceit. Time to be honest with Tina.

He wasn't always successful. Neither are you or I. But he stayed with his commitment, and Tina stayed with him. The wall was rebuilt, just like the one around Jerusalem, brick by brick.

THE WALL IS BUILT

"So the wall was completed on the twenty-fifth of Elul, in fifty-two days. When all our enemies heard about this, all the surrounding nations were afraid and lost their self-confidence, because they realized that this work had been done with the help of our God." [15]

"So the wall was completed." What a great line! Can't you just see Nehemiah writing that statement in his journal? I wish I could say that when we're rebuilding trust, those walls can be completed, but I don't know if the wall is *ever* completed. In fact, it's written that even though the wall around Jerusalem was completed in a relatively short period, they continued to patch it for some time afterward. [16]

What did Nehemiah's enemies do when they heard the wall was completed? "They lost their self-confidence." Why? Because "they realized the work had been done with the help of our God."

The more we rebuild the walls of our relationships, the more those who desire for those relationships to die will pull away. As we remain faithful and send the message that we're going to rebuild no matter what, our detractors will begin to back off. Why? Because they'll have to face the fact that we're not alone in rebuilding. God is in the center of the work. It was His desire for us to restore. He's the God of restoration and reconciliation. He's the God of closing loops.

LOOP THE LOOP

Choosing to close the loop. I wish I could say the process is easy. Clients often ask me after the first counseling appointment, "How long will this take?" Good question. No answer. Some people who come in just want clarification on an issue or a little feedback about something that's happened. But most people come in with hurts that take time to sort out and heal. I often explain that if they only want to be soothed, we can do that, but it doesn't lead to lasting change.

Change is painful. Band-Aids don't work. Closing loops takes time and effort. I know because I have a couple of open loops myself that need to be closed. I've tried, but to be honest, probably not enough. I haven't given up, though, and I continue to make efforts.

Where do you have open loops? Perhaps it's with your parents or your adult children. A large group of people would respond, "With my spouse." Maybe you can think of old friends you've lost contact with because of unresolved conflicts, and maybe you have to admit you've never confronted the people. For some reading this book, it would be with business associates, and for others with church friends. A few of you might say, "Grand slam, Gary. You hit them all."

It really doesn't matter whether you have one or several open loops. What does matter is that you try to close them.

I see three categories of open loops. In the next few pages, I want to address each of them. Try them on, think and pray about them, and see where your needs are.

OPEN LOOPS WITH OTHER PEOPLE

Most of this book has dealt with open loops in our interpersonal relationships. We've talked about mending relationships with friends, marriage partners, and children. It's fairly clear when we have conflicts with others that we need to resolve them in order to heal the relationship.

We've looked at how important it is to identify the offense and then express our hurt and anger to the person in a healthy manner. This process allows emotional intimacy to return. Loving confrontation and forgiveness can then occur, which will lead to rebuilding trust and healing.

OPEN LOOPS WITH OURSELVES

Forgiving others is so much easier for most people than forgiving themselves. Why? Because we tend to be hardest on ourselves. We know it's right to be gracious with other people. We're told not to hold grudges, to give people a break, to let things go. The clichés are endless. But who really talks to us about letting ourselves go, about experiencing the release of our self-doubts and self-criticism so we can heal?

Guilt and self-blame tend to diminish our success in forgiving ourselves. When we've done something that we or others perceive as wrong, we continue to beat ourselves up. We carry the blame with us everywhere we go. When we continue to hold on to these self-abusing hammers, we're completely disregarding God's greatest gift: grace.

Charles Swindoll, in his book *The Grace Awakening*, explained,

> This day—this very moment—millions
> are living their lives in shame, fear, and
> intimidation who should be free,
> productive individuals. The tragedy is
> they think it is the way they should be.
> They have never known the truth that
> could set them free. They are victim-
> ized, existing as if living on death row
> instead of enjoying the beauty and fresh
> air of the abundant life Christ modeled
> and made possible for all of His follow-
> ers to claim. Unfortunately, most don't
> have a clue to what they are missing.
> The whole package, in a word, is
> grace. [1]

Grace is a totally undeserved gift. So why do we
have so much trouble receiving it? We feel we need to
earn it. But that's the whole beauty of grace: It *can't* be
earned. Many of us need to exercise grace with
ourselves.

You know that conflict you're carrying? You
know that mistake you made last week or maybe last
decade? Confess it and let it go. Find a quiet place,
take the time, and share it. Maybe you need to
explain it to a friend, and maybe that friend needs to
be God. But share it. And as you do, pray that God
will help you to let it go. We can't go back in a time

machine and change the situation. We can only lay aside our pride and ask others for forgiveness, including ourselves.

AN OPEN LOOP WITH GOD

Sometimes I wonder why so many counselors and psychologists leave the critical step of forgiveness out of their formulas for resolving conflict. Perhaps Christians understand it more clearly because they've personally experienced the power and grace of God's forgiveness. Without His forgiveness, we're stuck with the biggest open loop of them all, and we lack His vital resources for dealing with the rest of our open loops.

Stan knew the pain and broken heart of a horrible loss. A drunk driver ended his wife's life prematurely, leaving Stan alone with their daughter, Bethany. He and Bethany always assumed they would have a lifetime to build memories with Mom, but the memories were cut short.

As I listened to Stan describe pain so intense I could hardly imagine it, I sensed that the only way he could face the loss was through a relationship with God. Stan needed the strength, hope, and joy that only He can give. But Stan said he was confused about how to relate to God in a personal way. Here's how I tried to help him understand:

God created us to enjoy a perfect relationship with Him. But the very first people chose to disobey Him, and that introduced sin to our world and alienated the human race from a holy God. Throughout the millennia since then, we've tried to win back God's favor by doing good works. But no amount of doing good can ever close the gap between us and Him. By ourselves, we can never be good enough.

So God, in His grace, sent His Son, Jesus, to earth in the form of a man. Here He lived a perfect life and then died on the cross, taking upon Himself the penalty for our sins and so making it possible for us to be reconciled to God. The Bible tells us, "For God so loved the world, that He gave His only begotten Son, that whoever believes in Him should not perish, but have eternal life." [2] And Jesus told us that belief in Him is the *only* way to peace with God: "I am the way, and the truth, and the life; no one comes to the Father, but through Me." [3]

When we put our trust in Jesus Christ, we become part of God's family and have His resources and promises to draw upon as we work to resolve conflicts and mend relationships. [4] We're not alone anymore in trying to lead lives full of peace and love.

If you realize you've never closed the loop with God, I urge you to do it now. This is the most important loop, the most important relationship, of all. You can do this by praying the simple prayer I used when, at the age of 21, I recognized my own need for a personal relationship with a loving God:

"Jesus, I need You. I believe You died for me on the cross and were resurrected. Thank You for paying for my sins. I now invite You into my life and accept You as my Lord and Savior. Thank You for forgiving me of my sins and giving me eternal life. I turn my life over to You and ask that You direct it. Amen."

Simple? Yes. But if you pray that prayer sincerely, you'll have eternal life. Regardless of what you've done, you will be forgiven.

Note how similar seeking forgiveness from other people is to seeking forgiveness from God. *Forgiveness* is really a one-word definition of Christianity.

THE QUESTION WE ALL ASK: "CAN I DO IT?"

Can I do it? Can I really mend my broken relationships? That's the question that nags at us, isn't it? We tend to ask fearfully, *What if I go to him and he shuts me out?* or *They don't care about me, so what's the use?*

Those are fair questions, but let me give you this encouragement: You *can* do it. Because I say so? No, because God wants us to resolve our conflicts and learn to reconcile with others, ourselves, and Him.

Read what Paul said in the book of Romans:

Therefore, since we have been justified through faith, we have peace with God through our Lord Jesus Christ, through whom we have gained access by faith into this grace in which we now stand. And we rejoice in the hope of the glory of God. Not only so, but we also rejoice in our sufferings, because we know that suffering produces perseverance; perseverance, character; and character, hope. And hope does not disappoint us, because God has poured out his love into our hearts by the Holy Spirit, whom he has given us.[5]

What do those words tell us about closing loops? Look at the key issues they cover.

First, we've been "justified through faith." By faith in Jesus Christ, we have peace with God.

In that relationship, we can "rejoice in the hope of the glory of God." We can also rejoice "in our sufferings." Even during the hard times, we can find joy in God. Why? Because He'll see us through them. The verse doesn't say to be glad *for* the sufferings—it says to rejoice *in* the sufferings. Jesus is our hope, not our bank accounts or what type of hood ornaments we have on our cars.

As we rejoice in the sufferings we encounter, we

know it will lead to perseverance. That means we'll develop a lifestyle of hanging in there even when we don't know how we're going to get out of a seemingly intolerable situation. Perseverance is the fine art of keeping our heads down in the midst of a blinding snow. We don't stick our heads *in* the snow, but we keep them down as we keep moving forward, knowing God will sustain us. During a blizzard, it seems as if the snow will never stop, but it will. We just need to stay obedient as the storm quiets.

In our perseverance we'll develop character. My dad always said I had character (or was it that I *was* a character?). Character suggests integrity. How is character developed? Not through days on the beach, sipping lemonade with the world in the palms of our hands. Instead, character is shaped as we encounter trials (like those involved in the reconstruction of a marriage) and remain obedient.

And what does character lead to? Hope. What a great word for this generation! Anybody out there need to know that if we hang in there we'll develop character and have hope? I do. Without the hope, we're lost. But with the sure hope of God's love and support for now and through eternity, we have a tremendous sense of security.

Loops can close. What does it take? We need to be willing to humble ourselves. We need to let go of our pride so we can reach out to others. We need to put the process of reconciliation that God created for us to work in all our broken relationships.

Take the first step today. It is possible. It works. Go for it!

STUDY GUIDE

Group leaders, please note:

This study guide was written with the individual user in mind. If you want to use it in a group setting, such as a Sunday school class, be aware that some of the questions deal with personal and/or private matters. These may need to be rephrased in order for group members to feel comfortable in responding verbally.

Session 1 (chapters 1-2)

1. In your own words, define a "moving violation."
2. What are some of the common types of moving violations in everyday life?
3. Why is conflict inevitable in human relationships?
4. What are some of the reasons we find it so hard to resolve conflicts even with loved ones?
5. Think back to a past conflict with another person that has been resolved. Who took the first step to work things out? Why?
6. As you look at the steps involved in "closing the loop" on a conflict (p. 11), which one seems the hardest to you? Why?

7. What price does the person who was hurt have to pay to reconcile a relationship?

8. What price does the person who committed the offense have to pay?

9. What special price does the person taking the initiative in the healing process have to pay?

10. On pages 13-18, Dr. Rosberg tells the story of the prodigal son from Luke 15. Read that story again, and then answer these questions:

    a. What had to happen in the young man's thinking before he turned toward home?

    b. Why do you suppose the loving father didn't go looking for his child in the far country?

    c. Assuming the father represents God in this story, what picture does it give you of His attitude toward conflict resolution?

11. Think of a current conflict you have with another person. On a scale from 1 (not at all willing) to 10 (very willing), how willing are you at this point to take the steps necessary to work things out in that situation? Circle the number below that best reflects your determination.

    1 2 3 4 5 6 7 8 9 10

    Why did you choose that number?

12. In your prayers over the next week, ask God to make you aware of any damaged relationships you need to mend.

Session 2 (chapter 3)

1. Why does conflict tend to take us by surprise?
2. What are some potential dangers of trying to avoid conflict at all costs?
3. What are some potential dangers of pretending conflict doesn't exist when it really does?
4. Think of a recent conflict you've had with someone. What were some of the differences between the two of you that contributed to the conflict?
5. On page 35, Dr. Rosberg suggests that if an offense is dealt with immediately, "it may not have any lasting consequences." In your experience, how many hurts are resolved right away? Why isn't the percentage higher?
6. Think of a married couple you know who have experienced conflict because of differing family backgrounds—perhaps you and your spouse if you're married. What issues or decisions have they argued over? Have they been able to resolve those issues? If so, how?
7. Why is it that personality differences can seem appealing *before* marriage but often produce tension in the relationship afterward?
8. When a conflict is produced by a difference in values that are important to both parties, what are some keys to finding a solution to the disagreement?

9. Dr. Rosberg says that one area in which men and women differ is their view of sexuality. What are some other areas of difference between the two genders?

10. First Corinthians 7:3-5 gives husbands and wives instruction regarding their sexual relationship. Read those verses, and then answer these questions:

    a. What does this passage require of a husband and wife?

    b. What conflicts can arise from how it is interpreted and applied?

    c. What are some other biblical passages that help us understand how this and all other aspects of a marriage should be conducted?

Session 3 (chapter 4)

1. Which of the "voices" described in chapter 4—our culture, the publishing world, TV, friends, secular counseling, and the church—do you think has the greatest influence on your approach to conflict resolution? Why?

2. In your own words, describe briefly the message of popular secular books and magazines regarding problems in relationships.

3. What are your three favorite TV programs? As you watch them over the next week, note how

the characters handle anger and other emotions.
Afterward, answer these questions:

    a. Were you surprised by what you saw in this new light?

    b. Are the models of conflict resolution they provide healthy or unhealthy? Explain.

4. In light of that evaluation, what changes, if any, might you want to make in your TV viewing habits? Why?

5. When you discuss conflicts with friends, what kinds of advice do you usually get?

6. What part do you think God can play in your efforts to reconcile a relationship?

7. Why does secular counseling tend to see God as part of the problem rather than part of the solution?

8. Read Ephesians 5:18-33; then answer the following:

    a. What attitude does this passage suggest husbands and wives should bring to their efforts to resolve differences?

    b. Why do husbands and wives (and friends and loved ones generally) often not display such an attitude?

    c. In terms of how disagreements are resolved, what might be some of the characteristics of a relationship in which that kind of attitude prevailed?

Session 4 (chapter 5)

1. What traits of your parents do you recognize in your own attitudes, opinions, and behaviors?

2. Which of those are helpful to you in resolving conflicts? Which are harmful? Why?

3. In your own words, summarize the basic problem with the "good" family when it comes to handling conflict (pp. 73-75).

4. In your own words, what's wrong with the way the "religious" family deals with differences (pp. 76-79)?

5. How would you describe the problems of the "wounded" family in resolving conflict (pp. 79-82)?

6. What are some of the good things the Blakes did in handling their dinnertime conflict (pp. 82-85)?

7. Think of a family you know that fits one of the three unhealthy categories described in chapter 5. How has it handled conflict? What has been the result?

8. In which of the four categories (the three unhealthy families plus the one healthy family) would you put your birth family? Why?

9. If you are or have been married, in which category would your spouse's (or ex's) birth family fit? If you're single, in which category does your best friend's family belong? Why?

10. In which category would you place your own present-day family? Why?

11. On pages 85-86, Dr. Rosberg quotes Psalm 78:5-7. Reread that passage, and then answer these questions:

   a. What do those verses suggest is a parent's responsibility?

   b. What do they suggest is a child's responsibility?

   c. Which commands of God will help us in resolving disagreements with our loved ones and others?

12. What steps can you take in the next week to make your family a more truly biblical one? In the next month? In the next year?

Session 5 (chapter 6)

1. What things make you the most angry? Why?

2. Why does anger usually follow being hurt? Are those reasons good or bad?

3. Think of someone you know who tends to express anger inappropriately. How do others respond to that person? Why?

4. If you haven't already done so, take the Rosberg Anger Inventory on pages 94-98. Did the results surprise you? Why or why not?

5. What's the difference between anger that's justifiable and anger that's not?

6. Which of the three kinds of "hot potatoes" is your anger usually in the form of (pp. 98-105)? How do you know?

7. Review the four common responses to anger on pages 106-11. How do people who use each of those responses hurt themselves? How do their responses affect the potential for resolution of conflicts with others?

8. In your own words, explain the negative effects of either venting or stuffing anger.

9. Genesis 4:1-12 tells the story of a time when Cain became very angry. Read those verses; then answer the following:

    a. Why did Cain get angry?

    b. Was his anger justified?

    c. How did he handle his anger?

    d. What were the results of his anger?

10. On a scale from 1 (very poorly) to 10 (extremely well), how well do you think you handle your anger? Circle the number below that best reflects your life in this area:

1 2 3 4 5 6 7 8 9 10

Now circle below the way you think *the person closest to you* (spouse, parent, best friend) would rate you:

1 2 3 4 5 6 7 8 9 10

If there's a discrepancy between the two numbers, what do you think accounts for it?

11. What is the positive purpose of anger?

Session 6 (chapter 7)

1. Why do we sometimes try to avoid making hard choices?

2. Think of a recent time when you had to decide whether to try to resolve a conflict with someone. What criteria did you use in choosing? What conclusion did you reach? Why?

3. If you haven't already done so, take the "Conflict-Resolution Survey" on pages 122-26 to learn your current style of handling disputes.

4. Did the results of that survey surprise you? Why or why not?

5. In your own words, describe briefly the strengths and weaknesses of each of the four conflict-resolution styles epitomized in "I Love Lucy" (pp. 127-30).

6. As Dr. Rosberg points out on page 131, each of those four styles tends to place a higher priority on either the relationship or being in control of the situation. Which do you think is more important? Why?

7. In discussing the Lucy Ricardo approach, Dr. Rosberg describes Lucy as a master of manipulation.

Think of a time when you knew someone was trying to manipulate you. How did it make you feel? How did you respond? Why?

8. From the brief description of the Ward Cleaver approach on page 132, what were two key characteristics of his conflict-resolution style?

9. In Joshua 24:14-15, Joshua called on the people of Israel to make a critical choice, and he stated the decision that he had made himself. Read those verses, and then answer these questions:

   a. What choice did Joshua ask the people to make?

   b. What decision had he made?

   c. Have you made the same choice? If not, will you do so today?

   d. How might such a commitment affect your decisions about whether to resolve the conflicts in your life?

Session 7 (chapters 8-10)

1. In your own words, what is a "red light" in the area of relationships and conflict resolution?

2. On a scale from 1 (very proud) to 10 (extremely humble), how proud do you think you are? Circle the number below that best represents your level of pride.

1 2 3 4 5 6 7 8 9 10

Why did you choose that number? How do you think the person closest to you would rate you? Why?

3. Is there some past event or attitude that causes you recurring guilt? What keeps you from admitting and repenting of it? What first steps could you take toward resolving that situation?

4. On a scale from 1 (not hard at all) to 10 (very hard), how hard do you work at your most important relationships? Circle your answer below.

1 2 3 4 5 6 7 8 9 10

Why did you pick that number? What number would the person closest to you choose for you? Why?

5. To what extent do defensiveness and secrets exist in either the family of your birth or your present family? Why? How do you know?

6. Proverbs 1:7, 9:10, and 15:33 speak of the "fear of the Lord." Read those verses, and then answer the following:

   a. What do those passages tell us about fearing God?

   b. How does such fear demonstrate wisdom?

   c. Can a person who does not fear God be truly wise? Why or why not?

   d. How can a healthy fear of God help us in resolving conflicts?

7. Do you have someone with whom you can talk candidly about your fears and problems? If your answer is yes and you are married, is that person your spouse? Why or why not? If your answer is no, where and how can you begin to develop such a friendship?

8. How close do you let others get to you? Why? How would the person closest to you answer that on your behalf? Why?

9. Does the thought of achieving greater success in your relationships—and needing to make changes in your life as a result (e.g., spending more time with others)—cause you to feel excited or afraid? Why?

10. To which of the fears discussed in chapter 9 do you relate most closely? Why?

11. In the section titled "The Fine Art of Slaying Dragons" (pp. 168-70), Dr. Rosberg suggests how to handle our fears about relationships. How can you apply his counsel to your greatest fear?

12. In what ways do you try to control others who are close to you? Why?

13. In your own words, how does a desire for control work against the resolution of conflict in a home?

Session 8 (chapter 11)

1. As you understand it, what is a nonnegotiable relationship?

2. Which relationships in your life are nonnegotiable? Why?

3. How might a determination that divorce is not an option affect a married couple's mind-set toward conflict in their relationship? Why?

4. Which of the three ingredients of restored relationships (pp. 200-207) is hardest for you? Why?

5. Which of the three is easiest for you? Why?

6. On page 205, Dr. Rosberg quotes Philippians 2:3-4, which speaks about humility. Read that passage again, and then answer these questions:

   a. Are those verses in conflict with the idea of having a healthy self-esteem? Why or why not?

   b. How do we look to the interests of others in a proper way?

   c. How does humility's opposite, pride, affect our willingness and ability to resolve disagreements?

7. On a scale from 1 (threadbare) to 10 (strong and tight), how secure is the safety net under your most important relationships? Circle your answer below.

   1 2 3 4 5 6 7 8 9 10

   Why did you choose that number?

8. Read the story of Phil and Susan on pages 208-12. What mistakes had Susan made? What mistakes had Phil made?

9. If you had been in Phil's place when Susan asked if he wanted her to leave, what do you think you would have said and done? Why?

10. How long do you think it should take Phil and Susan to rebuild their relationship and their trust in each other? Why?

11. What can you do in the next week or month to strengthen your commitment to your most important relationships?

Session 9 (chapters 12-13)

1. What are some of the things that tend to "clog your heart" and create a need for it to be cleared?

2. In your setting, what are some places where you can get away for a time to regain perspective?

3. Think about a conflict you're currently experiencing with another person. What sin might you need to confess in that situation? Why?

4. Regarding that same conflict, is your present attitude one of restoration or strife? Why?

5. On page 225, Dr. Rosberg asks a series of questions about your background and its influence on today's conflicts. If you haven't already done so, read and answer those questions.

6. On pages 230-31, Dr. Rosberg tells about a banker who used a telephone pole as a reminder to prepare himself mentally for interaction with his

family while he drove home each evening. What could serve as a similar marker for you?

7. Think of a time when you were in conflict with someone and you betrayed the other person's confidence. What was the result?

8. Are you in a friendship or group relationship where you're held accountable for how you handle things like conflict? If so, how has that affected your life? If not, with whom might you start to develop such a relationship? (Perhaps a group at your church?)

9. Do you tend to deal with your anger in a timely way? Why or why not? What personal policy might you establish to help you do a better job in this area?

10. Think of the last time you got really angry with someone. Then, with that situation in mind, ask yourself the questions Dr. Rosberg lists on page 250 regarding your self-talk at that time. How do your answers affect your understanding of what was going on then?

11. Read Matthew 5:38-48, a well-known passage about loving our enemies. Then answer the following:

    a. What do those verses say about our natural human desire for revenge?

    b. Why is it so hard for us to follow Jesus' teaching in this area?

    c. Practically speaking, how do we go about loving someone who has hurt us or in some other way made us angry?

12. Of all the strategies for handling anger provided in chapter 13, which might be of the greatest immediate help to you? Why?

Session 10 (chapter 14)

1. On a scale from 1 (total lack) to 10 (excellent), how would you rate the quality of communication in your home? Circle your answer below.

1 2 3 4 5 6 7 8 9 10

Why did you choose that number? What number do you think the person closest to you would pick? Why?

2. How long has it been since you asked the people closest to you, "How am I doing?" and "What do you need from me?" If it has been a while, plan a time for doing that in the near future.

3. Why do you think women tend to talk more than men? How can we, as Dr. Rosberg recommends, "save some of our word power for our families" each day?

4. What's a good occasional (e.g., once a week or month) setting for you and the person closest to you to have deep communication? If you're

married, what's the best time and place for daily, uninterrupted conversation?

5. In the section "Third and Long" (pp. 276-79), Dr. Rosberg describes three levels of communication. At which of those levels is most of your conversation with the person closest to you? Why? How often do the two of you get to the third level of expressing needs? Why?

6. How good a listener would you say you are? Choose your answer from the following:

___ Lousy
___ Not too good
___ Okay
___ Better than average
___ Excellent

How would the person closest to you rate you? Why?

7. On page 280, Dr. Rosberg quotes James 1:19-20. Read those verses again, and then answer these questions:

 a. What kind of attitude toward the other person does "quick to listen, slow to speak" demonstrate?

 b. How do you feel when someone really listens to you?

 c. How do you feel when the other person clearly *isn't* listening to you?

8. How would you describe the communication style

of your spouse (or the person closest to you if you're unmarried)? How well do you accommodate yourself to that style? How could you do it better?

9. What are some signs that a person may be sending an unspoken message along with a spoken one? How might you increase your sensitivity to such underlying issues?

10. Dr. Rosberg outlines seven techniques for improving communication in chapter 14 of the text. Pick one where you see a need to grow better, and plan how to begin working on that in the next week.

Session 11 (chapter 15)

1. Think back to your most recent conflict with another person. How do you think praying together might have affected the atmosphere? How might it have influenced the end result?

2. On pages 299-300, Dr. Rosberg offers four guidelines for choosing a setting for loving confrontation. Which of those are you most likely to violate? Why? How can you do a better job of picking the right time and place?

3. When we're having a disagreement with someone, why do we tend to bring up more than one issue at a time?

4. In your own words, why is it vital to focus on just one issue at a time in a loving confrontation?

5. Recall your last run-in with another person. How gentle were you in expressing your point of view? How might the conversation have been affected if you had been more gentle?

6. Think of someone at home, work, or church with whom you have occasional conflicts. Write out a couple of things it might help to say to that person in the form of *I* messages.

7. Besides tossing a pillow on the floor (see pp. 308-9), how might you depersonalize conflicts with the person closest to you?

8. What kinds of issues are typically involved in your disagreements with others? What does the Bible have to say about those issues?

9. Why do we so easily develop tunnel vision in conflict situations? How can we generate other options in those times?

10. In Matthew 5:23-24, Jesus spoke about dealing with conflict face to face. Read that passage, and then answer the following:

    a. What importance did Jesus place on such confrontation? How can you tell?

    b. In what spirit does He suggest such a confrontation should take place?

    c. With whom might you need to apply those verses now? Why?

Session 12 (chapters 16-18)

1. Whom do you need to release from a past offense committed against you? Why?

2. Why do we find it so hard to trust God in this area and forgive as He commands?

3. On pages 329-30, Dr. Rosberg paraphrases the parable of the unmerciful servant from Matthew 18:21-35. Read that passage of Scripture; then answer these questions:

    a. How much does this parable suggest God has forgiven us?

    b. Why do you think the unmerciful servant was unwilling to forgive his fellow servant?

    c. Why is it so important to God that we forgive others (see v. 35)?

4. How does the reminder that God has forgiven you (see pp. 337-38) affect your willingness to forgive others who have hurt you? Why?

5. In the story of Arnie and his family (pp. 339-43), it was Arnie's daughter, Melissa, who convinced him to take steps to be reconciled with his mother. For whom might you play the same role, gently urging the person to act before it's too late?

6. In your own words, how do we forgive a person without forgetting the offense he or she committed against us?

7. Why are our feelings often at odds with our need to forgive others or ourselves?

8. If we wait for the other party to initiate reconciliation or to at least respond to our overtures before we forgive, what's likely to happen? Why?

9. As you understand it, what are some of the dangers inherent in trying to grant forgiveness too quickly?

10. Think of the last time someone admitted to you that he or she had been wrong and was sorry. How did it make you feel about that person? About your relationship with that individual? Why?

11. Whose forgiveness do you need to seek? In this situation, what do you need to repent of? When will you ask for this person's forgiveness?

12. When you grant forgiveness to someone who has hurt you, do you tend to give it grudgingly or graciously? How do you know?

13. Think of someone with whom you're at odds right now. Have you given or asked for forgiveness (whichever is appropriate) yet? What other steps toward reconciliation might you take? Whether or not reconciliation seems likely, make that a matter for prayer.

Session 13 (chapters 19-20)

1. In your own words, why is rebuilding trust a necessary step beyond forgiveness?

2. After reviewing the story of Tina and Roger on pages 378-80, what practical things do you think Roger could do to demonstrate his growing trustworthiness to Tina?

3. Why do we tend to pray last rather than first when we have a broken relationship or any other problem?

4. Why is it so hard for us to communicate our needs honestly to others? What benefits do we gain from doing so?

5. Does the adage "Ignorance is bliss" ever apply when it comes to the state of our relationships with others? Why or why not?

6. Think of a relationship of yours that's damaged to some degree. How can you challenge the other person to join you in working to rebuild the trust between you?

7. What type of criticism or resistance can you anticipate getting as you try to rebuild that relationship? How might you overcome that?

8. First Peter 5:8-10 speaks of Satan, who more than anyone wants to keep people from being reconciled (see pp. 394-95). Read those verses, and then consider the following:

   a. How does the passage describe Satan?

   b. How does it say we should respond to him?

   c. What resources and motivation are we offered?

9. Which of the eight steps to rebuilding a wall of trust do you think would be the easiest for you? Why?

10. Which of the eight steps would be the hardest for you? Why?

11. Which of your open loops is in greatest need of repair? What step(s) can you take in the next week to begin closing that loop? In the next month?

12. What remaining fears or doubts do you have about your ability to close that loop? Take them to the Lord in prayer. And if you need further encouragement, discuss them with a mature, positive Christian friend.

NOTES

Chapter 2

1. Luke 15:20, 24, NASB.
2. Luke 15:13, NASB.
3. Luke 15:14–16, NASB.
4. Luke 15:17–19, NASB.
5. Luke 15:20–24, NASB.

Chapter 3

1. For more information, write to Charles Boyd, 21 Toulouse Ct., Little Rock, AR 72212.
2. Gary Smalley and John Trent, *The Two Sides of Love* (Wheaton, Ill.: Tyndale, 1990).
3. James Dobson, *Straight Talk* (Dallas: Word, 1991), p. 183.
4. Gary Smalley with John Trent, *Love Is a Decision* (Dallas: Word, 1989), p. 146.

Chapter 4

1. Kim France, "Sleeping with the Enemy," *Mademoiselle*, October 1991, p. 146.
2. Sue Bowders, "Salvaging the Troubled Relationship: When It's Up to You," *Cosmopolitan*, September 1991, p. 146.

3. Ibid.

4. Ibid.

5. Peter Gerstenzang, "Good Ways to Say Bad Things," *Cosmopolitan*, December 1991, p. 90.

6. U.S. Bureau of the Census, *Statistical Abstract of the United States: 1990* (110th ed.); Washington, D.C., 1990, p. 86.

7. Sandy Rovner, "Mental Health Group Seeks Changes in Way Soap Operas Deal with Anger," *Des Moines Register*, April 14, 1991, p. 8E.

8. Ibid.

9. Ephesians 5:25–30.

10. Robert Lewis and William Hendricks, *Rocking the Roles* (Colorado Springs, Colo.: NavPress, 1991), p. 68.

11. See Proverbs 11:14.

Chapter 5

1. Matthew 13:3–9.

2. Matthew 13:4.

3. *Family Life Conference Manual*, Campus Crusade for Christ, 1988, p. 19.

4. Dennis Rainey, *Lonely Husbands, Lonely Wives* (Dallas: Word, 1989), p. 51.

5. Matthew 13:5–6.

6. Stephen Arterburn and Jack Felton, *Toxic Faith* (Nashville: Oliver-Nelson, 1991), p. 31.

7. See Revelation 3:14–16.

8. Matthew 13:7.

9. Matthew 13:8.

10. Psalm 78:5–7, NASB.

11. Quotation by Charles Swindoll taken from a brochure published by the Family Ministry of Campus Crusade for Christ, 1985.

Chapter 6

1. "I Thought I'd Explode When . . . Chalk It Up! A weekly mini page just for kids," *Des Moines Register*, October 17, 1990.

2. Charles Swindoll, "Anger: The Burning Fuse of Hostility" (booklet). The material in this booklet originally appeared in *Three Steps Forward, Two Steps Back* (Nashville: Nelson, 1980), p. 3.

3. Matthew McKay, Peter D. Rogers, and Judith McKay, *When Anger Hurts* (Oakland: New Harbinger, 1989), p. 20.

4. Ibid., p. 22.

5. Ibid., p. 35.

6. Les Carter, *Good 'n' Angry* (Grand Rapids, Mich.: Baker, 1983), p. 35.

7. Stephen Arterburn and Jack Felton, *Toxic Faith* (Nashville: Oliver-Nelson, 1991), p. 108.

Chapter 8

1. Proverbs 16:18.

2. Cited in Wayne Martinsdale and Jerry Root, eds., *The Quotable Lewis* (Wheaton, Ill.: Tyndale, 1989), p. 318.

3. Bruce Narramore and Bill Counts, *Freedom from Guilt* (Santa Ana, Calif.: Vision House, 1974), p. 10.

4. 2 Corinthians 7:8–10.

5. Les Carter, *Will the Defense Please Rest?* (Grand Rapids, Mich.: Baker, 1986), p. 54.

6. Barbara Sullivan, *The Control Trap* (Minneapolis: Bethany House, 1991), p. 102.

7. Sandra D. Wilson, *Released from Shame* (Downers Grove, Ill.: InterVarsity, 1990), p. 10.

8. Pat Springle, *Codependency: A Christian Perspective* (Houston: Rapha, 1989), p. 103.

9. 2 Corinthians 12:9.

10. Ephesians 4:22–24, NASB.

Chapter 9

1. Frank Minirth, Paul Meier, and Don Hawkins, *Worry-Free Living* (Nashville: Nelson, 1989), pp. 208–9.

2. 2 Corinthians 7:5.

Chapter 10

1. Galatians 5:22–23.

2. Gary Smalley and John Trent, *The Language of Love* (Wheaton, Ill.: Tyndale, 1988), p. 17.

3. Revelation 3:20.

Chapter 11

1. C. S. Lewis, *The Problem of Pain* (New York: Collier, 1962), p. 93.

2. 2 Corinthians 2:9.

3. See Genesis 22:1–19.

4. Matthew 4:19.

5. See Matthew 18:21–22.

6. Psalm 27:14, NASB.

7. Joshua 1:2–9, NASB.

8. Philippians 2:3–4.

9. See 1 Corinthians 13.

10. See John 13:1–17.

11. Matthew 3:11.

12. Luke 15:19.

13. "Let the Walls Come Down." Words and music by Jon
    Mohr. © Copyright 1991 Jonathan Mark Music. All
    rights reserved. Used by permission.

Chapter 12

1. Psalm 139:23–24.

2. Matthew 5:9.

3. Larry Crabb, *Inside Out* (Colorado Springs, Colo.:
   NavPress, 1988), p. 29.

4. Tim Kimmel, *Little House on the Freeway* (Portland,
   Ore.: Multnomah, 1987), p. 31.

5. Bill and Lynne Hybels, *Fit to Be Tied* (Grand Rapids,
   Mich.: Zondervan, 1991), p. 178.

6. Ibid.

7. Matthew 18:15, NASB.

Chapter 13

1. Ephesians 4:26–27, NASB.
2. Archibald Hart in Tim LaHaye and Bob Phillips, *Anger Is a Choice* (Grand Rapids, Mich.: Zondervan, 1982), pp. 102–3.
3. Charles Swindoll, "Anger: The Burning Fuse of Hostility" (booklet). The material in this booklet originally appeared in *Three Steps Forward, Two Steps Back* (Nashville: Nelson, 1980), p. 3.
4. Matthew 7:5.
5. James 3:5, NASB.
6. Dennis and Barbara Rainey, *Building Your Mate's Self-Esteem* (San Bernardino, Calif.: Here's Life, 1986), p. 104.
7. Proverbs 15:1.
8. Dave Boehi, "Let Your Mind Dwell . . . ," *Worldwide Challenge*, September/October 1985, p. 7.
9. 1 Peter 3:9.
10. The story of "Chad" is a popular illustration used by speakers. Source unknown.

Chapter 14

1. Gary Smalley with John Trent, *Love Is a Decision* (Dallas: Word, 1989), p. 44.
2. James 1:19–20.

Chapter 15

1. Colossians 4:2.
2. Proverbs 12:18, NASB.

3. Kevin Miller, "Are Men Bad Listeners?" *Marriage Partnership*, Summer 1990, p. 26.
4. 1 Thessalonians 5:11.

Chapter 16
1. See Matthew 18:21–35.
2. Dwight L. Carlson, *Overcoming Hurts and Anger* (Eugene, Ore.: Harvest House, 1981), p. 126.
3. Lewis B. Smedes, *Forgive and Forget* (San Francisco: Harper & Row, 1984), p. 133.
4. Adolph Coors IV, "The Power of Forgiveness: No Right to Hate," Full Gospel Business Men's *VOICE*, December 1988, p. 11.
5. Ibid., p. 12.
6. Ephesians 4:32.
7. Jerry Bridges, *Transforming Grace* (Colorado Springs, Colo.: NavPress, 1990), p. 205.
8. Hebrews 4:15–16.
9. Philip Yancey, "An Unnatural Act," *Christianity Today*, April 18, 1991, p. 37.

Chapter 17
1. Lewis B. Smedes, *Forgive and Forget* (San Francisco: Harper & Row, 1984), p. 39.
2. Jeremiah 31:34.
3. Romans 12:18.
4. Ephesians 4:26, NASB.
5. Smedes, *Forgive and Forget*, p. 95.

Chapter 18

1. Malachi 4:6, NASB.
2. 2 Corinthians 7:9–10, NASB.
3. See 1 Peter 3:9.
4. David Stoop and James Masteller, *Forgiving Our Parents, Forgiving Ourselves* (Ann Arbor, Mich.: Vine Books, 1991), p. 263.

Chapter 19

1. See 2 Chronicles 36:15–21.
2. Nehemiah 1:3.
3. Nehemiah 1:4.
4. See Nehemiah 1:5–11.
5. James 5:16, NASB.
6. See Nehemiah 2:2.
7. Nehemiah 2:4–5.
8. Nehemiah 2:8.
9. Nehemiah 2:17–18.
10. Nehemiah 4:6.
11. Nehemiah 4:1–3.
12. Nehemiah 4:4.
13. Nehemiah 4:10.
14. Nehemiah 4:16–18.
15. Nehemiah 6:15–16.
16. See D. Guthrie and J. A. Motyer, *The New Bible Commentary: Revised* (Grand Rapids, Mich.: Eerdmans, 1970), p. 407.

Chapter 20

1. Charles R. Swindoll, *The Grace Awakening* (Dallas: Word, 1990), p. 4.
2. John 3:16, NASB.
3. John 14:6, NASB.
4. See John 1:12; Philippians 4:13.
5. Romans 5:1–5.

For speaking and conference information regarding The Rosbergs, America's Family Coaches, or for information about video and audio tapes of their speaking events, write or call:

The Rosbergs—America's Family Coaches
1200 35th Street, Suite 507
West Des Moines, IA 50266
1-888-ROSBERG
rosbergs@aol.com
You can also visit America's Family Coaches online at www.rosbergs.com.